Mometrix
TEST PREPARATION

WEST-E®

Early Childhood Special Education (071) Secrets Study Guide

WEST–E and Washington Educator Skills Tests–Endorsements are trademarks of the Washington Professional Educator Standards Board and Pearson Education, Inc. or its affiliate(s). This product was developed by Mometrix Test Preparation. It was not developed in connection with Pearson Education, Inc., nor was it reviewed, approved or endorsed by these agencies.

Dear Future Exam Success Story

First of all, **THANK YOU** for purchasing Mometrix study materials!

Second, congratulations! You are one of the few determined test-takers who are committed to doing whatever it takes to excel on your exam. **You have come to the right place.** We developed these study materials with one goal in mind: to deliver you the information you need in a format that's concise and easy to use.

In addition to optimizing your guide for the content of the test, we've outlined our recommended steps for breaking down the preparation process into small, attainable goals so you can make sure you stay on track.

We've also analyzed the entire test-taking process, identifying the most common pitfalls and showing how you can overcome them and be ready for any curveball the test throws you.

Standardized testing is one of the biggest obstacles on your road to success, which only increases the importance of doing well in the high-pressure, high-stakes environment of test day. Your results on this test could have a significant impact on your future, and this guide provides the information and practical advice to help you achieve your full potential on test day.

Your success is our success

We would love to hear from you! If you would like to share the story of your exam success or if you have any questions or comments in regard to our products, please contact us at **800-673-8175** or **support@mometrix.com**.

Thanks again for your business and we wish you continued success!

Sincerely,
The Mometrix Test Preparation Team

Need more help? Check out our flashcards at:
http://MometrixFlashcards.com/WEST

Copyright © 2026 by Mometrix Media LLC. All rights reserved.
Printed in the United States of America

Table of Contents

Introduction _____ 1
Secret Key #1 – Plan Big, Study Small _____ 2
Secret Key #2 – Make Your Studying Count _____ 3
Secret Key #3 – Practice the Right Way _____ 4
Secret Key #4 – Pace Yourself _____ 6
Secret Key #5 – Have a Plan for Guessing _____ 7
Test-Taking Strategies _____ 10
Understanding Young Children with Disabilities _____ 15
   Health Needs in Early Childhood _____ 15
   Types of Disabilities and Exceptionalities and their Implications _____ 21
   Factors that Affect Health and Development _____ 32
   Overview of Human Developmental Theories _____ 35
   Cognitive Development _____ 39
   Social and Emotional Development _____ 42
   Physical Development _____ 45
   Language Development _____ 46
   Developmental Delays _____ 50
   Chapter Quiz _____ 51
Assessment and Program Development _____ 52
   Screening in Early Childhood _____ 52
   Special Education Services in Early Childhood _____ 57
   Assessment Methodology _____ 59
   Developmental Screening _____ 71
   Individualized Education Programs _____ 75
   Collaborating with IEP Team Members _____ 80
   Behavior Assessment and Intervention _____ 83
   Chapter Quiz _____ 86
Delivering Specially Designed Instruction to Promote Development and Learning _ 87
   Adapting Instruction to Individual Needs _____ 87
   Modifications, Accommodations, and Adaptations _____ 88
   Social and Functional Living Skills _____ 94
   Life Stage Transitions _____ 97
   Instructional Design for Students with Disabilities _____ 99
   Special Education Settings _____ 104
   Learning Environments for Students with Disabilities _____ 107
   Behavioral Issues for Students with Disabilities _____ 111
   Crisis Prevention and Management _____ 112
   Planning and Service Delivery _____ 113
   Chapter Quiz _____ 121

Foundations and Professional Practice _____ 122
Roles and Responsibilities within the Local Education System _____ 122
Professional Development _____ 126
Team Teaching and Professional Collaboration _____ 130
Family Involvement and Collaboration _____ 132
Disability Education Laws _____ 139
Chapter Quiz _____ 151

WEST-E Practice Test _____ 152
Answer Key and Explanations _____ 170
How to Overcome Test Anxiety _____ 179
Online Resources _____ 185

Introduction

Thank you for purchasing this resource! You have made the choice to prepare yourself for a test that could have a huge impact on your future, and this guide is designed to help you be fully ready for test day. Obviously, it's important to have a solid understanding of the test material, but you also need to be prepared for the unique environment and stressors of the test, so that you can perform to the best of your abilities.

For this purpose, the first section that appears in this guide is the **Secret Keys**. We've devoted countless hours to meticulously researching what works and what doesn't, and we've boiled down our findings to the five most impactful steps you can take to improve your performance on the test. We start at the beginning with study planning and move through the preparation process, all the way to the testing strategies that will help you get the most out of what you know when you're finally sitting in front of the test.

We recommend that you start preparing for your test as far in advance as possible. However, if you've bought this guide as a last-minute study resource and only have a few days before your test, we recommend that you skip over the first two Secret Keys since they address a long-term study plan.

If you struggle with **test anxiety**, we strongly encourage you to check out our recommendations for how you can overcome it. Test anxiety is a formidable foe, but it can be beaten, and we want to make sure you have the tools you need to defeat it.

Secret Key #1 – Plan Big, Study Small

There's a lot riding on your performance. If you want to ace this test, you're going to need to keep your skills sharp and the material fresh in your mind. You need a plan that lets you review everything you need to know while still fitting in your schedule. We'll break this strategy down into three categories.

Information Organization

Start with the information you already have: the official test outline. From this, you can make a complete list of all the concepts you need to cover before the test. Organize these concepts into groups that can be studied together, and create a list of any related vocabulary you need to learn so you can brush up on any difficult terms. You'll want to keep this vocabulary list handy once you actually start studying since you may need to add to it along the way.

Time Management

Once you have your set of study concepts, decide how to spread them out over the time you have left before the test. Break your study plan into small, clear goals so you have a manageable task for each day and know exactly what you're doing. Then just focus on one small step at a time. When you manage your time this way, you don't need to spend hours at a time studying. Studying a small block of content for a short period each day helps you retain information better and avoid stressing over how much you have left to do. You can relax knowing that you have a plan to cover everything in time. In order for this strategy to be effective though, you have to start studying early and stick to your schedule. Avoid the exhaustion and futility that comes from last-minute cramming!

Study Environment

The environment you study in has a big impact on your learning. Studying in a coffee shop, while probably more enjoyable, is not likely to be as fruitful as studying in a quiet room. It's important to keep distractions to a minimum. You're only planning to study for a short block of time, so make the most of it. Don't pause to check your phone or get up to find a snack. It's also important to **avoid multitasking**. Research has consistently shown that multitasking will make your studying dramatically less effective. Your study area should also be comfortable and well-lit so you don't have the distraction of straining your eyes or sitting on an uncomfortable chair.

The time of day you study is also important. You want to be rested and alert. Don't wait until just before bedtime. Study when you'll be most likely to comprehend and remember. Even better, if you know what time of day your test will be, set that time aside for study. That way your brain will be used to working on that subject at that specific time and you'll have a better chance of recalling information.

Finally, it can be helpful to team up with others who are studying for the same test. Your actual studying should be done in as isolated an environment as possible, but the work of organizing the information and setting up the study plan can be divided up. In between study sessions, you can discuss with your teammates the concepts that you're all studying and quiz each other on the details. Just be sure that your teammates are as serious about the test as you are. If you find that your study time is being replaced with social time, you might need to find a new team.

Secret Key #2 – Make Your Studying Count

You're devoting a lot of time and effort to preparing for this test, so you want to be absolutely certain it will pay off. This means doing more than just reading the content and hoping you can remember it on test day. It's important to make every minute of study count. There are two main areas you can focus on to make your studying count.

Retention

It doesn't matter how much time you study if you can't remember the material. You need to make sure you are retaining the concepts. To check your retention of the information you're learning, try recalling it at later times with minimal prompting. Try carrying around flashcards and glance at one or two from time to time or ask a friend who's also studying for the test to quiz you.

To enhance your retention, look for ways to put the information into practice so that you can apply it rather than simply recalling it. If you're using the information in practical ways, it will be much easier to remember. Similarly, it helps to solidify a concept in your mind if you're not only reading it to yourself but also explaining it to someone else. Ask a friend to let you teach them about a concept you're a little shaky on (or speak aloud to an imaginary audience if necessary). As you try to summarize, define, give examples, and answer your friend's questions, you'll understand the concepts better and they will stay with you longer. Finally, step back for a big picture view and ask yourself how each piece of information fits with the whole subject. When you link the different concepts together and see them working together as a whole, it's easier to remember the individual components.

Finally, practice showing your work on any multi-step problems, even if you're just studying. Writing out each step you take to solve a problem will help solidify the process in your mind, and you'll be more likely to remember it during the test.

Modality

Modality simply refers to the means or method by which you study. Choosing a study modality that fits your own individual learning style is crucial. No two people learn best in exactly the same way, so it's important to know your strengths and use them to your advantage.

For example, if you learn best by visualization, focus on visualizing a concept in your mind and draw an image or a diagram. Try color-coding your notes, illustrating them, or creating symbols that will trigger your mind to recall a learned concept. If you learn best by hearing or discussing information, find a study partner who learns the same way or read aloud to yourself. Think about how to put the information in your own words. Imagine that you are giving a lecture on the topic and record yourself so you can listen to it later.

For any learning style, flashcards can be helpful. Organize the information so you can take advantage of spare moments to review. Underline key words or phrases. Use different colors for different categories. Mnemonic devices (such as creating a short list in which every item starts with the same letter) can also help with retention. Find what works best for you and use it to store the information in your mind most effectively and easily.

Secret Key #3 – Practice the Right Way

Your success on test day depends not only on how many hours you put into preparing, but also on whether you prepared the right way. It's good to check along the way to see if your studying is paying off. One of the most effective ways to do this is by taking practice tests to evaluate your progress. Practice tests are useful because they show exactly where you need to improve. Every time you take a practice test, pay special attention to these three groups of questions:

- The questions you got wrong
- The questions you had to guess on, even if you guessed right
- The questions you found difficult or slow to work through

This will show you exactly what your weak areas are, and where you need to devote more study time. Ask yourself why each of these questions gave you trouble. Was it because you didn't understand the material? Was it because you didn't remember the vocabulary? Do you need more repetitions on this type of question to build speed and confidence? Dig into those questions and figure out how you can strengthen your weak areas as you go back to review the material.

Additionally, many practice tests have a section explaining the answer choices. It can be tempting to read the explanation and think that you now have a good understanding of the concept. However, an explanation likely only covers part of the question's broader context. Even if the explanation makes perfect sense, **go back and investigate** every concept related to the question until you're positive you have a thorough understanding.

As you go along, keep in mind that the practice test is just that: practice. Memorizing these questions and answers will not be very helpful on the actual test because it is unlikely to have any of the same exact questions. If you only know the right answers to the sample questions, you won't be prepared for the real thing. **Study the concepts** until you understand them fully, and then you'll be able to answer any question that shows up on the test.

It's important to wait on the practice tests until you're ready. If you take a test on your first day of study, you may be overwhelmed by the amount of material covered and how much you need to learn. Work up to it gradually.

On test day, you'll need to be prepared for answering questions, managing your time, and using the test-taking strategies you've learned. It's a lot to balance, like a mental marathon that will have a big impact on your future. Like training for a marathon, you'll need to start slowly and work your way up. When test day arrives, you'll be ready.

Start with the strategies you've read in the first two Secret Keys—plan your course and study in the way that works best for you. If you have time, consider using multiple study resources to get different approaches to the same concepts. It can be helpful to see difficult concepts from more than one angle. Then find a good source for practice tests. Many times, the test website will suggest potential study resources or provide sample tests.

Practice Test Strategy

If you're able to find at least three practice tests, we recommend this strategy:

Untimed and Open-Book Practice

Take the first test with no time constraints and with your notes and study guide handy. Take your time and focus on applying the strategies you've learned.

Timed and Open-Book Practice

Take the second practice test open-book as well, but set a timer and practice pacing yourself to finish in time.

Timed and Closed-Book Practice

Take any other practice tests as if it were test day. Set a timer and put away your study materials. Sit at a table or desk in a quiet room, imagine yourself at the testing center, and answer questions as quickly and accurately as possible.

Keep repeating timed and closed-book tests on a regular basis until you run out of practice tests or it's time for the actual test. Your mind will be ready for the schedule and stress of test day, and you'll be able to focus on recalling the material you've learned.

Secret Key #4 – Pace Yourself

Once you're fully prepared for the material on the test, your biggest challenge on test day will be managing your time. Just knowing that the clock is ticking can make you panic even if you have plenty of time left. Work on pacing yourself so you can build confidence against the time constraints of the exam. Pacing is a difficult skill to master, especially in a high-pressure environment, so **practice is vital**.

Set time expectations for your pace based on how much time is available. For example, if a section has 60 questions and the time limit is 30 minutes, you know you have to average 30 seconds or less per question in order to answer them all. Although 30 seconds is the hard limit, set 25 seconds per question as your goal, so you reserve extra time to spend on harder questions. When you budget extra time for the harder questions, you no longer have any reason to stress when those questions take longer to answer.

Don't let this time expectation distract you from working through the test at a calm, steady pace, but keep it in mind so you don't spend too much time on any one question. Recognize that taking extra time on one question you don't understand may keep you from answering two that you do understand later in the test. If your time limit for a question is up and you're still not sure of the answer, mark it and move on, and come back to it later if the time and the test format allow. If the testing format doesn't allow you to return to earlier questions, just make an educated guess; then put it out of your mind and move on.

On the easier questions, be careful not to rush. It may seem wise to hurry through them so you have more time for the challenging ones, but it's not worth missing one if you know the concept and just didn't take the time to read the question fully. Work efficiently but make sure you understand the question and have looked at all of the answer choices, since more than one may seem right at first.

Even if you're paying attention to the time, you may find yourself a little behind at some point. You should speed up to get back on track, but do so wisely. Don't panic; just take a few seconds less on each question until you're caught up. Don't guess without thinking, but do look through the answer choices and eliminate any you know are wrong. If you can get down to two choices, it is often worthwhile to guess from those. Once you've chosen an answer, move on and don't dwell on any that you skipped or had to hurry through. If a question was taking too long, chances are it was one of the harder ones, so you weren't as likely to get it right anyway.

On the other hand, if you find yourself getting ahead of schedule, it may be beneficial to slow down a little. The more quickly you work, the more likely you are to make a careless mistake that will affect your score. You've budgeted time for each question, so don't be afraid to spend that time. Practice an efficient but careful pace to get the most out of the time you have.

Secret Key #5 – Have a Plan for Guessing

When you're taking the test, you may find yourself stuck on a question. Some of the answer choices seem better than others, but you don't see the one answer choice that is obviously correct. What do you do?

The scenario described above is very common, yet most test takers have not effectively prepared for it. Developing and practicing a plan for guessing may be one of the single most effective uses of your time as you get ready for the exam.

In developing your plan for guessing, there are three questions to address:

- When should you start the guessing process?
- How should you narrow down the choices?
- Which answer should you choose?

When to Start the Guessing Process

Unless your plan for guessing is to select C every time (which, despite its merits, is not what we recommend), you need to leave yourself enough time to apply your answer elimination strategies. Since you have a limited amount of time for each question, that means that if you're going to give yourself the best shot at guessing correctly, you have to decide quickly whether or not you will guess.

Of course, the best-case scenario is that you don't have to guess at all, so first, see if you can answer the question based on your knowledge of the subject and basic reasoning skills. Focus on the key words in the question and try to jog your memory of related topics. Give yourself a chance to bring the knowledge to mind, but once you realize that you don't have (or you can't access) the knowledge you need to answer the question, it's time to start the guessing process.

It's almost always better to start the guessing process too early than too late. It only takes a few seconds to remember something and answer the question from knowledge. Carefully eliminating wrong answer choices takes longer. Plus, going through the process of eliminating answer choices can actually help jog your memory.

Summary: Start the guessing process as soon as you decide that you can't answer the question based on your knowledge.

How to Narrow Down the Choices

The next chapter in this book (**Test-Taking Strategies**) includes a wide range of strategies for how to approach questions and how to look for answer choices to eliminate. You will definitely want to read those carefully, practice them, and figure out which ones work best for you. Here though, we're going to address a mindset rather than a particular strategy.

Your odds of guessing an answer correctly depend on how many options you are choosing from.

Number of options left	5	4	3	2	1
Odds of guessing correctly	20%	25%	33%	50%	100%

You can see from this chart just how valuable it is to be able to eliminate incorrect answers and make an educated guess, but there are two things that many test takers do that cause them to miss out on the benefits of guessing:

- Accidentally eliminating the correct answer
- Selecting an answer based on an impression

We'll look at the first one here, and the second one in the next section.

To avoid accidentally eliminating the correct answer, we recommend a thought exercise called **the $5 challenge**. In this challenge, you only eliminate an answer choice from contention if you are willing to bet $5 on it being wrong. Why $5? Five dollars is a small but not insignificant amount of money. It's an amount you could afford to lose but wouldn't want to throw away. And while losing

$5 once might not hurt too much, doing it twenty times will set you back $100. In the same way, each small decision you make—eliminating a choice here, guessing on a question there—won't by itself impact your score very much, but when you put them all together, they can make a big difference. By holding each answer choice elimination decision to a higher standard, you can reduce the risk of accidentally eliminating the correct answer.

The $5 challenge can also be applied in a positive sense: If you are willing to bet $5 that an answer choice *is* correct, go ahead and mark it as correct.

Summary: Only eliminate an answer choice if you are willing to bet $5 that it is wrong.

Which Answer to Choose

You're taking the test. You've run into a hard question and decided you'll have to guess. You've eliminated all the answer choices you're willing to bet $5 on. Now you have to pick an answer. Why do we even need to talk about this? Why can't you just pick whichever one you feel like when the time comes?

The answer to these questions is that if you don't come into the test with a plan, you'll rely on your impression to select an answer choice, and if you do that, you risk falling into a trap. The test writers know that everyone who takes their test will be guessing on some of the questions, so they intentionally write wrong answer choices to seem plausible. You still have to pick an answer though, and if the wrong answer choices are designed to look right, how can you ever be sure that you're not falling for their trap? The best solution we've found to this dilemma is to take the decision out of your hands entirely. Here is the process we recommend:

Once you've eliminated any choices that you are confident (willing to bet $5) are wrong, select the first remaining choice as your answer.

Whether you choose to select the first remaining choice, the second, or the last, the important thing is that you use some preselected standard. Using this approach guarantees that you will not be enticed into selecting an answer choice that looks right, because you are not basing your decision on how the answer choices look.

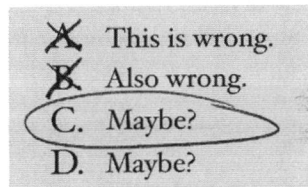

This is not meant to make you question your knowledge. Instead, it is to help you recognize the difference between your knowledge and your impressions. There's a huge difference between thinking an answer is right because of what you know, and thinking an answer is right because it looks or sounds like it should be right.

Summary: To ensure that your selection is appropriately random, make a predetermined selection from among all answer choices you have not eliminated.

Test-Taking Strategies

This section contains a list of test-taking strategies that you may find helpful as you work through the test. By taking what you know and applying logical thought, you can maximize your chances of answering any question correctly!

It is very important to realize that every question is different and every person is different: no single strategy will work on every question, and no single strategy will work for every person. That's why we've included all of them here, so you can try them out and determine which ones work best for different types of questions and which ones work best for you.

Question Strategies

⊘ READ CAREFULLY

Read the question and the answer choices carefully. Don't miss the question because you misread the terms. You have plenty of time to read each question thoroughly and make sure you understand what is being asked. Yet a happy medium must be attained, so don't waste too much time. You must read carefully and efficiently.

⊘ CONTEXTUAL CLUES

Look for contextual clues. If the question includes a word you are not familiar with, look at the immediate context for some indication of what the word might mean. Contextual clues can often give you all the information you need to decipher the meaning of an unfamiliar word. Even if you can't determine the meaning, you may be able to narrow down the possibilities enough to make a solid guess at the answer to the question.

⊘ PREFIXES

If you're having trouble with a word in the question or answer choices, try dissecting it. Take advantage of every clue that the word might include. Prefixes can be a huge help. Usually, they allow you to determine a basic meaning. *Pre-* means before, *post-* means after, *pro-* is positive, *de-* is negative. From prefixes, you can get an idea of the general meaning of the word and try to put it into context.

⊘ HEDGE WORDS

Watch out for critical hedge words, such as *likely, may, can, often, almost, mostly, usually, generally, rarely,* and *sometimes*. Question writers insert these hedge phrases to cover every possibility. Often an answer choice will be wrong simply because it leaves no room for exception. Be on guard for answer choices that have definitive words such as *exactly* and *always*.

⊘ SWITCHBACK WORDS

Stay alert for *switchbacks*. These are the words and phrases frequently used to alert you to shifts in thought. The most common switchback words are *but, although,* and *however*. Others include *nevertheless, on the other hand, even though, while, in spite of, despite,* and *regardless of*. Switchback words are important to catch because they can change the direction of the question or an answer choice.

ⓥ Face Value

When in doubt, use common sense. Accept the situation in the problem at face value. Don't read too much into it. These problems will not require you to make wild assumptions. If you have to go beyond creativity and warp time or space in order to have an answer choice fit the question, then you should move on and consider the other answer choices. These are normal problems rooted in reality. The applicable relationship or explanation may not be readily apparent, but it is there for you to figure out. Use your common sense to interpret anything that isn't clear.

Answer Choice Strategies

ⓥ Answer Selection

The most thorough way to pick an answer choice is to identify and eliminate wrong answers until only one is left, then confirm it is the correct answer. Sometimes an answer choice may immediately seem right, but be careful. The test writers will usually put more than one reasonable answer choice on each question, so take a second to read all of them and make sure that the other choices are not equally obvious. As long as you have time left, it is better to read every answer choice than to pick the first one that looks right without checking the others.

ⓥ Answer Choice Families

An answer choice family consists of two (in rare cases, three) answer choices that are very similar in construction and cannot all be true at the same time. If you see two answer choices that are direct opposites or parallels, one of them is usually the correct answer. For instance, if one answer choice says that quantity x increases and another either says that quantity x decreases (opposite) or says that quantity y increases (parallel), then those answer choices would fall into the same family. An answer choice that doesn't match the construction of the answer choice family is more likely to be incorrect. Most questions will not have answer choice families, but when they do appear, you should be prepared to recognize them.

ⓥ Eliminate Answers

Eliminate answer choices as soon as you realize they are wrong, but make sure you consider all possibilities. If you are eliminating answer choices and realize that the last one you are left with is also wrong, don't panic. Start over and consider each choice again. There may be something you missed the first time that you will realize on the second pass.

ⓥ Avoid Fact Traps

Don't be distracted by an answer choice that is factually true but doesn't answer the question. You are looking for the choice that answers the question. Stay focused on what the question is asking for so you don't accidentally pick an answer that is true but incorrect. Always go back to the question and make sure the answer choice you've selected actually answers the question and is not merely a true statement.

ⓥ Extreme Statements

In general, you should avoid answers that put forth extreme actions as standard practice or proclaim controversial ideas as established fact. An answer choice that states the "process should be used in certain situations, if..." is much more likely to be correct than one that states the "process should be discontinued completely." The first is a calm rational statement and doesn't even make a definitive, uncompromising stance, using a hedge word *if* to provide wiggle room, whereas the second choice is far more extreme.

☑ Benchmark

As you read through the answer choices and you come across one that seems to answer the question well, mentally select that answer choice. This is not your final answer, but it's the one that will help you evaluate the other answer choices. The one that you selected is your benchmark or standard for judging each of the other answer choices. Every other answer choice must be compared to your benchmark. That choice is correct until proven otherwise by another answer choice beating it. If you find a better answer, then that one becomes your new benchmark. Once you've decided that no other choice answers the question as well as your benchmark, you have your final answer.

☑ Predict the Answer

Before you even start looking at the answer choices, it is often best to try to predict the answer. When you come up with the answer on your own, it is easier to avoid distractions and traps because you will know exactly what to look for. The right answer choice is unlikely to be word-for-word what you came up with, but it should be a close match. Even if you are confident that you have the right answer, you should still take the time to read each option before moving on.

General Strategies

☑ Tough Questions

If you are stumped on a problem or it appears too hard or too difficult, don't waste time. Move on! Remember though, if you can quickly check for obviously incorrect answer choices, your chances of guessing correctly are greatly improved. Before you completely give up, at least try to knock out a couple of possible answers. Eliminate what you can and then guess at the remaining answer choices before moving on.

☑ Check Your Work

Since you will probably not know every term listed and the answer to every question, it is important that you get credit for the ones that you do know. Don't miss any questions through careless mistakes. If at all possible, try to take a second to look back over your answer selection and make sure you've selected the correct answer choice and haven't made a costly careless mistake (such as marking an answer choice that you didn't mean to mark). This quick double check should more than pay for itself in caught mistakes for the time it costs.

☑ Pace Yourself

It's easy to be overwhelmed when you're looking at a page full of questions; your mind is confused and full of random thoughts, and the clock is ticking down faster than you would like. Calm down and maintain the pace that you have set for yourself. Especially as you get down to the last few minutes of the test, don't let the small numbers on the clock make you panic. As long as you are on track by monitoring your pace, you are guaranteed to have time for each question.

☑ Don't Rush

It is very easy to make errors when you are in a hurry. Maintaining a fast pace in answering questions is pointless if it makes you miss questions that you would have gotten right otherwise. Test writers like to include distracting information and wrong answers that seem right. Taking a little extra time to avoid careless mistakes can make all the difference in your test score. Find a pace that allows you to be confident in the answers that you select.

ⓘ Keep Moving

Panicking will not help you pass the test, so do your best to stay calm and keep moving. Taking deep breaths and going through the answer elimination steps you practiced can help to break through a stress barrier and keep your pace.

Final Notes

The combination of a solid foundation of content knowledge and the confidence that comes from practicing your plan for applying that knowledge is the key to maximizing your performance on test day. As your foundation of content knowledge is built up and strengthened, you'll find that the strategies included in this chapter become more and more effective in helping you quickly sift through the distractions and traps of the test to isolate the correct answer.

Now that you're preparing to move forward into the test content chapters of this book, be sure to keep your goal in mind. As you read, think about how you will be able to apply this information on the test. If you've already seen sample questions for the test and you have an idea of the question format and style, try to come up with questions of your own that you can answer based on what you're reading. This will give you valuable practice applying your knowledge in the same ways you can expect to on test day.

Good luck and good studying!

Understanding Young Children with Disabilities

Transform passive reading into active learning! After immersing yourself in this chapter, put your comprehension to the test by taking a quiz. The insights you gained will stay with you longer this way. Scan the QR code to go directly to the chapter quiz interface for this study guide. If you're using a computer, simply visit the online resources page at **mometrix.com/resources719/westeearchsped** and click the Chapter Quizzes link.

Health Needs in Early Childhood

EFFECT OF MATURATIONAL FACTORS ON THE DEVELOPMENT AND LEARNING

Many physiological factors affect the development of babies and young children. These dictate which kinds of learning activities are appropriate or ineffective for certain ages. For example, providing a newborn with visual stimuli from several feet away is wasted, as newborns cannot yet focus on distant objects. Adults cannot expect infants younger than about 5 months to sit up unsupported, as they have not yet developed the strength for it. Adults cannot expect toddlers who have not yet attained stable walking gaits to hop or balance upon one foot successfully. It is not coincidental that first grade begins at around 6 years: younger children cannot physically sit still for long periods and have not developed long enough attention spans to prevent distraction. This is also why kindergarten classes feature varieties of shorter-term activities and more physical movement. Younger children also have not yet developed the self-regulation to keep from shouting out on impulse, getting up and running around, etc.—behaviors disruptive to formal schooling but developmentally normal.

NUTRITIONAL FACTORS IN DIET AFFECTING EARLY CHILDHOOD DEVELOPMENT

Babies are typically nourished via the mother's milk or infant formula, and then with baby food; however, young children mostly eat the same foods as adults by the age of 2 years. Though they eat smaller quantities, young children have similar nutritional needs to those of adults. Calcium can be more important in early childhood to support the rapid bone growth occurring during this period; young children should receive 2–3 servings of dairy products and/or other calcium-rich foods. For all ages, whole-grain foods are nutritionally superior for their fiber and nutrients than refined flours, which have had these removed. Refined flours provide "empty calories," causing wider blood-sugar fluctuations and insulin resistance—type 2 diabetes risks—than whole grains, which stabilize blood sugar and offer more naturally occurring vitamins and minerals. Darkly and brightly colored produce are most nutritious. Adults should cut foods into small, bite-sized pieces to prevent choking in young children, who have not yet perfected their biting, chewing, and swallowing skills.

CONSIDERATIONS FOR EARLY CHILDHOOD NUTRITION

Raw or lightly steamed vegetables are best because excess heat destroys nutrients and frying adds fat calories. Fresh, in-season and flash-frozen fruits are more nutritious and less processed than canned. Adults should monitor young children's diets to limit highly processed produce, which can have excessive sugar, salt, or preservatives. Good protein sources include legumes, nuts, lean poultry, and fish. Serving nut butters instead of whole nuts is safer, but spread thinly on whole-grain breads, crackers, or vegetable pieces, because young children can choke on large globs of nut butter as well. Omega-3 fatty acids from salmon, mackerel, herring, flaxseeds, and walnuts control inflammation, prevent heart arrhythmias, and lower blood pressure. Monounsaturated fats from avocados, olives, peanuts, and their oils, as well as canola oil, prevent heart disease, lower bad cholesterol, and raise good cholesterol. Polyunsaturated fats from nuts and seeds and from corn, soy, sesame, sunflower, and safflower oils lower cholesterol. These fats/oils should be served in moderation, and saturated fats should be avoided.

Considerations for Feeding Young Children

Saturated fats from meats and full-fat dairy should be limited; they can cause health problems like high cholesterol, cardiovascular disease, obesity, and diabetes. Trans fats are produced chemically by hydrogenating normally liquid unsaturated fats and converting them to solid, saturated fats as in margarine and shortening used in many baked goods. These are considered even unhealthier than regular saturated fats and should be avoided. (The words *partially hydrogenated* in the ingredients signal trans fats.) Infants derive enough water from their mother's milk or from formula, but young children should be given plenty of water and/or milk in "sippy cups" to stay hydrated. The common practice of giving young children fruit juice should be avoided. Even without added sugars, fruit juices crowd out room in small stomachs for food nutrients and cause dental cavities and weaken permanent teeth before they erupt. Children can also gain weight, as juice calories do not replace food calories the way actual fruit does with its fiber and solids. Young children should eat two-thirds of adult-sized portions.

Characteristics of Young Children's Nutritional Needs

Young children have smaller stomachs than adults and cannot eat as much at one time as teens or adults. However, it is common practice for today's restaurants to provide oversized portions. The historical tradition of encouraging young children to "clean their plates" is ill-advised, considering these excessive portions and the abundance of food in America today. Adults can help young children by teaching them instead to respond to their own bodies' signals and eat only until they are satisfied. Adults can also place smaller portions of food on young children's plates and request to-go containers at restaurants to take leftovers home. Because young children cannot eat a lot at once, they must maintain their blood sugar and energy throughout the day by snacking between meals. However, "snack foods" need not be high in sugar, salt, and unhealthy fats. Cut pieces of fresh fruits and vegetables, whole-grain crackers and low-fat cheeses, and portable yogurt tubes make good snacks for young children.

Development of Nutritious Eating Habits and Attitudes

Early childhood is an age range often associated with "finicky" eaters. Adults can experiment by substituting different foods that are similar sources of protein or other nutrients to foods young children dislike. Preparing meals to look like happy faces or animals or to have appealing designs can entice young children to eat varied foods. Engaging children age-appropriately in selecting and preparing meals with supervision can also motivate them to consume foods when they have participated in their preparation. Adults should model healthy eating habits for young children, who imitate admired adults' behaviors. Early childhood is when children form basic food-related attitudes and habits and so is an important time for influencing these. Children are exposed to unhealthy foods in advertising, at school, in restaurants, and with friends, so adult modeling and guidance regarding healthy choices are important to counteract these influences. However, adults should also impart the message early that no foods are "bad" or forbidden, allowing some occasional indulgences in small amounts to prevent the development of eating disorders.

SLEEP QUALITY AND BLOOD SUGAR CONTROL IN CHILDREN WITH TYPE 1 DIABETES

Researchers find blood sugar stability problematic for many children with type 1 (juvenile) diabetes, despite all efforts by parents and children to follow diabetic health care rules, because of sleep differences. Diabetic children spend more time in lighter than deeper stages of sleep compared to nondiabetic children. This results in higher levels of blood sugar and poorer school performance. Lighter sleep and resulting daytime sleepiness tend to increase blood sugar levels. Sleep apnea is a sleep disorder that causes a person's breathing to be interrupted often during sleeping. These breathing interruptions result in poorer sleep quality, fatigue, and daytime sleepiness. Sleep apnea has previously been associated with type 2 diabetes—historically adult-onset, though now children are developing it, too. It is now known that apnea is also associated with type 1 diabetes in children: roughly one-third of diabetic children studied have sleep apnea, regardless of their weight (being overweight can contribute to apnea). Sleep apnea is additionally associated with much higher blood sugars in diabetic children.

GENERAL SLEEP NEEDS AND BEHAVIORS OF YOUNG CHILDREN

Sleep allows the body to become repaired and recharged for the day and is vital for young children's growth and development. Children aged 2–5 years generally need 10–12 hours of sleep daily. Children 5–7 years old typically need 9–11 hours of sleep. Their sleep schedules should be fairly regular. While occasionally staying up later or missing naps for special events is not serious, overall inconsistent/disorganized schedules cause lost sleep and lethargic and/or cranky children. Some young children sleep fewer hours at night but need long daytime naps, while others need longer, uninterrupted nighttime sleep but seldom nap. Young children are busy exploring and discovering new things; they have a lot of energy and are often excited even when tired. Because they have not developed much self-regulation, they need adult guidance to calm down enough to go to sleep and will often resist bedtimes. Adults should plan bedtime routines. These can vary, but their most important aspect is consistency. Children then expect routines' familiar steps, and anticipating these steps comfort them.

COMPONENTS AND CHARACTERISTICS OF GOOD BEDTIME ROUTINES

Bedtime routines serve as transitions from young children's exciting, adventurous daytime activities to the tranquility needed for healthful rest. Adults should begin routines by establishing and enforcing a rule that daytime activities like rough-and-tumble physical play or TV-watching stop at a specific time. While preschoolers may be less interested in video games than older children, establishing limits early will help parents enforce stopping these activities at bedtime when they are older, too. Bath time is one good way to begin bedtime routines. Toys and games make baths fun, and bath washes with lavender and other soothing ingredients are now available to relax young children. Also, since young children eat smaller meals, healthy bedtime snacks are important. Too much or too little food will disrupt sleep, and too much liquid can cause bedwetting. Adults should plan nighttime snacks appropriately for the individual child. Bedtime reading promotes interest in books and learning and adult-child/family bonding, and calms children. Singing lullabies, hugging, and cuddling also support bonding, relax children, and make them feel safe and secure.

HELPING YOUNG CHILDREN TRANSITION FROM CRIBS TO REGULAR BEDS

One of young children's significant transitions from infancy is moving from a crib to a "big bed." Some become very motivated to escape cribs. For example, some bright, adventurous toddlers and even babies have untied padded crib bumpers, stacked them, and climbed out of the crib. For such children, injury is a greater danger from a crib than a bed. Others, whose cognitive and verbal skills are more developed than motor skills, may stand or jump up and down, repeatedly calling, "Hey, I'm up!" until a parent comes. These children should be moved to regular beds, with guardrails and/or body pillows to prevent rolling and falling-out accidents. If a child is moved to a bed to free the crib for a new baby, this should be done weeks ahead of the infant's arrival if possible, to separate these two significant life events. Most young children are excited about "grown-up" beds. Some, if hesitant, can sleep in the crib and nap in the bed for a gradual transition until ready for the bed full-time.

Considerations in Children's Bedrooms and Family Beds

The majority of early childhood experts think young children should not have adults in their rooms every night while they fall asleep. They believe this can interfere with young children's capacity for "self-soothing" and falling asleep on their own, making them dependent on an adult presence to fall asleep. Parents/caregivers are advised to help children relax until sleepy, and then leave, saying "Good night" and "I love you." Young children frequently feel more comfortable going to bed with a favorite blanket or stuffed animal and/or a night light. Regardless, fears and nightmares are still fairly common in early childhood. "Family beds" (i.e., children sleeping in the same bed or adjacent beds with parents) are subject to controversy. However, this is traditional in many developing countries and was historically so in America. Whatever the individual family choice, it should be consistent, as young children will be frustrated by inconsistent practices and less likely to develop good sleeping habits.

Hygiene in Early Childhood
Importance of Hand-Washing

A major change during early childhood is that hygiene transforms from something adults do for children to something children learn to do themselves. Toddlers are typically learning toilet-training, getting many germs on their hands. Preschoolers today are also often exposed to germs in daycare or school settings. Adults must explain to young children using concrete, easily understood terms how germs spread, how hand-washing removes germs, and when and how to wash their hands. Adults also need to remind children frequently to wash their hands until it becomes a habit. Hand-washing should be required before eating, after toileting, after being outdoors, after sneezing/coughing, and after playing with pets. Because young children have short attention spans and can be impatient, they are unlikely to wash long or thoroughly enough. Adults can encourage this by teaching children to sing "Happy Birthday" or other 15- to 20-second songs/verses while washing, both assuring optimal hand-washing duration and making the process more fun.

Bathing

While infants are bathed by adults, by the time they are toddlers or preschoolers, they generally have learned to sit in a bathtub and wash themselves. However, regardless of their ability to bathe, young children should never be left unsupervised by adults in the bath. Young children can drown very quickly, even in an inch of water; an adult should always be in the bathroom. Also, adults should not let young children run bathwater: they are likely to make it too cold or hot. Adults can prevent scalding accidents by turning down the water heater temperature. The adult should adjust water temperature and test it on his or her own inner arm (an area with more sensitive skin). Parents/caregivers should choose baby shampoos, soaps, and washes that do not irritate young eyes or skin, and keep adult bath products out of children's reach and sight. Very active children may need to bathe daily; others suffering dry, itchy skin should bathe every other day and/or have parents/caregivers apply mild moisturizing lotion.

Promoting and Teaching Dental Hygiene

Even while young children still have their deciduous teeth ("baby" teeth), dental hygiene practices can affect their permanent adult teeth before they erupt. For example, excessive sugar can weaken adult teeth before they even appear above the gumline. Adults should not only teach young children how important it is to brush their teeth twice and floss once daily at a minimum, they should also model these behaviors. Children are far more likely to imitate parents' dental hygiene practices than do what parents only tell them but do not do themselves. Integrating tooth brushing into morning and bedtime routines promotes the habit. Adults can help motivate resistant children with entertaining toothbrushes that play music, spin, light up, and/or have cartoon illustrations. Young children have not developed the fine motor skills sufficient for flossing independently and will need adult supervision until they are older. Individual flossers are easier for them to use with help than traditional string dental floss.

Exercise Benefits for Young Children

Young children need daily physical exercise to strengthen their bones, lungs, hearts, and other muscles. Throwing, catching, running, jumping, kicking, and swinging actions develop young children's gross motor skills. Children sleep better with regular physical activity and are at less risk for obesity. Playing actively with other children also develops social skills, including empathy, sharing, cooperation, and communication. Family playtimes strengthen bonding and let parents model positive exercise habits. Outdoor play is fun for youngsters; running and laughing lift children's moods. Pride at physical attainments moreover boosts children's self-images and self-esteem. At least 60 minutes of physical activity most days is recommended for children. This includes jungle gyms, slides, swings, and other playground equipment; family walks, bike-riding, playing backyard catch, baseball, football, or basketball; adult-supervised races or obstacle courses; and age-appropriate community sports activities/leagues. Adults should plan and supervise activities to prevent injuries. They should also provide repeated sunscreen applications for outdoor activities to prevent sunburn and long-term skin damage.

Exposure to Media and Optimal Environmental Conditions for Leisure Activities

Preschool-aged children are not yet cognitively able to distinguish between reality and fantasy. Therefore, overly violent or intense content in TV or other media can frighten them. Additionally, exposure to video violence has been proven to increase aggressive behaviors in young children. Moreover, using TV as a babysitter for long times excludes more cognitively stimulating and interactive pursuits. Parents/caregivers can provide young children with paints, crayons, and modeling clay. They can play board games and simple card games, do puzzles, sing songs, and read stories with young children. Pretend/make-believe play develops during early childhood, so adults can encourage their playing "house," "dress-up," or "auto shop." Park/playground trips afford outdoor play and physical activity/exercise. Visiting local museums, zoos, or planetariums combine education and entertainment with outings. In multiple-child families, it is important for each child to get some one-on-one time with parents regularly, even in unstructured activities like going to the hardware store with Daddy or keeping Mommy company while she washes dishes.

Economically Deprived and Culturally Diverse Environments

Historically, research on the effects of poverty has been focused on the disadvantages coming from a lack of necessary resources and the presence of risk factors. Due to the lack of resources, children in economically deprived communities commonly have fewer stimulating toys, less diverse verbal interaction, and commonly inadequate nutrition. Other risk factors often include unhealthy family environments, medical illness without treatment, and insufficient social-services, such as education, policing, and medical care. However, more recent research also identifies poverty's advantages, including opportunities for young children to play with peers and older children with little adult intervention, promoting empathy, cooperation, self-control, self-reliance, and sense of belonging; experience with multiple teaching styles, especially modeling, observation, and imitation; and language acquisition within a culturally-specific context through rich cultural traditions of stories, songs, games, and toys. These findings illuminate the resiliency or stress resistance of some children. Recent research also identifies protective factors against risk factors. These protections contribute to child resiliency, including the child's personality traits; having stable, supportive, cohesive family units; and having external support systems promoting positive values and coping skills.

INFLUENCE OF CULTURES AND CULTURAL VALUES ON EARLY CHILDHOOD DEVELOPMENT

The culture in a society influences and determines one's individual values, as do both historical and current social and political occurrences. One's values then influence the ways in which children are valued and raised. American educators can understand the "American" perspective on early childhood better through understanding cultural diversity. Americans tend to fixate on their own culture's beliefs of truth as the only existing reality, but depending on personal histories and values and current conditions, there can actually be multiple right ways of doing things. For example, Western cultures value children's early attainment of independence and individuality, but Eastern cultures value interdependence and group harmony more than individualism. In affluent societies, letting children explore the environment early and freely is valued, but in poor and/or developing societies, parents protect children, keeping them close and even carrying them while working, and thus do not value early freedom and exploration.

EFFECT OF AGE, ETHNICITY, AND INCOME ON HEALTH AND SCHOOL OUTCOMES

Research traces many variations in well-being and health to early childhood. These differences come from inequities in service access and treatment, congenital health problems, and early exposure to greater familial and community risk factors. Child groups at risk that are overrepresented in the American population include young children, low-income children, and minority children. These risk factors also carry a high correlation with one another as minority groups tend to be overrepresented below the **federal poverty level (FPL)** and low-income families statistically carry the highest birth rate. Childhood poverty has long-lasting effects on students' developmental, socioeconomic, and academic success. Furthermore, the earlier a student is in poverty, the more likely they are to encounter the adverse effects of poverty, as they may miss certain milestones or lack the support needed to keep up with their peers.

ENVIRONMENT, SOCIAL AND EMOTIONAL SUPPORT, SELF-IMAGE, AND SUCCESS

Researchers have recently found that a child's sense of self is significant in predicting success in life. Even when a child's family environment involves multiple stressors, having a good relationship with one parent mitigates a child's psychosocial risks. As a child grows older, a close, supportive, lasting relationship with an adult outside the family can confer similar protection. Such relationships promote self-esteem in a child. Children with positive self-esteem are more able to develop feelings of control, mastery, and self-efficacy to achieve tasks, and they are more able to manage stressful life experiences. Such children demonstrate more initiative in forming relationships and accomplishing tasks. They reciprocally derive more positive experiences from their environments. Children with positive self-concepts pursue, develop, and sustain experiences and relationships that support success. Their positive self-images are further enhanced by these successes, generating additional supportive relationships and experiences. While we often hear about negative cycles of poverty, abuse, or failure, positive cycles of success can be equally as self-perpetuating.

INDIVIDUALISTIC VERSUS COLLECTIVISTIC CULTURES

Anthropologists have classified various world cultures along a continuum of how individualistic or interdependent their structures and values are. Investigating these differences is found to afford much insight and application for early childhood education. The predominant culture in America is considered very individualistic. Children are encouraged to assert themselves and make their own choices to realize their highest potentials, with the ultimate goal of individual self-fulfillment. Collectivistic/sociocentric cultures, however, place the highest importance on group well-being; if collective harmony is disrupted by individual assertiveness, such self-assertion is devalued. Some educators characterize this contrast as the difference between standing out (individualist) and fitting in (collectivist). Researchers note that when asked to finish "I am…" statements, members of interdependent cultures tend to supply a family role, religion, or organization (e.g., "a father/a Buddhist"), whereas members of individualistic cultures cite personal qualities (e.g., "intelligent/hardworking"). Research finds American culture most individualistic, Latin American and Asian cultures most interdependent, and European cultures in the middle.

HEALTH STATISTICS RELATED TO RACE AND ETHNICITY

Children are at higher risk for inadequate development when they are born prematurely or with low birth weights. Recent research found racial and ethnic disparities in these birth conditions. For example, average rates of low birth weights between 2018 and 2020 were almost double for African Americans as for whites (14 percent versus 6.9 percent). Latinos had similar but slightly higher risk than whites for low birth weight (7.5 percent versus 6.9 percent). Native American/Alaska Natives had slightly higher risk than whites (8.1 percent versus 6.9 percent), as did Asian/Pacific Islanders (8.6 percent versus 6.9 percent). The CDC reported that in 2017 and 2018, the prevalence of obesity among different racial groups varied greatly. Non-Hispanic Asians reported the lowest average 17.4 percent of obesity, whereas non-Hispanic White demonstrated a 42.2 percent obesity rate, followed by 44.8 percent for Hispanic and 49.6 percent for Non-Hispanic Black adults. These two statistics demonstrate a sample of correlated health risks present among varied socioeconomic groups.

Types of Disabilities and Exceptionalities and their Implications

CAUSES OF INTELLECTUAL DISABILITIES IN BABIES AND YOUNG CHILDREN

INFECTIONS

Congenital cytomegalovirus (CMV) is passed to fetuses from mothers, who may be asymptomatic. About 90% of newborns are also asymptomatic; 5–10% of these have later problems. Of the 10% born with symptoms, 90% will have later neurological abnormalities, including intellectual disabilities. **Congenital rubella**, or German measles, is also passed to fetuses from unvaccinated and exposed mothers, causing neurological damage, including blindness or other eye disorders, deafness, heart defects, and intellectual disabilities. **Congenital toxoplasmosis** is passed to fetuses by infected mothers, who can be asymptomatic, with a parasite from raw or undercooked meat that causes intellectual disabilities, vision or hearing loss, and other conditions. Encephalitis is brain inflammation caused by infection, most often viral. **Meningitis** is inflammation of the meninges, or membranes, covering the brain and is caused by viral or bacterial infection; the bacterial form is more serious. Both encephalitis and meningitis can cause intellectual disabilities. Maternal **human immunodeficiency virus** (HIV) and **acquired immunodeficiency syndrome** (AIDS) can be passed to fetuses, destroying immunity to infections, which can cause intellectual disabilities. **Maternal listeriosis**, a bacterial infection from contaminated food, animals, soil, or water, can cause meningitis and intellectual disabilities in surviving fetuses and infants.

ENVIRONMENTAL, NUTRITIONAL, AND METABOLIC INFLUENCES

Environmental deprivation syndrome results when developing children are deprived of necessary environmental elements—physical, including adequate nourishment (malnutrition); climate or temperature control (extremes of heat or cold); hygiene, like changing and bathing; and so on. It also includes lack of adequate cognitive stimulation, which can stunt a child's intellectual development, and neglect in general. Malnutrition results from starvation; vitamin, mineral, or nutrient deficiency; deficiencies in digesting or absorbing foods; and some other medical conditions. **Environmental radiation**, depending on dosage and time of exposure, can cause intellectual disabilities. **Congenital hypothyroidism** (underactive thyroid) can cause intellectual disabilities, as can hypoglycemia (low blood sugar) from inadequately controlled diabetes or occurring independently and infant **hyperbilirubinemia**. Bilirubin, a waste product of old red blood cells, is found in bile made by the liver and is normally removed by the liver; excessive bilirubin buildup in babies can cause intellectual disabilities. **Reye's syndrome**, caused by aspirin given to children with flu or chicken pox, or following these viruses or other upper respiratory infections, or from unknown causes, produces sudden liver and brain damage and can result in intellectual disabilities.

Genetic Abnormalities and Syndromes Affecting the Nervous System

Rett syndrome is a nervous system disorder causing developmental regression, particularly severe in expressive language and hand function. It is associated with a defective protein gene on an X chromosome. Having two X chromosomes, females with the defect on one of them can survive; with only one X chromosome, males are either miscarried, stillborn, or die early in infancy. Rett syndrome produces many symptoms, including intellectual disabilities. **Tay-Sachs disease**, an autosomal recessive disorder, is a nervous system disease caused by a defective gene on chromosome 15, resulting in a missing protein for breaking down gangliosides, chemicals in nerve tissues that build up in cells, particularly brain neurons, causing damage. Tay-Sachs is more prevalent in Ashkenazi Jews. The adult form is rare; the infantile form is commonest, with nerve damage starting in utero. Many symptoms, including intellectual disabilities, appear at 3 to 6 months, and death occurs by 4 to 5 years. Tuberous sclerosis, caused by genetic mutations, produces tumors damaging the kidneys, heart, skin, brain, and central nervous system. Symptoms include intellectual disabilities, seizures, and developmental delays.

Genetic or Inherited Metabolic Disorders

- **Adrenoleukodystrophy** is an X-linked genetic trait. Some female carriers have mild forms, but it affects more males more seriously. It impairs metabolism of very long-chain fatty acids, which build up in the nervous system (as well as adrenal glands and male testes). The childhood cerebral form, manifesting at ages 4 to 8, causes seizures, visual and hearing impairments, receptive aphasia, dysgraphia, dysphagia, intellectual disabilities, and other effects.
- **Galactosemia** is an inability to process galactose, a simple sugar in lactose, or milk sugar. By-product buildup damages the liver, kidneys, eyes, and brain.
- **Hunter syndrome, Hurler syndrome, and Sanfilippo syndrome** each cause the lack of different enzymes; all cause an inability to process mucopolysaccharides or glycosaminoglycans (long sugar-molecule chains). Hurler and Sanfilippo (but not Hunter) syndromes are autosomal recessive traits, meaning both parents must pass on the defect. All cause progressive intellectual disabilities.
- **Lesch Nyhan syndrome**, affecting males, is a metabolic deficiency in processing purines. It causes hemiplegia, varying degrees of intellectual disabilities, and self-injurious behaviors.
- **Phenylketonuria** (PKU), an autosomal recessive trait, causes lack of the enzyme to process dietary phenylalanine, resulting in intellectual disabilities.

PRESCRIPTION DRUGS, SUBSTANCES OF ABUSE, SOCIAL DRUGS, AND DISEASES

- **Warfarin**, a prescription anticoagulant drug to thin the blood and prevent excessive clotting, can cause microcephaly (undersized head) and intellectual disabilities in an infant when the mother has taken it during pregnancy.
- **Trimethadione**, the prescription antiseizure drug, can cause developmental delays in babies when it has been taken by pregnant mothers.
- **Maternal abuse of solvent chemicals** during pregnancy can also cause microcephaly and intellectual disabilities.
- **Maternal crack cocaine abuse** during pregnancy can cause severe and profound intellectual disabilities and many other developmental defects in fetuses, which become evident when they are newborns.
- **Maternal alcohol abuse** can cause fetal alcohol syndrome, which often includes intellectual disabilities, among many other symptoms.
- **Maternal rubella** (German measles) virus can cause intellectual disabilities as well as visual and hearing impairments and heart defects.
- **Maternal herpes simplex virus** can cause microcephaly, intellectual disabilities, and microphthalmia (small or no eyes).
- **The varicella** (chicken pox) **virus** in pregnant mothers can also cause intellectual disabilities as well as muscle atrophy in babies.

CHARACTERISTICS OF INFANTS AND YOUNG CHILDREN WITH INTELLECTUAL DISABILITIES

Newborns with intellectual disabilities, especially of greater severity, may not demonstrate normal reflexes, such as rooting and sucking reflexes, necessary for nursing. They may not show other temporary infant reflexes such as the Moro, Babinski, swimming, stepping, or labyrinthine reflexes, or they may demonstrate weaker versions of some of these. In some babies, these reflexes will exist but persist past the age when they normally disappear. Babies with intellectual disabilities are likely to display developmental milestones at later-than-typical ages. The ages when they do display milestones vary according to the severity of the disability and by individual. Young children with intellectual disabilities are likely to walk, self-feed, and speak later than normally developing children. Those who learn to read and write do so at later ages. Children with mild intellectual disabilities may lack curiosity and have quiet demeanors; those with profound intellectual disabilities are likely to remain infantile in abilities and behaviors throughout life. Intellectually disabled children will score below normal on standardized IQ tests and adaptive behavior rating scales.

POTENTIAL VARIABLES CAUSING LEARNING DISABILITIES

LDs are basically neurological disorders. Though they are more specific to particular areas of learning than global disorders like intellectual disabilities, scientific research has found correlations between LDs and many of the same factors that cause intellectual disabilities, including prenatal influences like excessive alcohol or other drug consumption, diseases, and so on. Once babies are born, glandular disorders, brain injuries, exposure to secondhand smoke or other toxins, infections of the central nervous system, physical trauma, or malnutrition can cause neurological damage resulting in LDs. Hypoxia and anoxia (oxygen loss) before, during, or after birth is a cause, as are radiation and chemotherapy. These same influences often cause behavioral disorders as well as LDs. Another factor is genetic: Both LDs and behavior disorders have been observed to run in families. While research has not yet identified specific genetic factors, heritability does appear to be a component in influencing learning and behavioral disorders.

Types of Neurological Damage Found in Children with LDs and ADHD

Various neurological research studies have revealed that children diagnosed with LDs and ADHD have at least one of several kinds of structural damage to their brains. Scientists have found smaller numbers of cells in certain important regions of the brains of some children with learning and behavioral disorders. Some of these children are found to have brain cells of smaller than normal size. In some cases, dysplasia is discovered; that is, some brain cells migrate into the wrong area of the brain. In some children with learning and behavioral disorders, blood flow is found to be lower than normal to certain regions in the brain. Also, the brain cells of some children with learning and behavioral disabilities show lower levels of glucose metabolism; glucose (blood sugar) is the brain's main source of fuel, so inadequate utilization of glucose can affect the brain's ability to perform some functions related to cognitive processing, as in LDs, and to attention and impulse control, as in ADHD.

Behavioral Variations and Characteristics of ADHD

While the chief symptoms associated with ADHD are inattentiveness, impulsive behavior, distractibility, and excessive physical activity, there is considerable variation among individual children having ADHD. For example, the degree of severity of this condition can vary widely from one child to the next. In addition, each child can vary in how much he or she exhibits each of these primary characteristics. Some children might not appear to behave very impulsively but show severe deficits in attention. Some may focus better, but only for short periods, and are very easily distracted. Some display very disruptive behavior, while others do not but may daydream excessively, not attending to programming. In general, children who have ADHD can show deficits in following rules and directions. Also, when their developmental skills are evaluated or observed, they are likely to demonstrate inconsistencies in performance over time. To identify or select specific intervention methods and strategies, professionals should use a comprehensive evaluation to obtain information about the child's specific behaviors in his or her natural environment that need remediation.

Types and Characteristics of Learning Disabilities

Dyslexia is the most common subcategory of specific learning disability that primarily affects reading but can also interfere with writing and speaking. Characteristics include reversing letters and words, for example, confusing *b* and *d* in reading and writing; reading *won* as *now*, confusing similar speech sounds like /p/ and /b/, and perceiving spaces between words in the wrong places when reading. **Dyscalculia** is difficulty doing mathematical calculations; it can also affect using money and telling time. Dysgraphia means difficulties specifically with writing, including omitting words in writing sentences or leaving sentences unfinished, difficulty putting one's thoughts into writing, and poor handwriting. **Central auditory processing disorder** causes difficulty perceiving small differences in words despite normal hearing acuity; for example, *couch* and *chair* may be perceived as *cow* and *hair*. Background noise and information overloads exacerbate the effects. Visual processing disorders affect visual perception despite normal visual acuity, causing difficulty finding information in printed text or from maps, charts, pictures, graphs, and so on; synthesizing information from various sources into one place; and remembering directions to locations.

> **Review Video: Disorders that Impair Reading and Writing**
> Visit mometrix.com/academy and enter code: 306758

Attachment Styles Identified in Toddlers by Mary Ainsworth

Mary Ainsworth worked with **John Bowlby**, discovering the first empirical evidence supporting his attachment theory. From her "strange situation" experiments, she identified secure, insecure and avoidant, insecure and resistant, and insecure and disorganized attachment styles. Securely attached children show normal separation anxiety when their mother leaves and happiness when she returns, avoid strangers when alone but are friendly when their mother is present, and use their mother as a safe base for environmental exploring. Insecure and resistant children show exaggerated separation anxiety, ambivalence, and resistance to their mother upon reuniting, fear strangers, cry more, and explore less than secure or avoidant babies. Insecure and avoidant children show no separation anxiety or stranger anxiety and little interest on reunions with their mother and are comforted equally by their mother or strangers. Insecure and disorganized types seem dazed and confused, respond inconsistently, and may mix resistant and ambivalent and avoidant behaviors. Secure styles are associated with sensitive, responsive caregiving and children's positive self-images and other images, resistant and ambivalent styles with inconsistent caregiving, and avoidant with unresponsive caregivers. Avoidant, resistant, and disorganized styles, associated with negative self-images and low self-esteem, are most predictive of emotional disturbances.

EMOTIONAL DISTURBANCES IN YOUNG CHILDREN CLASSIFIED AS ANXIETY DISORDERS

Anxiety disorders all share a common characteristic of overwhelming, irrational, and unrealistic fears and include:

- **Generalized anxiety disorder** (GAD) involves excessive worrying about anything or everything and free-floating anxiety.
- **Obsessive-compulsive disorder** (OCD) involves obsessive and preoccupied thoughts and compulsive or irresistible actions, including often bizarre rituals. Germ phobia, constant hand washing, repeatedly checking whether tasks are done or undone, and collecting things excessively are common.
- **Posttraumatic stress disorder** (PTSD) follows traumatic experiences/events. Children have frequent, extreme nightmares, crying, flashbacks wherein they vividly perceive or believe they are experiencing the traumatic event again, insomnia, depression, anxiety, and social withdrawal.
- **Panic Disorder** symptoms include panic attacks involving extreme fear and physical symptoms like a racing heart, cold hands and feet, pallor, hyperventilation, and feeling unable to move
- **Social phobia** includes fear and avoidance of day care, preschool, or other social settings
- **Specific phobias** are associated with specific objects, animals, or persons and are often triggered by traumatic experiences involving these

FACTORS CONTRIBUTING TO EMOTIONAL DISTURBANCES

Researchers have investigated **emotional disturbances** but have not yet established known causes for any. Some disturbances, for example, the major mental illness **schizophrenia**, seem to run in families and hence include a genetic component; childhood schizophrenia exists as a specific diagnosis. Factors contributing to emotional disturbances can be biological or environmental but more often are likely a combination of both. Dysfunctional family dynamics can often contribute to emotional disorders in children. Physical and psychological stressors on children can also contribute to the development of emotional problems. Some people have attributed emotional disturbances to diet, and scientists have also researched this but have not discovered proof of cause and effect. **Bipolar disorder** is often successfully treated with the chemical lithium, which affects sodium flow through nerve cells, so chemical imbalance may be implicated as an etiology. Pediatric bipolar disorder, which has different symptoms than adult bipolar disorder, correlates highly with histories of bipolar and other mood disorders or alcoholism in both parents.

Symptoms of Pediatric Bipolar Disorder

Bipolar disorder, formerly called manic-depressive disorder, has similar depressive symptoms in children as adults. However, children's mood swings often occur much faster, and children show more symptoms of anger and irritability than other adult manic symptoms. Bipolar children's most common symptoms include:

- Frequent mood swings
- Extreme irritability
- Protracted (up to several hours) tantrums or rages
- Separation anxiety
- Oppositional behavior
- Hyperactivity
- Impulsivity, and distractibility
- Restlessness and fidgetiness
- Silly, giddy, or goofy behavior
- Aggression
- Racing thoughts
- Grandiose beliefs or behaviors
- Risk-taking
- Depressed moods
- Lethargy
- Low self-esteem
- Social anxiety
- Hypersensitivity to environmental or emotional triggers
- Carbohydrate (sugar or starch) cravings
- Trouble getting up in the morning

Other common symptoms include bed-wetting (especially in boys), night terrors, pressured or fast speech, obsessive or compulsive behaviors, motor and vocal tics, excessive daydreaming, poor short-term memory, poor organization, learning disabilities, morbid fascinations, hypersexuality, bossiness and manipulative behavior, lying, property destruction, paranoia, hallucinations, delusions, and suicidal ideations. Less common symptoms include migraines, bingeing, self-injurious behaviors, and animal cruelty.

Conduct Disorder in Children

Factors contributing to conduct disorders in children include genetic predispositions, neurological damage, child abuse, and other traumatic experiences. Children with conduct disorders display characteristic emotional and behavioral patterns. These include aggression: They bully or intimidate others, often start physical fights, will use dangerous objects as weapons, exhibit physical cruelty to animals or humans, and assault and steal from others. Deliberate property destruction is another characteristic—breaking things or setting fires. Young children are limited in some of these activities by their smaller size, lesser strength, and lack of access; however, they show the same types of behaviors against smaller, younger, weaker, or more vulnerable children and animals, along with oppositional and defiant behaviors against adults. Also, while truancy is impossible or unlikely in preschoolers, and running away from home is less likely, young children with conduct disorders are likely to demonstrate some forms of seriously violating rules, another symptom of this disorder.

Symptoms of Childhood-Onset Schizophrenia

The incidence of childhood-onset schizophrenia is rare, but it does exist. One example of differential diagnosis involves distinguishing qualitatively between true auditory hallucinations and young children's "hearing voices" otherwise: in the latter case, a child hears his or her own or a familiar adult's voice in his or her head and does not seem upset by it, while in the former, a child may hear other voices, seemingly in his or her ears, and is frightened and confused by them. Tantrums, defiance, aggression, and other acting-out, externalized behaviors are less frequent in childhood-onset schizophrenia than internalized developmental differences, for example, isolation, shyness, awkwardness, fickleness, strange facial expressions, mistrust, paranoia, anxiety, and depression. Children demonstrate nonpsychotic symptoms earlier than psychotic ones. However, it is difficult to use prepsychotic symptoms as predictors due to variance among developmental peculiarities. While psychiatrists find the course of childhood-onset schizophrenia somewhat more variable than in adults, child symptoms resemble adult symptoms. Childhood-onset schizophrenia is typically chronic and severe, responds less to medication, and has a more guarded prognosis than adolescent- or adult-onset schizophrenia.

Diagnosing the Emotional Disturbances in Children as Psychotic Disorders

Psychosis is a general psychiatric category referring to thought disturbances or disorders. The most common symptoms are delusions (believing things that are not true) and hallucinations (seeing, hearing, feeling, tasting, or smelling things that are not there). While early childhood psychosis is rarer than at later ages, psychiatrists confirm it does occur. Moreover, prognosis is poorer for psychosis with onset in early childhood than in adolescence or adulthood. Causes can be from known metabolic or brain disorders or unknown. Younger children are more vulnerable to environmental stressors. Also, in young children, thoughts distorted by fantasy can be from normal cognitive immaturity, due to lack of experience and a larger range of normal functioning, or pathology; where they lie on this continuum must be determined by clinicians. Believing one is a superhero who can fly can be vivid imagination or delusional; having imaginary friends can be pretend play or hallucinatory. Other developmental disorders can also cloud differential diagnosis.

Visual Impairments

Developmental Characteristics of Infants and Young Children with Visual Impairments

Historically, it was thought that visually impaired children developed more slowly than normal; however, it is now known that ages for reaching developmental milestones are equally variable in visually impaired babies as in others and that they acquire milestones within equal age ranges. One developmental difference is in sequence: visually impaired children tend to utter their first words or subject-verb two-word sentences earlier than other children. Some visually impaired children also demonstrate higher levels of language development at younger-than-typical ages. For example, they may sing songs from memory or recall events from the past at earlier ages than other children. This is a logical development in children who must rely more on input to their hearing and other senses than to their vision when the latter is impaired. Totally blind babies reach for objects later, hence explore the environment later; hand use, eye-hand coordination, and gross and fine motor skills are delayed. Blind infants' posture control develops normally (rolling, sitting, all-fours, and standing), but mobility (raising on arms, pulling up, and walking) is delayed.

Causes of Visual Impairments in Babies and Young Children

Syndrome-related and other malformations like cleft iris or lens dislocation causing visual impairment can have prenatal origins. Cataracts clouding the eye's lens can be congenital, traumatic, or due to maternal rubella. Eyes can be normal, but impairment in the brain's visual cortex can cause visual impairment. Infantile glaucoma, like adult glaucoma, causes intraocular fluid buildup pressure and visual impairment. Conjunctivitis and other infections cause visual impairment. Strabismus and nystagmus are ocular-muscle conditions, respectively causing eye misalignments and involuntary eye movements. Trauma damaging the eyeball(s) is another visual impairment cause. The optic nerve can suffer from atrophy (dysfunction) or hypoplasia, that is, developmental regression, usually prenatally due to neurological trauma; acuity cannot be corrected. Refractive errors like nearsightedness, farsightedness, and astigmatism are correctable. Retinoblastoma, or behind-the-eye tumors, can cause blindness and fatality; surgical or chemotherapeutic treatment is usually required before age 2. Premature infants can have retinopathy of prematurity or retrolental fibroplasia. Cryotherapeutic treatment seems to stop disease progression. Its effects range from none to severe visual impairment (approximately 25% of children) to complete blindness.

IMPACTS OF BLINDNESS UPON COGNITIVE DEVELOPMENT

Blind children have more difficulty determining and confirming characteristics of things, hence defining concepts and organizing them into more abstract levels; their problem-solving is active but harder, and they construct different realities than sighted children. Blind babies typically acquire object permanence (the understanding that unseen objects still exist) a year later than normal; they learn to reach for objects only by hearing. Understanding cause-and-effect relationships is difficult without visual evidence. Blind babies and toddlers take longer to understand an object's constancy regardless of their orientation in space, affecting their ability to orient toys and their own hands. Blind children can identify object size differences and similarities, but classifying object differences and similarities in other attributes requires longer times and more exposures to various similar objects. Blind children's development of the abilities to conserve object properties like material or substance, weight, amount and volume, length, and liquid volume is later than normal.

EFFECTS OF BLINDNESS ON EMOTIONAL AND SOCIAL DEVELOPMENT

Blind babies and children are more dependent than others on adults, affecting development. With control of their inner realities but not of their outer environments, blind children may withdraw, seeking and responding less to social interaction. They may not readily develop concepts of the external world or self-concepts as beings separate from the world and the understanding that they can be both agents and recipients of actions relative to the environment. Mother-infant smiling initiates recognition, attachment, and communication in sighted babies; blind infants smile on hearing mother's voice at 2 months. Only tactile stimuli like tickling and nuzzling evoke regular smiling in blind babies. Missing facial expressions and other visual cues, blind children have more complicated social interactions. They often do not understand the basics of playing with others and seem emotionally ambivalent or uninterested and uncommunicative. Peers may reject or avoid them; adults often overprotect them. Self-help skills like chewing, scooping, self-feeding, teeth brushing, grooming, and toilet training are delayed in blind children.

HEARING IMPAIRMENTS

PREVALENCE AND ETIOLOGIES OF HEARING IMPAIRMENTS

Half or more (50% to 60%) of infant hearing losses have genetic origins—Down and other genetically based syndromes or the existence of parental hearing loss. About 25% or more of infant hearing losses are caused by maternal infections during pregnancy, such as cytomegalovirus (CMV), postnatal complications like blood transfusions or infection with meningitis, or traumatic head injuries. Included in this 25% or more are babies having nongenetic neurological disorders or conditions that affect their hearing. Malformations of the ears, head, or face can cause hearing loss in babies. Babies spending five days or longer in neonatal intensive care units (NICUs) or having complications while in the NICU are also more likely to suffer hearing loss. Around 25% of babies are diagnosed with hearing loss whose etiology is unknown.

Signs of Hearing Impairments

If an infant does not display a startle response to loud noises, this is a potential sign of hearing loss. This can also indicate other developmental disabilities, but because hearing loss is the most prevalent disability among newborns, hearing screening is a priority. Between birth and 3 or 4 months old, babies should turn toward the source of a sound; if they do not, it could indicate hearing loss. A child who does not utter first words like *mama* or *dada* by age 1 could have hearing impairment. When babies or young children do not turn their heads when their names are called, adults may mistake this for inattention or ignoring; however, children turning upon seeing adults, but not upon hearing their names, can indicate hearing loss. Babies and children who seem to hear certain sounds but not others may have partial hearing losses. Delayed speech-language development or unclear speech, not following directions, saying "Huh?" often, and wanting higher TV or music volumes can indicate hearing loss in children.

Speech and Language Impairments

Factors Contributing to Speech and Language Impairments

Some speech and language disorders in children have unknown causes. Others have known causes such as hearing loss: speech and language are normally acquired primarily through the auditory sense, so children with impaired hearing have delayed and impaired development of speech and language. Brain injuries, neurological disorders, viral diseases, and some medications can also cause problems with developing language or speech. Children with intellectual disabilities are more likely to have delayed language development, and their speech is also more likely to develop more slowly and to be distorted. Cerebral palsy causes neuromuscular weakness and incoordination of speech. When severe, it can cause the inability to produce recognizable speech sounds; some children without speech can still vocalize, and some cannot. A cleft palate or lip and other physical impairments affect speech. Inadequate speech-language modeling at home inhibits speech-language development. Vocal abuse in children (screaming, coughing, throat clearing, or excessive talking) can cause vocal nodules or polyps, causing voice disorders. Stuttering can be related to maturation, anxiety or stress, auditory feedback defects, or unknown causes.

Characteristics

In speech, most phonological disorders are articulatory; that is, children fail to pronounce specific speech sounds or phonemes correctly beyond the normal developmental age for achieving accuracy. Stuttering, disfluency, and rate and rhythm disorders cause children to repeat phonemes, especially initial word sounds; to repeat words; to prolong vowels or consonants; or to block, straining so hard to produce a sound that, pressure builds, but no sound issues. Their speech rates may also increase and decrease irregularly. Children with voice disorders can have voices that sound hoarse, raspy, overly nasal, higher- or lower-pitched than normal, overly weak or strident, and whispery or harsh. Hoarseness is common with vocal nodules and polyps. Cleft palate commonly causes hypernasality. In language, one of the most common impairments is delayed language development due to environmental deprivation, intellectual disabilities, neurological damage or defects, hearing loss, visual impairment, and so on. Children with neurological damage or disorders may exhibit aphasias, language disorders characterized by receptive difficulty with understanding spoken or written language, or expressive difficulty constructing spoken or written language.

Physical and Health Impairments
Examples of Physical and Health Impairments

In the special education field of early childhood education, "other health impairment" is a term referring to health and physical conditions that rob a child of strength, vitality, or alertness or that cause excessive alertness to environmental stimuli, all having the end result of impeding the child's ability to attend or respond to the educational environment. Health problems can be acute(short-term or temporary but serious) or chronic (long-term, persistent, or recurrent). Some examples of such health and physical impairments include cerebral palsy, spina bifida, amputations or missing limbs, muscular dystrophy, cystic fibrosis, asthma, rheumatic fever, sickle-cell anemia, nephritis or kidney disease, leukemia, Tourette syndrome, hemophilia, diabetes, heart disease, AIDS, and lead poisoning. All these conditions and others can interfere with a child's development and ability to attend and learn. In addition to seizure disorders, which often cause neurological damage, seizure-controlling medications also frequently cause drowsiness, interfering with attention and cognition. Attention deficit and attention deficit hyperactivity disorders (ADD and ADHD) limit attention span, focus, and concentration and thus are sometimes classified as health impairments requiring special education services.

Characteristics of Babies and Children with Physical and Health Impairments

The characteristics of children having various physical or health impairments can range from having no limitations to severe limitations in their activities. Children with cerebral palsy, for example, usually have deficiencies in gross and fine motor development and deficits in speech-language development. Physical and health conditions causing severe debilitation in some children not only seriously limit their daily activities but also cause multiple primary disabilities and impair their intellectual functioning. Other children with physical or health impairments function at average, above-average, or gifted intellectual and academic levels. An important consideration when working with babies and young children having physical or health impairments is handling and positioning them physically. Correctly picking up, holding, carrying, giving assistance, and physically supporting younger children and arranging play materials for them based on their impairment is not only important for preventing injury, pain, and discomfort; it also enables them to receive instruction better and to manipulate materials and perform most efficiently. Preschoolers with physical impairments also tend to have difficulty with communication skills, so educators should give particular attention to facilitating and developing these.

Developmental Delays
Factors Leading to Developmental Delays

Developmental delays can come from genetic or environmental causes or both. Infants and young children with intellectual disabilities are most likely to exhibit developmental delays. Their development generally proceeds similarly to that of normal children but at slower rates; milestones are manifested at later-than-typical ages. Sensory impairments such as with hearing and vision can also delay many aspects of children's development. Children with physical and health impairments are likely to exhibit delays in their motor development and performance of physical activities. Another factor is environmental: children deprived of adequate environmental stimulation commonly show delays in cognitive, speech-language, and emotional and social development. Children with autism spectrum disorders often have markedly delayed language and speech development; many are nonverbal. Autistic children also typically have impaired social development, caused by an inability or difficulty with understanding others' emotional and social nonverbal communications. When they cannot interpret these, they do not know how to respond and also cannot imitate them; however, they can often learn these skills with special instruction.

Characteristics Indicating Developmental Delays

Developmental delays mean that a child does not reach developmental milestones at the expected ages. For example, if most babies normally learn to walk between 12 and 15 months of age, a 20-month-old who is not beginning to walk is considered as having a developmental delay. Delays can occur in cognitive, speech-language, social-emotional, gross motor skill, or fine motor skill development. Signs of delayed motor development include stiff or rigid limbs, floppy or limp body posture for the child's age, using one side of the body more than the other, and clumsiness unusual for the child's age. Behavioral signs of children's developmental delays include inattention or shorter-than-normal attention span for the age, avoiding or infrequent eye contact, focusing on unusual objects for long times or preferring objects over social interaction, excessive frustration when attempting tasks normally simple for children their age, unusual stubbornness; aggressive and acting-out behaviors; daily violent behaviors, rocking, excessive talking to oneself, and not soliciting love or approval from parents.

Traumatic Brain Injury (TBI)
IDEA's Legal Definition of Traumatic Brain Injury

TBI is defined by the **IDEA law** (the Individuals with Disabilities Education Act) as "an acquired injury to the brain from external physical force, resulting in total or partial functional disability or psychosocial impairment, or both, that adversely affect a child's educational performance." This definition excludes injuries from birth trauma, congenital injuries, and degenerative conditions. TBI is the foremost cause of death and disability in children (and teens) in the USA. The most common causes of TBI in children include falls, motor vehicle accidents, and physical abuse. In spite of the IDEA's definition, aneurysms and strokes are three examples of internal traumas that can also cause TBI in babies and young children. External head injuries that can result in TBI include both open and closed head injuries. Shaken baby syndrome is caused by forcibly shaking an infant. This causes the brain literally to bounce against the insides of the skull, causing rebound injuries, resulting in TBI and even death.

> **Review Video: Medical Conditions in Education**
> Visit mometrix.com/academy and enter code: 531058

Characteristics

TBI can impair a child's cognitive development and processing. It can impede the language development of children, which is dependent upon cognitive development. Children who have sustained TBI often have difficulties with attention, retention, and memory; reasoning, judgment, understanding abstract concepts, and thinking abstractly; and problem-solving abilities. TBIs can also impair a child's motor functions and physical abilities. The sensory and perceptual functions of children with TBI can be abnormal. Their ability to process information is often compromised. Their speech can also be affected. In addition, TBIs can impair a child's psychosocial behaviors. Memory deficits are commonest, tend to be more long-lasting, and are often area-specific; for example, a child may recall personal experiences but not factual information. Other common characteristics of TBI include cognitive inflexibility or rigidity, damaged conceptualization and reasoning, language loss or poor verbal fluency, problems with paying attention and concentrating, inadequate problem solving, and problems with reading and writing.

Etiologies and Characteristics of Multiple Disabilities

The term *multiple disabilities* refers to any combination of more than one disabling condition. For example, a child may be both blind and deaf due to causes such as having rheumatic fever in infancy or early childhood. Anything causing neurological damage before, during, or shortly after birth can result in multiple disabilities, particularly if it is widespread rather than localized. For example, infants deprived of oxygen or suffering traumatic brain injuries in utero, during labor or delivery, or postnatally can sustain severe brain damage. So can babies having encephalitis or meningitis and those whose mothers abused drugs prenatally. Infants with this type of extensive damage can often present with multiple disabilities, including intellectual disabilities, cerebral palsy, physical paralysis, mobility impairment, visual impairment, hearing impairment, and speech-language disorders. They may have any combination of or all of these disabilities as well as others. In addition to a difficulty or inability with normal physical performance, multiple disabled children often have difficulty acquiring and retaining cognitive skills and transferring or generalizing skills among settings and situations.

Prematurity or Preterm Birth

Babies born before 37 weeks' gestation are classified as **premature** or **preterm**. Premature infants can have difficulty with breathing, as their lungs are not fully developed, and with regulating their body temperatures. Premature infants may be born with pneumonia, respiratory distress, extra air or bleeding in the lungs, jaundice, sepsis or infection, hypoglycemia (low blood sugar), severe intestinal inflammation, bleeding into the brain or white-matter brain damage, or anemia. They have lower-than-normal birth weights, body fat, muscle tone, and activity. Additional typical characteristics of premature infants include apnea (interrupted breathing); lanugo (a coating of body hair that full-term infants no longer have); thin, smooth, shiny, translucent skin through which veins are visible; soft, flexible ear cartilage; cryptorchidism (undescended testicles) and small, non-ridged scrotums in males; enlarged clitorises in females; and feeding difficulties caused by weak or defective sucking reflexes or incoordination of swallowing with breathing.

Disabling Conditions Resulting from Premature Births

Physicians find it impossible to predict the long-term results of prematurity for any individual baby based on an infant's gestational age and birth weight. However, some related immediate and long-term effects can be identified. Generally, the lower the birth weight and the more prematurely a child is born, the greater the risk is for complications. Infants born at less than 34 weeks of gestation typically cannot coordinate their sucking and swallowing and may temporarily need feeding or breathing tubes or oxygen. They also need special nursery care until able to maintain their body temperatures and weights. Long-term complications of prematurity can include bronchopulmonary dysplasia, a chronic lung condition; delayed physical growth and development; delayed cognitive development; mental or physical delays or disabilities; and blindness, vision loss, or retinopathy of prematurity (formerly called retrolental fibroplasia). While some premature infants sustain long-term disabilities, some severe, other babies born prematurely grow up to show no effects at all; any results within this range can also occur.

Factors that Affect Health and Development

Heredity, Environment, and Behavior

Heredity, environment, and behavior contribute to overall health:

- **Hereditary** factors are traits passed within a family that can impact one's health in both negative and positive ways. For example, a family history of heart disease and cancer can negatively impact risk of disease, and a family history of long life can positively affect longevity.

- Environment refers to the **physical environment** (e.g., polluted air and water, unsafe home, etc.) and the social environment (e.g., substance abuse in the home, partner abuse, etc.). Both can impact health.
- **Behavior** refers to **personal** choices that impact health. These behaviors include decisions on tobacco and alcohol use, drinking and driving, and dietary choices.

These elements interact to positively and negatively impact health. For example, a person with a family history of cancer (**hereditary factor**) should avoid excessive sun exposure, eat a high-fiber/low-fat diet, and receive more frequent cancer screenings (**behaviors**) than a person without the hereditary risk. As another example, one who is aware of a family history of heart disease (**hereditary factor**) and therefore chooses to eat a balanced, low-fat, high-protein diet and exercise (**behavior**) can reduce their risk. As a final example, a person with a family history of lung disease (**hereditary factor**) may decide to live in an area with reduced air pollution (**environment**) and choose not to smoke tobacco (**behaviors**).

EFFECT OF NUTRITION ON GROWTH AND DEVELOPMENT

An adequate and **balanced diet** is a key element in proper growth and development. A balance of carbohydrates, proteins, fats, fiber, and minerals is necessary for the growth, development, functioning, and repair of the body. **Dietary deficiencies** of these nutritional building blocks can lead to health problems early in life with some that can extend into adulthood. For example, a diet consisting of whole grains with carbohydrates, fibers, and vitamins not only provides proper nutrition to growing bodies, but also provides energy allowing for increased exercise tolerance. A quality, balanced diet goes hand-in-hand with **physical activity** to maintain desired body weight and regulate blood sugars. Good dietary habits established early in life, when combined with physical activity, often extend into adulthood to maintain health as one ages.

EFFECT OF EXERCISE ON GROWTH AND DEVELOPMENT

Early development of bones and muscles are the foundation of proper growth. **Exercise** helps develop necessary bone mass and density, which can reduce the likelihood of osteoporosis and other bone diseases. Proper exercise also reduces the risk of heart disease and diabetes later in life. In addition to **disease prevention**, proper levels of exercise/physical activity increase coordination, balance, posture, and flexibility. It is recommended children aged 6–17 perform 60 minutes of aerobic exercise per day, combined with muscle strengthening exercises (e.g., pushups, rope climbing, etc.) and bone strengthening exercises (e.g., jumping, running, etc.) at least three times per week.

EFFECT OF SLEEP ON GROWTH AND DEVELOPMENT

Proper sleep directly impacts growth, stress hormones, the immune system, respiration, and cardiovascular function. **Lack of sleep** is linked to obesity, heart disease, and increased infections later in life. **Adequate sleep** is linked to improved exercise outcomes because of the increased time given for muscle recovery. In addition, **growth hormones** which are critical to proper growth and development are released during sleep. It is recommended that:

- **Preschool children** (3–5 years) should sleep 10–13 hours during each 24-hour period.
- **Elementary school children** (6–12) should sleep 9–12 hours during each 24-hour period.
- **Teenagers** (13–18) should sleep 8–10 hours each 24-hour period.
- **Adults** (18–60) should sleep 7 or more hours each 24-hour period.

Key signs that one is receiving **enough sleep** include the ability to sleep through the night with minimal interruption, and awakening rested and alert.

Relationship Between Diet and Exercise

Personal health behaviors often have the greatest impact upon lifetime health, and many of these behaviors begin early in life. One of these key behaviors is eating a **balanced diet**, like one based on the **Healthy Plate Model**. A healthy diet combined with adequate, regular exercise have a cumulative effect on reducing obesity, the leading cause of **morbidity and mortality** (i.e., disease and death) in the U.S. It is recommended that one participate in at least 150 minutes of moderate physical activity or 75 minutes of vigorous activity each week. This should include a balance between **aerobic** exercise (i.e., activities that make a person breath hard and sweat), and **strengthening** exercises (i.e., activities that focus on increasing muscle mass and flexibility).

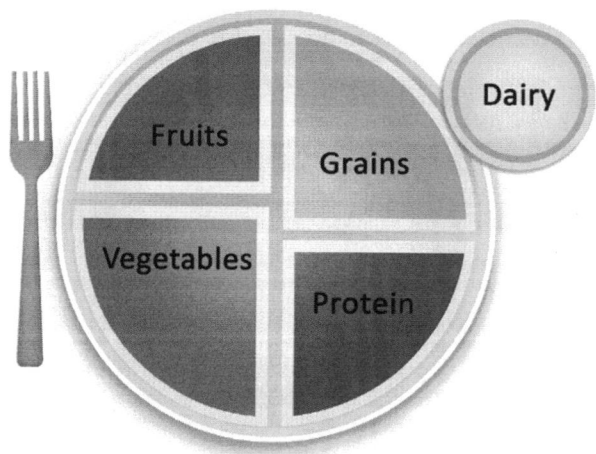

Common Changes Occurring in Puberty

The onset of **puberty** can occur as early as elementary school (8–12 years of age) or as late as high school (13–15 years of age) and can create a host of **physical and emotional** responses. Often these include changes in **personal hygiene** (e.g., increased showering due to body odor, use of feminine hygiene products in response to the start of the menstrual cycle). For females, puberty typically consists of beginning of the **menstrual cycle**, changes in body shape, breast tenderness, and hair growth. In males, puberty is characterized by acne, genital growth, hair growth, deepening of the voice, height and muscle growth, erections, and nocturnal emissions. Though the physical changes are the most obvious, the **emotional and social** impacts on personal health can be profound. Youth going through puberty often become more self-conscious, experience dramatic mood swings, develop a sexual interest in others, and experience changes in sleep patterns and energy levels. Given that sexuality is an uncomfortable topic for many parents, it is not uncommon for students to have little to no information about puberty. This creates further anxiety and confusion among many students.

Overview of Human Developmental Theories

Issues of Human Development

Historically, there have been a number of arguments that theories of human development seek to address. These ideas generally lie on a spectrum but are often essential concepts involved in developmental theories. For instance, the nature vs. nurture debate is a key concept involved in behaviorist camps of development, insisting that a substantial portion of a child's development may be attributed to his or her social environment.

- **Universality vs. context specificity**: Universality implies that all individuals will develop in the same way, no matter what culture they live in. Context specificity implies that development will be influenced by the culture in which the individual lives.
- **Assumptions about human nature** (three doctrines: original sin, innate purity, and tabula rasa):
  - Original sin says that children are inherently bad and must be taught to be good.
  - Innate purity says that children are inherently good.
  - Tabula rasa says that children are born as "blank slates" without good or bad tendencies and can be taught right and wrong.
- **Behavioral consistency**: Children either behave in the same manner no matter what the situation or setting or they change their behavior depending on the setting and who is interacting with them.
- **Nature vs. nurture**: Nature refers to the genetic influences on development. Nurture refers to the environmental and social influences on development.
- **Continuity vs. discontinuity**: Continuity states that development progresses at a steady rate and that the effects of change are cumulative. Discontinuity states that development progresses in a stair-step fashion and that the effects of early development have no bearing on later development.
- **Passivity vs. activity**: Passivity refers to development being influenced by outside forces. Activity refers to development influenced by the child him or herself and how he or she responds to external forces.
- **Critical vs. sensitive period**: The critical period is the window of time when the child will be able to acquire new skills and behaviors. The sensitive period refers to a flexible time period when a child will be receptive to learning new skills, even if it is later than the norm.

Theoretical Schools of Thought on Human Development

- **Behaviorist Theory** – This philosophy discusses development in terms of conditioning. As children interact with their environments, they learn what behaviors result in rewards or punishments and develop patterns of behaviors as a result. This school of thought lies heavily within the nurture side of the nature/nurture debate, arguing that children's personalities and behaviors are a product of their environments.
- **Constructivist Theory** – This philosophy describes the process of learning as one in which individuals build or construct their understanding from their prior knowledge and experiences in an environment. In constructivist thought, individuals can synthesize their old information to generate new ideas. This school of thought is similar to behaviorism in that the social environment plays a large role in learning. Constructivism, however, places greater emphasis on the individual's active role in the learning process, such as the ability to generate ideas about something an individual has not experienced directly.

- **Ecological Systems Theory** – This philosophy focuses on the social environments in and throughout a person's life. Ecological systems theorists attempt to account for all of the complexities of various aspects of a person's life, starting with close relationships, such as family and friends, and zooming out into broader social contexts, including interactions with school, communities, and media. Alongside these various social levels, ecological systems discuss the roles of ethnicity, geography, and socioeconomic status in development across a person's lifespan.
- **Maturationist Theory** – This philosophy largely focuses on the natural disposition of a child to learn. Maturationists lean heavily into the nature side of the nature/nurture argument and say that humans are predisposed to learning and development. As a result, maturationists propose that early development should only be passively supported.
- **Psychoanalytic Theory** – Psychoanalytic theorists generally argue that beneath the conscious interaction with the world, individuals have underlying, subconscious thoughts that affect their active emotions and behaviors. These subconscious thoughts are built from previous experiences, including developmental milestones and past traumas. These subconscious thoughts interact with conscious thoughts to form a person's desires, personality, attitudes, and habits.

Freud's Psychosexual Developmental Theory

Sigmund Freud was a neurologist who founded the psychoanalytic school of thought. He described the distinction between the conscious and unconscious mind and the effects of the unconscious mind on personality and behavior. He also developed a concept of stages of development, in which an individual encounters various conflicts or crises, called psychosexual stages of development. The way in which an individual handles these crises were thought to shape the individual's personality over the course of life. This general formula heavily influenced other psychoanalytic theories.

Erikson's Psychosocial Developmental Theory

Eric Erikson's psychosocial development theory was an expansion and revision of Freud's psychosexual stages. Erikson describes eight stages in which an individual is presented with a crisis, such as an infant learning to trust or mistrust his or her parents to provide. The choice to trust or mistrust is not binary, but is on a spectrum. According to the theory, the individual's resolution of the crisis largely carries through the rest of his or her life. Handling each of the eight conflicts well theoretically leads to a healthy development of personality. The conflicts are spaced out throughout life, beginning at infancy and ending at death.

Kohlberg's Stages of Moral Development

Kohlberg's stages of moral development are heavily influenced by Erikson's stages. He describes three larger levels of moral development with substages. In the first level, the **preconventional level**, morality is fully externally controlled by authorities and is motivated by the avoidance of punishment and pursuit of rewards. In the second level, the **conventional level**, the focus shifts to laws, social factors, and the pursuit of being seen by others as good or nice. In the third and final level, the **postconventional** or **principled level**, the individual looks beyond laws and social obligations to more complex situational considerations. A person in this stage might consider that a law may not always be the best for individuals or society and that a particular situation may warrant breaking the rule for the true good.

George Herbert Mead's Play and Game Stage Development Theory

George Herbert Mead was a sociologist and psychologist who described learning by stepping into **social roles**. According to his theory, children first interact with the world by imitating and playing by themselves. While engaged in this play, a child can experiment with concepts. Mead describes this development in terms of three stages characterized by increasing complexity of play. A child in the **preparatory stage** can **play** pretend and learn cooking concepts by pretending to cook. As a child develops socially, he or she learns to step in and out of increasingly abstract and complex **roles** and includes more interaction. This is known as the **play stage**, including early interactive roles. For instance, children may play "cops and robbers," which are more symbolically significant roles because they are not natural roles for children to play in society. As social understanding develops, children enter the **game stage**, in which the child can understand his or her own role and the roles of others in a game. In this stage, children can participate in more complex activities with highly structured rules. An example of a complex game is baseball, in which each individual playing has a unique and complex role to play. These stages are thought to contribute to an individual's ability to understand complex social roles in adulthood.

IVAN PAVLOV

Ivan Pavlov was a predecessor to the behaviorist school and is credited with being the first to observe the process of classical conditioning, also known as Pavlovian conditioning. Pavlov observed that dogs would begin salivating at the sound of a bell because they were conditioned to expect food when they heard a bell ring. According to classical conditioning, by introducing a neutral stimulus (such as a bell) to a naturally significant stimulus (such as the sight of food), the neutral stimulus will begin to create a conditioned response on its own.

JOHN B. WATSON

Watson is credited as the founder of behaviorism and worked to expand the knowledge base of conditioning. He is famous for his experiments, including highly unethical experiments such as the "Little Albert" experiment in which he used classical conditioning to cause an infant to fear animals that he was unfamiliar with. Watson proposed that psychology should focus only on observable behaviors.

B.F. SKINNER

Skinner expanded on Watson's work in behaviorism. His primary contributions to behaviorism included studying the effect of **reinforcement** and **punishment** on particular behaviors. He noted that stimuli can be both additive or subtractive and may be used to either increase or decrease behavior frequency and strengths.

LEV VYGOTSKY

Vygotsky's sociocultural theory describes development as a social process in which individuals mediate knowledge through social interactions and can learn by interacting with and watching others. Vygotsky's ideas have been widely adopted in the field of education, most notably his theory of the **zone of proximal development**. This theory describes three levels of an individual's ability to do tasks, including completely incapable of performing a task, capable with assistance, and independently capable. As an individual's experience grows, he or she should progress from less capable and independent to more capable and independent.

> **Review Video: Instructional Scaffolding**
> Visit mometrix.com/academy and enter code: 989759

BANDURA'S SOCIAL LEARNING THEORY

Albert Bandura's social learning theory argues against some of the behaviorist thoughts that a person has to experience stimulus and response to learn behaviors and, instead, posits that an individual can learn from other peoples' social interactions. Bandura would say that most learning takes place from observing and predicting social behavior, not through direct experience. This becomes a more efficient system for learning because people are able to learn information more synthetically.

Bowlby's Attachment Theory

Bowlby's attachment theory describes the impact that early connections have on lifelong development. Working from an evolutionary framework, Bowlby described how infants are predisposed to be attached to their caregivers because this increases chance of survival. According to Bowlby's theory, infants are predisposed to stay close to known caregivers and use them as a frame of reference to help with learning what is socially acceptable and what is safe.

Piaget's Cognitive Development Theory

Piaget's theory of cognitive development describes how as individuals develop, their cognitive processes are able to become more complex and abstract. In the early stages, an infant may be able to recognize an item, such as a glass of water, on sight only. As that individual grows, he or she is able to think, compare, and eventually develop abstract thoughts about that concept. According to Piaget, this development takes place in all individuals in predictable stages.

Maslow's Hierarchy of Needs

Maslow defined human motivation in terms of needs and wants. His **hierarchy of needs** is classically portrayed as a pyramid sitting on its base divided into horizontal layers. He theorized that, as humans fulfill the needs of one layer, their motivation turns to the layer above. The layers consist of (from bottom to top):

- **Physiological**: The need for air, fluid, food, shelter, warmth, and sleep
- **Safety**: A safe place to live, a steady job, a society with rules and laws, protection from harm, and insurance or savings for the future
- **Love/belonging**: A network consisting of a significant other, family, friends, co-workers, religion, and community
- **Esteem or self-respect**: The knowledge that you are a person who is successful and worthy of esteem, attention, status, and admiration

- **Self-actualization**: The acceptance of your life, choices, and situation in life and the empathetic acceptance of others, as well as the feeling of independence and the joy of being able to express yourself freely and competently

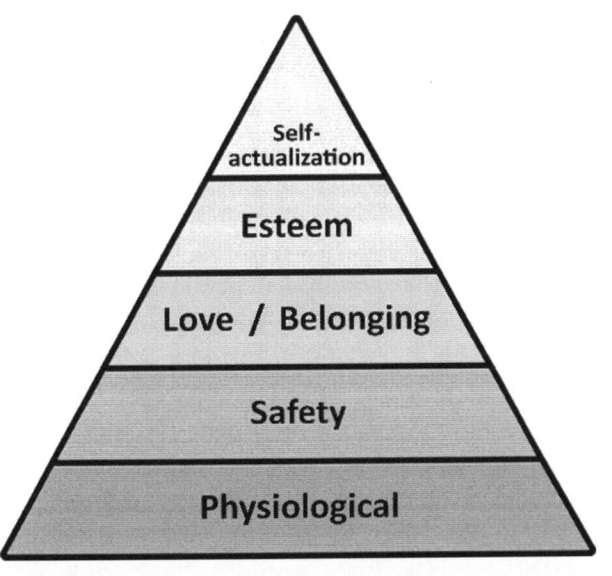

Review Video: **Maslow's Hierarchy of Needs**
Visit mometrix.com/academy and enter code: 461825

Cognitive Development

PIAGET'S THEORY OF COGNITIVE DEVELOPMENT

Jean Piaget's theory of cognitive development consists of four stages that a child moves through throughout life. The four stages are the **sensorimotor stage** (birth-2 years), **preoperational stage** (2-7 years), **concrete operational stage** (7-11 years), and **formal operational stage** (12 years and beyond). Piaget believed that the way children think changes as they pass through these stages. In the **sensorimotor stage**, infants exist in the present moment and investigate their world for the first time through their senses, reflexes, and actions. Key skills infants acquire during this stage include object permanence and self-recognition. In the **preoperational stage**, children learn to express ideas symbolically, including through language and pretend play. Markers of this stage include engaging in animism, egocentrism, and the inability to understand conservation (the knowledge that the quantity of something does not change when its appearance does). In the **concrete operational stage**, children develop logical thought and begin understanding conservation. The **formal operational stage** brings the ability to think abstractly and hypothetically. Piaget believed that children learn through experimenting and building upon knowledge from experiences. He asserted that educators should be highly qualified and trained to create experiences that support development in each of these stages.

Review Video: **Piaget's Cognitive Development Theory**
Visit mometrix.com/academy and enter code: 100376

Skills Typically Acquired at Each Stage of Cognitive Development

- **Sensorimotor:** Children in the sensorimotor stage gain an increasing awareness of their bodies and the world around them and acquire a wide range of skills as they mature from infancy to toddlerhood. Early skills at this stage include sucking, tasting, smiling, basic vocalizations, and **gross motor skills** such as kicking and grasping. These skills increase in complexity over time and come to include abilities such as throwing and dropping objects, crawling, walking, and using simple words or phrases to communicate. As children near the end of this stage, they are typically able to exhibit skills such as stacking, basic problem solving, planning methods to achieve a task, and attempting to engage in daily routines, such as dressing themselves or brushing their hair.
- **Preoperational:** This stage is marked by significant leaps in **cognition** and **gross motor skills**. Children in the preoperational stage are able to use increasingly complex language to communicate, and they develop skills like jumping, running, and climbing as they gain increasing control over their bodies. Preoperational children begin learning the basic categorization of alike objects, such as animals, flowers, or foods. This stage is also characterized by the development of pretend play and includes skills such as creating imaginary friends, role playing, and using toys or objects to symbolize something else, such as using a box as a pretend house.
- **Concrete operational:** In this stage, children begin developing **logical reasoning** skills that allow them to perform increasingly complex tasks. Concrete operational children are able to distinguish subcategories, including types of animals, foods, or flowers, and can organize items in ascending or descending order based upon characteristics like height, weight, or size. Children at this stage develop the understanding that altering the appearance of an object or substance does not change the amount of it. A classic example of this is the understanding that liquid transferred from one container to another retains its volume. This concept is known as **conservation**.
- **Formal operational:** The formal operational stage is characterized by the development of **abstract** and **hypothetical** cognitive skills. Children at this stage are able to solve increasingly complex math equations, hypothesize and strategically devise a plan for engaging in science experiments, and develop creative solutions to problems. They are also able to theorize potential outcomes to hypothetical situations as well as consider the nuances of differing values, beliefs, morals, and ethics.

Substages of the Sensorimotor Stage

Piaget's sensorimotor stage is divided into six substages. In each, infants develop new skills for representing and interacting with their world. In the first substage, infants interact **reflexively** and involuntarily to stimuli in the form of muscle jerking when startled, sucking, and gripping. Subsequent stages are circular, or repetitive, in nature and are based on interactions with the self and, increasingly, the environment. **Primary circular reactions**, or intentionally repeated actions, comprise the second substage. Infants notice their actions and sounds and purposefully repeat them, but these actions do not extend past the infant's body. Interaction with the environment begins in the third substage as infants engage in **secondary circular reactions**. Here, infants learn that they can interact with and manipulate objects within their environment to create an effect, such as a sound from pressing a button. They then repeat the action and experience joy in this ability. In the fourth substage, secondary circular reactions become coordinated as infants begin planning movements and actions to create an effect. **Tertiary circular reactions** allow for exploration in the fifth substage, as infants start experimenting with cause and effect. In the sixth substage, infants begin engaging in **representational thought** and recall information from memory.

EXAMPLES OF PRIMARY, SECONDARY, AND TERTIARY CIRCULAR REACTIONS

The following are some common examples of primary, secondary, and tertiary circular reactions:

- **Primary:** Primary circular reactions are repeated **bodily** actions that the infant finds enjoyable. Such actions include thumb sucking, placing hands or feet in the mouth, kicking, and making basic vocalizations.
- **Secondary:** Secondary circular reactions refer to repeated enjoyable interactions between the infant and objects within their **environment** in order to elicit a specific response. Such actions include grasping objects, rattling toys, hitting buttons to hear specific sounds, banging two objects together, or reaching out to touch various items.
- **Tertiary:** Tertiary circular reactions are intentional and planned actions using objects within the environment to **achieve a particular outcome**. Examples include stacking blocks and knocking them down, taking toys out of a bin and putting them back, or engaging in a repeated behavior to gauge a caretaker's reaction each time.

DEFINING CHARACTERISTICS OF THE PREOPERATIONAL STAGE OF DEVELOPMENT

The preoperational stage of development refers to the stage before a child can exercise operational thought and is associated with several defining characteristics including **pretend play**, **animism**, and **egocentrism**. As children learn to think and express themselves symbolically, they engage in pretend play as a means of organizing, understanding, and representing the world around them as they experience it. During this stage, children do not understand the difference between inanimate and animate objects and thus demonstrate animism, or the attribution of lifelike qualities to inanimate objects. Egocentrism refers to the child's inability to understand the distinction between him or herself and others and, consequentially, the inability to understand the thoughts, perspectives, and feelings of others. During the preoperational stage, the brain is not developed enough to understand **conservation**, which is the understanding that the quantity of something does not change just because its appearance changes. Thus, children in this stage exhibit **centration**, or the focusing on only one aspect of something at a time. Additionally, children struggle with **classification** during this stage, as they are not cognitively developed enough to understand that an object can be classified in multiple ways.

MILESTONES ACHIEVED DURING THE CONCRETE OPERATIONAL STAGE OF DEVELOPMENT

The concrete operational stage marks the beginning of a child's ability to think logically about the concrete world. In this stage, children develop many of the skills they lacked in the preoperational phase. For example, egocentrism fades as children in this stage begin to develop empathy and understand others' perspectives. Additionally, they develop an understanding of conservation, or the idea that the quantity of something does not change with its appearance. Children in this stage begin to learn to classify objects in more than one way and can categorize them based on a variety of characteristics. This allows them to practice **seriation**, or the arranging of objects based on quantitative measures.

DEVELOPMENT OF COGNITIVE ABILITIES IN THE FORMAL OPERATIONAL STAGE

In the formal operational stage, children can think beyond the concrete world and in terms of abstract thoughts and hypothetical situations. They develop the ability to consider various outcomes of events and can think more creatively about solutions to problems than in previous stages. This advanced cognitive ability contributes to the development of personal identity. In considering abstract and hypothetical ideas, children begin to formulate opinions and develop personal stances on intangible concepts, thus establishing individual character. The formal operational stage continues to develop through adulthood as individuals gain knowledge and experience.

LEV VYGOTSKY'S THEORY OF COGNITIVE DEVELOPMENT

Lev Vygotsky's theory on cognitive development is heavily rooted in a **sociocultural** perspective. He argued that the most important factors for a child's cognitive development reside in the cultural context in which the child grows up and social interactions that they have with adults, mentors, and more advanced peers. He believed that children learn best from the people around them, as their social interactions, even basic ones such as smiling, waving, or facial expressions, foster the beginning of more complex cognitive development. He is well-known for his concept of the **Zone of Proximal Development (ZPD)**, which is the gap between what a child can do independently and what the child can do with assistance from a more advanced individual or a collaborator. He believed that children could move through the ZPD and complete increasingly complicated tasks when receiving assistance from more cognitively advanced mentors. According to Vygotsky, children develop the most when passing through the ZPD. Vygotsky's contributions are heavily embedded in modern education and often take the form of teacher-led instruction and scaffolding to assist learners as they move through the ZPD.

Zone of Proximal Development

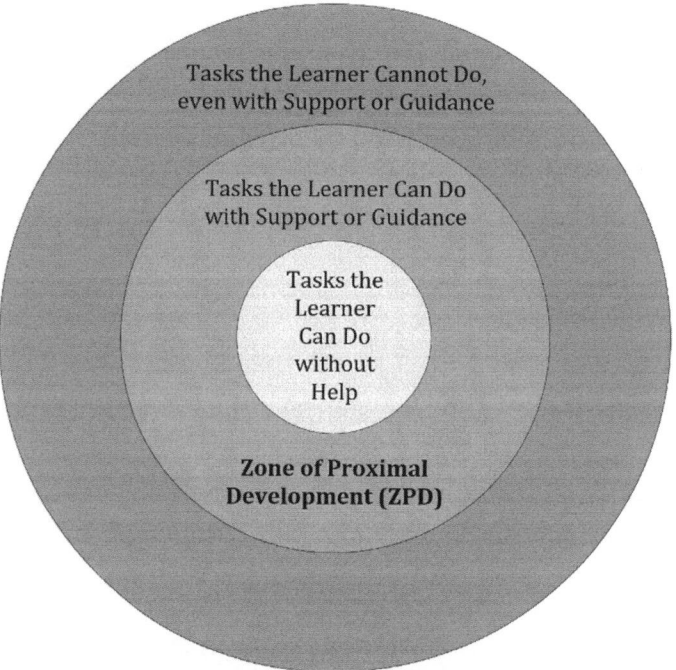

Review Video: **Zone of Proximal Development (ZPD)**
Visit mometrix.com/academy and enter code: 555594

Social and Emotional Development

ERIK ERIKSON'S EIGHT STAGES OF PSYCHOSOCIAL DEVELOPMENT

Erik Erikson defined eight predetermined stages of psychosocial development from birth to late adulthood in which an individual encounters a crisis that must be resolved to successfully transition to the next stage. The first is **trust vs. mistrust** (0-18 months), where the infant learns that the world is safe and that caregivers can be trusted to tend to his or her basic needs. The next stage is **autonomy vs. shame** (18 months-3 years), where children learn to control their actions and establish independence. In the **initiative vs. guilt stage** (3-5 years), children acquire a sense of purpose and initiative through social interactions. Next, children enter the **industry vs. inferiority stage** (6-11 years), where they develop mastery and pride in completing a task. The next stage is **identity vs. role confusion** (12-18 years), in which children explore and develop characteristics that will comprise their identities and determine their roles in society. The sixth stage is **intimacy vs. isolation** (19-40 years), where one forms relationships by sharing the identity developed in the previous stage with others. **Generativity vs. stagnation** (40-65 years) occurs in middle adulthood and focuses on contributing to society's next generation through finding one's life purpose. The last stage is **ego integrity vs. despair** (65 to death), in which one reflects on the productivity and success of his or her life.

EXPECTED BEHAVIORS AT EACH STAGE OF PSYCHOSOCIAL DEVELOPMENT

Stage	Examples of expected behaviors
Trust vs. mistrust	In this stage, the infant's primary goal is ensuring the fulfillment of his or her **basic needs**. Infants will cry or make other vocalizations to indicate to caregivers when they want something, such as to be fed or picked up. Separation anxiety from parents is also typical during this stage.
Autonomy vs. shame	Children in this stage begin attempting to perform daily tasks **independently**, such as making food, dressing themselves, bathing, or combing their hair. As children in this stage begin to realize they have a separate identity, they often begin attempting to assert themselves to parents and caregivers.
Initiative vs. guilt	Children at this stage often begin actively engaging and playing with other children. In play settings, these children will often assume **leadership roles** among a group of peers, create new games or activities, and devise their own rules for them. The initiative vs. guilt stage is also characterized by the development of feelings of sadness or guilt when making a mistake or hurting another's feelings.
Industry vs. inferiority	In this stage, children begin attempting to master concepts or skills with the intention of seeking **approval** and **acceptance** from others, particularly those older than themselves, in order to secure a feeling of competency. Children in this stage often become more involved in striving to succeed academically, extracurricular activities, and competitive sports.
Identity vs. role confusion	This stage is characterized by experimentation and uncertainty as young adolescents strive to establish an **independent identity**. Typical behaviors include interacting with new peer groups, trying new styles of dress, engaging in new activities, and considering new beliefs, values, and morals. As young adolescents in this stage are impressionable, they may potentially engage in risky or rebellious behavior as a result of peer pressure.
Intimacy vs. isolation	Individuals in this stage have typically established their identities and are ready to seek **long-term relationships**. This stage marks the development of a social network composed of close friends and long-term romantic partners.

Stage	Examples of expected behaviors
Generativity vs. stagnation	During this stage, individuals begin engaging in **productive** activities to benefit others and elicit personal fulfillment. Such activities include advancing in a career, parenting, or participating in community service projects.
Integrity vs. despair	This stage occurs at the end of one's life and is characterized by **reflection** upon lifetime accomplishments and positive contributions to society. Doing so allows the individual to assess whether his or her purpose was fulfilled and begin accepting death.

INCORPORATING LIFE SKILLS INTO CURRICULUM

In addition to academic achievement, the ultimate goal of education is to develop the whole child and provide a successful transition to independence and adulthood. Incorporating valuable life skills, such as decision-making, goal setting, organization, self-direction, and workplace communication, in early childhood through grade 12 is vital in ensuring students become productive contributors to society. Furthermore, the implementation of these life skills in early childhood is integral in allowing children to successfully progress in independence and maturity. The acquisition of such skills instills in students the self-motivation and ability to set goals, make decisions on how to effectively organize and manage time to complete them, and overcome obstacles. Additionally, teaching students to apply these skills promotes effective communication when working with others toward a goal. Through incorporating life skills into curriculum, teachers instill a growth mindset and foster self-empowered, confident lifelong learners with the necessary tools to navigate real-life situations and achieve success as they transition to adulthood. In the classroom, activities that promote leadership skills, cooperative learning, goal setting, self-monitoring, and social interaction foster an increasing sense of independence as children develop.

EXTERNAL ENVIRONMENTAL FACTORS ON SOCIAL AND EMOTIONAL DEVELOPMENT

Social and emotional development is heavily influenced by a child's home environment. Children learn social and emotional skills such as self-regulation, self-awareness, coping, and relationship building through modeling from parents and caregivers. A positive and supportive home environment is integral for proper social and emotional development. External factors, including lack of affection and attention, parental divorce, and homelessness, pose profound negative impacts on this development. In terms of social development, such external factors could lead to attachment or abandonment issues as well as distrust. Furthermore, children exposed to negative environmental factors could struggle in forging relationships, cooperating, and following societal rules. Emotionally, negative impacts on development cause aggression, poor self-regulation, insecurity, anxiety, isolation, and depression. Since developmental domains are interconnected, the impacts that external factors have on social and emotional development ultimately damage cognitive and physical development. Underdeveloped social skills impair cognitive development because the inability to properly interact with peers impedes the ability to learn from them. Additionally, inadequate emotional skills can inhibit concentration and understanding in school, thus inhibiting cognitive development. Physically, struggling to interact with others leads to impaired development of gross and fine motor skills as well as large muscle development that would be achieved through play.

Physical Development

PHYSICAL CHANGES OCCURRING IN EARLY CHILDHOOD THROUGH ADOLESCENCE

EARLY CHILDHOOD

As children pass through stages of development from early childhood through middle childhood and adolescence, they experience significant physical changes. Children in early childhood experience rapid growth in height and weight as they transition away from physical characteristics of infancy. In this stage, children begin to gain independence as they develop and improve upon gross and fine motor skills. Throughout early childhood, children develop the ability to walk and run, and as they mature through this stage, they learn to throw, catch, climb, and hop. Of the locomotive skills listed, walking comes first, running and climbing can develop simultaneously, and hopping or jumping comes last. They improve in their fine motor skills and learn to hold and manipulate small objects such as zippers and buttons and can grasp writing utensils to create shapes, letters, and drawings with increasing accuracy.

MIDDLE CHILDHOOD

Physical growth varies for individual children in middle childhood, as some children begin experiencing prepubescent bodily changes. Children in middle childhood experience further improvements and refinements of gross and fine motor skills and coordination. Significant physical and appearance changes occur in adolescence as children enter puberty. These changes often occur quickly, resulting in a period of awkwardness and lack of coordination as adolescents adjust to this rapid development.

IMPACT OF EXTERNAL FACTORS ON PHYSICAL DEVELOPMENT

As children pass through physical development stages from early childhood to adolescence, it is important that environmental factors are supportive of proper growth and health. Physical development can be hindered by external factors, such as poor nutrition, lack of sleep, prenatal exposure to drugs, and abuse, as these can cause significant and long-lasting negative consequences. Exposure to such factors can lead to stunted physical growth, impaired brain development and function, poor bone and muscle development, and obesity. Furthermore, the negative impacts from such external factors ultimately impedes cognitive, social, and emotional development. Impaired brain development and function negatively affect cognitive development by impacting the ability to concentrate and grasp new concepts. In terms of emotional development, physical impairments due to external factors can cause a child to become depressed, withdrawn, aggressive, prone to low self-esteem, and unable to self-regulate. Improper physical growth and health impacts social development in that physical limitations could hinder a child's ability to properly interact with and play with others. Impacted brain development and function can limit a child's ability to understand social cues and norms.

Language Development

STAGES OF LANGUAGE DEVELOPMENT

The first stage of language development and acquisition, the **pre-linguistic stage**, occurs during an infant's first year of life. It is characterized by the development of gestures, making eye contact, and sounds like cooing and crying. The **holophrase** or **one-word sentence stage** develops in infants between 10 and 13 months of age. In this stage, young children use one-word sentences to communicate meaning in language. The **two-word sentence stage** typically develops by the time a child is 18 months old. Each two-word sentence usually contains a noun or a verb and a modifier, such as "big balloon" or "green grass." Children in this stage use their two-word sentences to communicate wants and needs. **Multiple-word sentences** form by the time a child is two to two and a half years old. In this stage, children begin forming sentences with subjects and predicates, such as "tree is tall" or "rope is long." Grammatical errors are present, but children in this stage begin demonstrating how to use words in appropriate context. Children ages two and a half to three years typically begin using more **complex grammatical structures**. They begin to include grammatical structures that were not present before, such as conjunctions and prepositions. By the age of five or six, children reach a stage of **adult-like language development**. They begin to use words in appropriate context and can move words around in sentences while maintaining appropriate sentence structure. Language development and acquisition has a wide range of what is considered normal development. Some children do not attempt to speak for up to two years and then may experience an explosion of language development at a later time. In these cases, children often emerge from their silent stage with equivalent language development to babies who were more expressive early on. A child who does not speak after two years, however, may be exhibiting signs of a developmental delay.

ORAL LANGUAGE DEVELOPMENT

Oral language development begins well before students enter educational environments. It is learned first without formal instruction, with **environmental factors** being a heavy influence. Children tend to develop their own linguistic rules as a result of genetic disposition, their environments, and how their individual thinking processes develop. Oral language refers to both speaking and listening. Components of oral language development include phonology, syntax, semantics, morphology, and pragmatics. **Phonology** refers to the production and recognition of sounds. **Morphology** refers to how words are formed from smaller pieces, called morphemes. **Semantics** refers to the meaning of words and phrases and has overlap with morphology and syntax, as morphemes and word order can both change the meaning of words. Semantic studies generally focus on learning and understanding vocabulary. **Syntax** refers to how words and morphemes are combined to make up meaningful phrases. In English, word order is the primary way that many components of grammar are communicated. Finally, **pragmatics** refers to the practical application of language based on various social situations. For instance, a college student is likely to use different vocabulary, complexity, and formality of language when speaking with a professor than when speaking with his or her peer group. Each of these five components of language are applied in oral language. Awareness and application of these components develops over time as students gain experience and education in language use. **Oral language development** can be nurtured by caregivers and teachers well before children enter educational environments. Caregivers and teachers can promote oral language development by providing environments full of language development opportunities. Additionally, teaching children how conversation works, encouraging interaction among children, and demonstrating good listening and speaking skills are good strategies for nurturing oral language development.

> **Review Video: Components of Oral Language Development**
> Visit mometrix.com/academy and enter code: 480589

Helping Students Develop Oral Language Abilities

Children pick up oral language skills in their home environments and build upon these skills as they grow. Early language development is influenced by a combination of genetic disposition, environment, and individual thinking processes. Children with **oral language acquisition difficulties** often experience difficulties in their **literacy skills**, so activities that promote good oral language skills also improve literacy skills. **Strategies** that help students develop oral language abilities include developing appropriate speaking and listening skills; providing instruction that emphasizes vocabulary development; providing students with opportunities to communicate wants, needs, ideas, and information; creating language learning environments; and promoting auditory memory. Developing appropriate speaking and listening skills includes teaching turn-taking, awareness of social norms, and basic rules for speaking and listening. Emphasizing **vocabulary development** is a strategy that familiarizes early learners with word meanings. Providing students with opportunities to **communicate** is beneficial for developing early social skills. Teachers can create **language learning environments** by promoting literacy in their classrooms with word walls, reading circles, or other strategies that introduce language skills to students. Promoting **auditory memory** means teaching students to listen to, process, and recall information.

> **Review Video: Types of Vocabulary Learning (Broad and Specific)**
> Visit mometrix.com/academy and enter code: 258753

Helping Students Monitor Errors in Oral Language

Oral language is the primary way people communicate and express their knowledge, ideas, and feelings. As oral language generally develops, their **speaking and listening skills** become more refined. This refinement of a person's language is called fluency, which can be broken down into the subdisciplines of language, reading, writing, speaking, and listening. **Speaking fluency** usually describes the components of rate, accuracy, and prosody. **Rate** describes how fast a person can speak, and **prosody** describes the inflection and expressions that a person puts into speech. **Accuracy** describes how often a person makes an error in language production. In early stages of language development, individuals generally do not have enough language knowledge to be able to monitor their own speech production for errors and require input from others to notice and correct their mistakes. As an individual becomes more proficient, he or she will be able to monitor his or her own language usage and make corrections to help improve fluency. In the classroom, the teacher needs to be an active component of language monitoring to help facilitate growth. Teachers can monitor **oral language errors** with progress-monitoring strategies. Teachers can also help students monitor their own **oral language development** as they progress through the reading curriculum. Students can monitor their oral language by listening to spoken words in their school and home environments, learning and practicing self-correction skills, and participating in reading comprehension and writing activities. Students can also monitor oral language errors by learning oral language rules for phonics, semantics, syntax, and pragmatics. These rules typically generalize to developing appropriate oral language skills.

EXPRESSIVE AND RECEPTIVE LANGUAGE

Expressive language refers to the aspects of language that an individual produces, generally referring to writing and speaking. **Receptive language** refers to the aspects of language that an individual encounters or receives and generally refers to reading and listening. Both expressive and receptive language are needed for communication from one person to another.

	Expressive	Receptive
Written	Writing	Reading
Oral	Speaking	Listening

EXPRESSIVE LANGUAGE SKILLS

Expressive language skills include the ability to use vocabulary, sentences, gestures, and writing. People with good **expressive language skills** can label objects in their environments, put words in sentences, use appropriate grammar, demonstrate comprehension verbally by retelling stories, and more. This type of language is important because it allows people to express feelings, wants, needs, thoughts, ideas, and individual points of view. Strong expressive language skills include pragmatic knowledge, such as using gestures and facial expressions or using appropriate vocabulary for the listener or reader and soft skills, such as checks for comprehension, use of analogies, and grouping of ideas to help with clarity. Well-expressed language should be relatively easy for someone else to comprehend.

RECEPTIVE LANGUAGE SKILLS

Receptive language refers to a person's ability to perceive and understand language. Good receptive language skills involve gathering information from the environment and processing it into meaning. People with good **receptive language skills** perceive gestures, sounds, words, and written information well. Receptive language is important for developing appropriate communication skills. Instruction that targets receptive language skills can include tasks that require sustained attention and focus, recognizing emotions and gestures, and listening and reading comprehension. Games that challenge the players to communicate carefully, such as charades or catchphrase, can be a great way to target receptive language skills. As one student tries to accurately express an idea with words or gestures, the rest of the class must exercise their receptive language skills. Lastly, focusing on **social skills and play skills instruction** encourages opportunities for children to interact with their peers or adults. This fosters receptive language skills and targets deficits in these skills.

STAGES OF LITERACY DEVELOPMENT

The development of literacy in young children is separated into five stages. Names and ranges of these stages sometimes vary slightly, but the stage milestones are similar. Stage 1 is the **Emergent Reader stage**. In this stage, children ages 6 months to 6 years demonstrate skills like pretend reading, recognizing letters of the alphabet, retelling stories, and printing their names. Stage 2 is the **Novice/Early Reader stage** (ages 6–7 years). Children begin to understand the relationships between letters and sounds and written and spoken words, and they read texts containing high-frequency words. Children in this stage should develop orthographic conventions and semantic knowledge. In Stage 3, the **Decoding Reader stage**, children ages 7–9 develop decoding skills in order to read simple stories. They also demonstrate increased fluency. Stage 4 (ages 8–15 years) is called the **Fluent, Comprehending/Transitional Reader stage**. In this stage, fourth to eighth graders read to learn new ideas and information. In Stage 5, the **Expert/Fluent Reader stage**, children ages 16 years and older read more complex information. They also read expository and narrative texts with multiple viewpoints.

> **Review Video: Stages of Reading Development**
> Visit mometrix.com/academy and enter code: 121184

RELATIONSHIP BETWEEN LANGUAGE DEVELOPMENT AND EARLY LITERACY SKILLS

Language development and early literacy skills are interconnected. **Language concepts** begin and develop shortly after birth with infant/parent interactions, cooing, and then babbling. These are the earliest attempts at language acquisition for infants. Young children begin interacting with written and spoken words before they enter their grade school years. Before they enter formal classrooms, children begin to make **connections** between speaking and listening and reading and writing. Children with strong speaking and listening skills demonstrate strong literacy skills in early grade school. The development of **phonological awareness** is connected to early literacy skills. Children with good phonological awareness recognize that words are made up of different speech sounds. For example, children with appropriate phonological awareness can break words (e.g., "bat" into separate speech sounds, "b-a-t"). Examples of phonological awareness include rhyming (when the ending parts of words have the same or similar sounds) and alliteration (when words all have the same beginning sound). Success with phonological awareness (oral language) activities depends on adequate development of speech and language skills.

PROMOTING LITERACY DURING THE EARLY STAGES OF LITERACY DEVELOPMENT

Teachers and parents can implement strategies at different stages of literacy development in order to build **good reading skills** in children with and without disabilities. During the **Emergent Reader stage**, teachers and parents can introduce children to the conventions of reading with picture books. They can model turning the pages, reading from left to right, and other reading conventions. Book reading at this stage helps children begin to identify letters, letter sounds, and simple words. Repetitive reading of familiar texts also helps children begin to make predictions about what they are reading. During the **Novice/Early Reader** and **Decoding Reader stages**, parents and teachers can help children form the building blocks of decoding and fluency skills by reading for meaning and emphasizing letter-sound relationships, visual cues, and language patterns. In these stages, increasing familiarity with sight words is essential. In the **Fluent, Comprehending/Transitional Reader stage**, children should be encouraged to read book series, as the shared characters, settings, and plots help develop their comprehension skills. At this stage, a good reading rate (fluency) is an indicator of comprehension skills. **Expert/Fluent readers** can independently read multiple texts and comprehend their meanings. Teachers and parents can begin exposing children to a variety of fiction and non-fiction texts before this stage in order to promote good fluency skills.

> **Review Video: Phonics (Encoding and Decoding)**
> Visit mometrix.com/academy and enter code: 821361
>
> **Review Video: Fluency**
> Visit mometrix.com/academy and enter code: 531179

Developmental Delays

DEVELOPMENTAL DIFFERENCES ENCOUNTERED AND STRATEGIES TO ADDRESS THEM

Cognitive, physical, social, and emotional milestones through which children pass as they mature are approximate, and development in any domain depends on the individual child as well as countless environmental factors that comprise each child's unique situation; therefore, a teacher will encounter multiple variations in cognitive, physical, social, and emotional development in students that pose significant implications for instructional planning. Cognitively, a teacher will encounter several intelligences and learning styles. Teachers will encounter students with various learning disabilities, gifted and talented students, or English Language Learners. Physically, students grow and develop at individual rates, and teachers will encounter students with varying physical abilities or limitations. Social developmental differences vary as well and are heavily influenced by environmental factors. Variances in social cues, norms, relationship building, and communication are based on a child's culture and environment. Emotional development, such as self-regulation and coping, are also impacted by environment. Such an array of differences requires a teacher to be trained to recognize the prior knowledge and learning needs of his or her students in order to effectively teach to those differences. Strategies to achieve this include adjusting curriculum, activities, and assessments to match individual student needs, providing necessary scaffolds, and differentiating instruction to access learners of all abilities.

EFFECT OF DEVELOPMENTAL DELAYS ON LEARNING EXPERIENCES AND ASSESSMENTS

Developmental delays in any domain pose significant potential impacts on learning experiences and assessments through affecting comprehension and participation. A delay in cognitive development could impact information processing times, information retention, and the ability to understand complex ideas, thus hindering comprehension and ultimately impacting the willingness to participate. A student with a physical developmental delay may struggle with fine and gross motor skills that prevent effective participation in class activities that would improve comprehension of new instruction. Students with social developmental delays may have difficulty properly expressing a need for assistance, thus potentially discouraging participation and overall comprehension. Furthermore, students with social or emotional developmental delays may be withdrawn, depressed, anxious, or have behavioral issues that impede their self-motivation and ability to focus, thus affecting comprehension and willingness to participate. These potential impacts can have long-lasting consequences on students' overall learning experiences, and early recognition is imperative for instilling the proper accommodations for each student.

ACCOMMODATIONS TO ASSIST STUDENTS WITH DEVELOPMENTAL DELAYS

In order to create an equitable and inclusive environment, the teacher must have an understanding of the developmental characteristics of each student. Furthermore, the teacher must be able to use this knowledge to make the proper accommodations to the curriculum, instruction, and assessments in such a way that addresses individual needs and abilities across the domains of development. Modifications should be specific to the student and his or her individual needs and should provide the necessary support to allow for success in learning. Such accommodations may include scaffolding to break instruction into smaller, more manageable pieces, extended work time for assignments and assessments, shorter work periods with frequent breaks, reduced ratio of students to teacher, individualized instruction, and preferential seating based on the student's need for proximity. Additionally, students may require accommodations to address physical developmental delays, including scribes, text to speech for assignments, or enlarged fonts. Providing accommodations to address individual needs in the four areas of development allows for the teacher to effectively assess student progress and ultimately allows for success in learning.

Recognizing Signs of Developmental Delays or Impairments

Although each child develops at a different pace, there are often indicators that a student is not developing at a similar rate as his or her peers. Developmental delays or impairments can be cognitive, physical, emotional, or social. Some common indicators of developmental delays include lower-than-average assessment scores, difficulty concentrating and retaining new information, difficulty socializing or communicating with others, limited vocabulary compared to others in the same age group, clumsiness, and difficulty holding small objects. Delays can be difficult to detect, but a teacher can recognize signs through observing students and analyzing their progress across subject areas compared to their peers. Early recognition and detection are beneficial in early intervention and developing treatment plans for these students that can improve their progress both inside and outside of the classroom.

Chapter Quiz

Ready to see how well you retained what you just read? Scan the QR code to go directly to the chapter quiz interface for this study guide. If you're using a computer, simply visit the online resources page at **mometrix.com/resources719/westeearchsped** and click the Chapter Quizzes link.

Assessment and Program Development

Transform passive reading into active learning! After immersing yourself in this chapter, put your comprehension to the test by taking a quiz. The insights you gained will stay with you longer this way. Scan the QR code to go directly to the chapter quiz interface for this study guide. If you're using a computer, simply visit the online resources page at **mometrix.com/resources719/westeearchsped** and click the Chapter Quizzes link.

Screening in Early Childhood

SCREENING FOR PARTICULAR DELAY CRITERION

Initial screenings are required, but if a young child has been screened for developmental disorders or delays within the past 6 months and no changes have been observed or reported, repeat screening may be waived. Hearing and vision screenings are mandatory when screening young children. Formal developmental measures are also required, which may include screening tests of motor skills development, cognitive development, social-emotional development, and self-help skills development. Formal screening tests of speech-language development are also required. Additional tests recommended during screening include informal measures. For example, checklists, rating scales, and inventories may be used to screen a child's behavior, mood, and performance of motor skills, cognitive skills, self-help skills, and social and emotional skills. On checklists, parents or caregivers check whether the child does or does not demonstrate listed behaviors, or assessors may complete them via parent or caregiver interviews or interviewing and observing the child. Rating scales ask parents, caregivers, and assessors to rate a child's behaviors, affect, mood, and so on, within a range of numbered and labeled descriptions. Inventories list demonstrated skills and needs. Behavioral observations and existing records and information are also used.

> **Review Video: Developmental Screening Strategies**
> Visit mometrix.com/academy and enter code: 100353

FEATURES OF DEVELOPMENTAL SCREENINGS AND EVALUATIONS

If a child's development is suspected of being delayed—for example, the child is not reaching developmental milestones during expected age ranges—a developmental screening may be administered. Screening tests are quickly performed and yield more general results. The hospital or doctor's office may give a questionnaire to the parent or caregiver to complete for a screening. Alternatively, a health or education professional may administer a screening test to the child. Screening tests are not intended to diagnose specific conditions or give details; they are meant to identify children who may have some problem. Screenings can overidentify or under-identify developmental delays in children. Hence, if the screening identifies a child as having developmental delays, the child is then referred for a developmental evaluation—a much longer, more thorough, comprehensive, in-depth assessment using multiple tests, administered by a psychologist or other highly-trained professional. Evaluation provides a profile of a child's strengths and weaknesses in all developmental domains. Determination of needs for early intervention services or treatment plans is based on evaluation results.

Developmental Evaluation Data Types

The child's social history should be obtained, which is typically done by a social worker. Details of the child's developmental progress up until present day; the family's composition, socioeconomic status, and situation; and the child's and family's health and medical histories and status should be emphasized. A physician's or nurse's medical assessment is required, including a **physical examination** and, if indicated, a specialist's examination. A psychologist typically assesses intellectual and **cognitive development**; at least one such test is generally required. At least one test of adaptive behavior is also required to assess **emotional-social development**. **Self-help skills** are evaluated; this may be included within cognitive, adaptive behavior, or programming assessments. **Communication skills** are typically evaluated by a speech-language pathologist. Both receptive and expressive language must be tested comprehensively rather than simply by single-word vocabulary tests. As indicated, **speech articulation** is also tested. At least one test of **motor skills**, typically administered by a physical or occupational therapist, is required. **Programming** evaluation requires at least one criterion-referenced or curriculum-based measure, typically administered by an educator.

Child Find

Child Find is an ongoing process with the aim of locating, identifying, and referring young children with disabilities and their families as early as possible for service programs. This process consists of activities designed to raise public awareness and screenings and evaluations to identify and diagnose disabilities. The federal IDEA law mandates under Part B that disabled children are guaranteed early childhood special education services and under Part C that infants and toddlers at risk for developmental delays are guaranteed early intervention programs. (Eligibility guidelines vary by US state.) The IDEA requires school districts to find, identify, and evaluate children with disabilities in their attendance areas. School districts have facilitated this Child Find process by establishing community-informed referral networks whose members refer children who may have exceptional educational needs (EENs). Network members typically include parents, doctors, birth-to-3 programs, child care programs, Head Start programs, public health agencies, social service agencies, and any other community members with whom the young children come into contact.

Current Collaborative Approaches and Models of Screening

Historically, the tradition was to conduct kindergarten screenings of children entering schools around age 5. However, in recent years, school districts have developed community referral networks to assist in the processes of Child Find, screening, evaluation, and referral for early intervention and early childhood special education and related services. Current models are more informal, proactive, and collaborative. Cooperative educational interagency service efforts give parents information about normal early childhood development and available community resources and offer opportunities for developmental screenings of their young children. Specific procedures are governed by individual US state laws. Generally, district networks implementing current models send developmental review forms to parents to complete in advance, and then they attend a developmental screening at a community site. Parents discuss normal early childhood growth and development with program staff, while, in the same room, trained professionals observe their children as they play. Children's vision and hearing are also screened. Parents can discuss their children's current development with psychologists, early childhood educators, or counselors. Thereafter, they can learn about community resources.

Defining Developmental Delays in Infants and Toddlers

The IDEA Part C specifies the areas of development that states must include in **defining developmental delays**. However, individual states must identify the criteria they use to determine eligibility, including pertinent diagnostic instruments, procedures, and functional levels. States currently use quantitative and qualitative measures. Quantitative criteria for developmental delay include the difference between chronological age and performance level, expressed as a percentage of chronological age; performance at a given number of months below chronological age; or number of standard deviations (SDs) below mean of performance on a norm-referenced test. Qualitative criteria include the development considered atypical or delayed for established norms or observed behaviors considered atypical. At least one state differentially defines delay according to a child's age in months, with the rationale that a 25% delay, for example, is very different for a 1-year-old than a 3-year-old. Quantitative criteria for defining delay and determining eligibility vary widely among states. A 25% or 20% delay (2 SDs below mean in 1+ areas or 1.5 SD below mean in 2+ areas) is some common state criteria.

Risk Factors in Infants and Toddlers

Scientists find that developmental outcomes for children are not reliably predicted by any one risk factor or event. **Developmental risk** increases with increased biological, medical, or environmental risk factors. However, researchers have found some variables that afford resiliency in children to offset risk factors. These can include the child's basic temperament, the child having high self-esteem, the child having a good emotional relationship with at least one parent, and the child having experiences of successful learning. These findings indicate that assessments should include criteria for multiple biological and environmental risk factors, for cumulative biological and environmental risk factors, and for protective or resilience factors, considering all of these in the context of change occurring over time. Under the IDEA, US states have the option to provide early intervention services to children considered at risk for adverse developmental outcomes as well as those already identified with them. Some states apply multiple-risk models, requiring three to five risk factors for service eligibility. Some states also determine eligibility with less DD when biological, medical, or environmental risk factors also exist.

Resources on Early Intervention and Preschool Special Education Services

Military families stationed both in the United States and overseas who have young special needs children can seek information and assistance from the federally funded organization Specialized Training of Military Families (STOMP). The staff of STOMP is composed of parents having special needs children themselves, who also have been trained to work with other parents of special needs children. STOMP staff members are spouses of military personnel who thus understand the unique, specialized circumstances and needs of military families. Another government agency, the US Department of Defense, includes the office of the Department of Defense Education Activity (DoDEA) and provides comprehensive guidance to military families with special needs children who are eligible to receive, or are receiving, free appropriate public education (FAPE) as mandated by the IDEA law, whether that education is located in the United States or in other countries.

Providing Special Education Services for Preschoolers

If parents observe that their preschooler is not attaining developmental milestones within the expected age ranges or does not seem to be developing in the same way as most other children, they should seek **evaluation** for possible developmental delay or disability. Although 3-to-5-year-olds are likely not in elementary school yet, the elementary school in a family's school district is still the best first contact because the IDEA law specifies that school districts must provide special education services at no family cost to eligible children, including preschoolers. Another excellent source of more information about special education is the National Dissemination Center for Children with Disabilities (NICHCY) of the US Department of Education's Office of Special Education Programs. They partner with nonprofit organizations like the Academy for Educational Development (AED) to produce useful documents for families with special needs children. NICHCY supplies state resource sheets listing main contacts regarding special education services in each US state. Families can obtain these sheets at NICHCY's website or by telephone.

INFORMATION SOURCES FOR EVALUATION

Under the IDEA (Individuals with Disabilities Education Act), evaluation information sources include: physicians' reports, the child's medical history, developmental test results, current classroom observations and assessments (when applicable), completed developmental and behavioral checklists, feedback and observations from parents and all other members of the evaluation team, and any other significant records, reports, and observations regarding the child. Under the IDEA, the parents are involved in the evaluation, along with at least one regular education teacher and special education teacher, if the child has these, and any special education service provider working with the child—for children receiving early intervention services from birth through age 2 and transitioning to preschool special education, it may be an early intervention service provider; a school administrator knowledgeable about children with disabilities, special education policies, regular education curriculum, and resources available; a psychologist or educator who can interpret evaluation results and discuss indicated instruction; individuals with special expertise or knowledge regarding the child (recruited by school or parents); when appropriate, the child; and other professionals, for example, physical or occupational therapists, speech therapists, medical specialists, and so on.

INFORMAL ASSESSMENT INSTRUMENTS

Early childhood teachers assess pre-K children's performance in individual, small-group, and whole-class activities throughout the day using informal tools that are teacher-made, school-, program-, or district-furnished, or procured by school systems from commercial educational resources. For classroom observations, teachers might complete a form based on their observations during class story or circle time, organized using three themes per day, each targeting different skills—social-emotional, math, alphabet knowledge, oral language, or emergent writing. They note the names of children demonstrating the specified skill and those who might need follow-up, and provide needed one on one interventions daily. For individual observations, teachers might fill out a chart divided into domains like physical development, oral language development, math, emergent reading, emergent writing, science and health, fine arts, technology and media, social studies, social-emotional development, and approaches to learning, noting one child's strengths and needs in each area per chart. In addition to guided observation records, teachers complete checklists, keep anecdotal and running records, and assemble portfolio assessments of children's work. Tracking children's progress informs responsive instructional planning.

> **Review Video: Assessment Reliability and Validity**
> Visit mometrix.com/academy and enter code: 424680

DIFFERENCES BETWEEN SCREENING AND ASSESSMENT INSTRUMENTS

A variety of screening and assessment instruments exist for early childhood measurement. Some key areas where they differ include which developmental domains are measured by an instrument; for which applications an instrument is meant to be used; to which age ranges an instrument applies; the methods by which a test or tool is administered; the requirements for scoring and interpreting a test, scale, or checklist; whether an instrument is appropriate for use with ethnically diverse populations; and whether a tool is statistically found to have good validity and reliability. Early childhood program administrators should choose instruments that can measure the developmental areas pertinent to their program; support their program's established goals; and include all early childhood ages served in their program. Instruments' administration, scoring, and interpretation methods should be congruent with program personnel's skills. Test/measure administration should involve realistic time durations. Instruments/tools should be appropriate to use with ethnically diverse and non-English-speaking children and families. Tests should also be proven psychometrically accurate and dependable enough.

> **Review Video: Early Childhood Developmental Domains**
> Visit mometrix.com/academy and enter code: 100380

TYPICAL APPLICATIONS OF SCREENING AND ASSESSMENT INSTRUMENTS

The ways in which screening and assessment instruments applicable to early childhood education are used include a wide range of variations. For example, early childhood education programs typically need to identify children who might have developmental disorders or delays. Screening instruments are used to identify those children showing signs of possible problems who need assessments, not to diagnose problems. Assessment instruments are used to develop and/or confirm diagnoses of developmental disorders or delays. Assessment tools are also used to help educators and therapists plan curricular and treatment programs. Another important function of assessment instruments is to determine a child's eligibility for a given program. In addition, once children are placed in early childhood education programs, assessment tools can be used to monitor their progress and other changes occurring over time. Moreover, program administrators can use assessment instruments to evaluate children's achievement of the learning outcomes that define their program goals, and, by extension, the teachers' effectiveness in furthering children's achievement of those outcomes.

FORMAL ASSESSMENT INSTRUMENTS

Formal assessment instruments are typically standardized tests, administered to groups. They give norms for age groups/developmental levels for comparison. They are designed to avoid administrator bias and capture children's responses only. Their data can be scaled and be reported in aggregate to school/program administrators and policymakers. The Scholastic Early Childhood Inventory (SECI) is a formal one-on-one instrument to assess children's progress in four domains found to predict kindergarten readiness: phonological awareness, oral language development, alphabet knowledge, and mathematics. Other instruments measuring multiple developmental domains include:

- **The Assessment, Evaluation, and Programming System** (0–6 years) for planning intervention
- **The Bayley Scale for Infant Development** (1–42 months) for assessing developmental delays
- **The Brigance Diagnostic Inventory of Early Development** (0–7 years) for planning instruction
- **The Developmental Profile II** (0–6 years) to assess special needs and support IEP development
- **The Early Coping Inventory** (4–36 months)
- **Early Learning Accomplishment Profile** (0–36 months), both for planning interventions
- **The Infant-Toddler Developmental Assessment** (0–42 months) to screen for developmental delays

SCREENING AND ASSESSMENT INSTRUMENTS MEASURING DEVELOPMENT

The available screening and assessment instruments for early childhood development cover a wide range in scope and areas of focus. Some measures are comprehensive, assessing young children's progress in many developmental domains, including sensory, motor, physical, cognitive, linguistic, emotional, and social. Some other instruments focus exclusively on only one domain, such as language development or emotional-social development. Some instruments even focus within a domain upon only one of its facets, (e.g., upon attachment or temperament within the domain of emotional-social development). In addition, some tools measure risk and resiliency factors influencing developmental delays and disorders. Programs like Head Start that promote general early childhood development should select comprehensive assessment instruments. Outreach programs targeting better identification of children having untreated and/or undetected mental health problems should choose instruments assessing social-emotional development. Clinics treating children with regulatory disorders might select an instrument measuring temperament. Prevention programs helping multiple-needs families access supports and services could use a measure for risk and resiliency factors. Multifaceted early childhood programs often benefit most from using several instruments in combination.

AGE RANGES INCLUDED IN VARIOUS SCREENING AND ASSESSMENT INSTRUMENTS

An important consideration for screening and assessment in early childhood is that early childhood development is very dynamic and occurs rapidly. Hence, screening and assessment instruments must be sensitive to such frequent and pronounced developmental changes. Some instruments target specific age ranges like 0–36 months. Others cover wider ranges, such as children aged 2–16 years. The latter may have internal means of application to smaller age ranges; for example, sections respectively for 3–6-month-old babies, 7–12-month-olds, and 12–18-month-olds. Or they indicate different scoring and interpretation criteria by age; for example, some screening tools specify different numbers of test items depending on the child's age to indicate a need for assessment. Choosing screening and assessment instruments covering the entire age range served in an early childhood education program is advantageous—not only because they can be used with all child ages in the program but also because they can be administered and readministered at the beginning and end of programs and/or in between, to compare and monitor changes, which is difficult with separate, age-specific tests.

Special Education Services in Early Childhood

SPECIAL EDUCATION SERVICES FOR PRESCHOOL CHILDREN

Special education for preschoolers is education specifically designed to meet the individual needs of a child aged 3 to 5 years with a disability or developmental delay. The specialized design of this instruction can include adaptations to the content, the teaching methods, and the way instruction is delivered to meet a disabled child's unique needs. Special education for preschoolers includes various settings, such as in the home, classrooms, hospitals, institutions, and others. It also includes a range of related services, such as speech-language pathology services, specialized physical education instruction, early vocational training, and training in travel skills. The school district's special education system provides evaluation and services to eligible preschoolers free of charge. Evaluation's purposes are to determine whether a child has a disability under the IDEA's definitions and determine that child's present educational needs.

POST-EVALUATION AND THE INDIVIDUALIZED EDUCATION PROGRAM

After a preschool child is evaluated, the parents and involved school personnel meet to discuss the evaluation results. Parents are included in the group that decides whether the child is eligible for special education services based on those results. For eligible children, the parents and school personnel will develop an IEP. Every child who will receive special education services must have an IEP. The main purposes of the IEP are (1) to establish reasonable educational goals for the individual child and (2) to indicate what services the school district will provide to the child. The IEP includes a statement of the child's present levels of functioning and performance. It also includes a list of more general instructional goals for the child to achieve through school and parental support along with more specific learning objectives reflecting those goals and specifying exactly what the child will be able to demonstrate, under what circumstances, how much of the time—for example, a percentage of recorded instances—and within what time period (e.g., 1 year).

Individualized Education Program Goals and Objectives

In an IEP, the goals are more global, describing a skill for the child to acquire or a task to master. The objectives are more specific articulations of achievements that will demonstrate the child's mastery of the goal. For example, if a goal is for the child to increase his or her functional communicative vocabulary, a related objective might be for the child to acquire x number of new words in x length of time; another related objective could be for the child to use the words acquired in 90% of recorded relevant situations. If the goal is for the child to demonstrate knowledge and discrimination of colors, one objective might be for the child to identify correctly a red, yellow, and blue block 95% of the time when asked to point out each color within a group of blocks. Progress toward or achievement of some objectives may be measured via formal tests; with preschoolers, many others are measured via observational data collection.

Progress Monitoring, Updating, and Revising IEPs

Once a child has been identified with a disability, has been determined eligible for special education and related services under the IDEA, and has had an IEP developed and implemented, the child's progress must be monitored. Monitoring methods may be related to evaluation methods. For example, if a child identified with problem behaviors was initially evaluated using a behavioral checklist, school personnel can use the same checklist periodically, comparing its results to the baseline levels of frequency and severity originally obtained. If an affective disorder or disturbance was identified and instruments like the Beck Depression Inventory or Anxiety Inventory were used, these can be used again periodically; reduced symptoms would indicate progress. If progress with IEP goals and objectives is less or greater than expected, the IEP team meets and may revise the program. This can include specifying shorter or longer times to achieve some goals and objectives; lowering or raising requirements proving too difficult or easy; resetting successive objective criteria in smaller or larger increments; changing teaching methods, content, or materials used; and so on.

Assessment Methodology

ASSESSMENT METHODS

Effective teaching requires multiple methods of assessment to evaluate student comprehension and instructional effectiveness. Assessments are typically categorized as diagnostic, formative, summative, and benchmark and are applicable at varying stages of instruction. **Diagnostic** assessments are administered before instruction and indicate students' prior knowledge and areas of misunderstanding to determine the path of instruction. **Formative** assessments occur continuously to measure student engagement, comprehension, and instructional effectiveness. These assessments indicate instructional strategies that require adjustment to meet students' needs in facilitating successful learning and include strategies like checking for understanding, observations, total participation activities, and exit tickets. **Summative** assessments are given at the end of a lesson or unit to evaluate student progress in reaching learning targets and identify areas of misconception for reteaching. Such assessments can be given in the form of exams and quizzes or be project-based activities in which students demonstrate their learning through hands-on, personalized methods. Additionally, portfolios serve as valuable summative assessments in allowing students to demonstrate their progress over time and provide insight regarding individual achievement. **Benchmark** assessments occur less frequently and encompass large portions of curriculum. These assessments are intended to evaluate the progress of groups of students in achieving state and district academic standards.

ASSESSMENT TYPES

- **Diagnostic:** These assessments can either be formal or informal and are intended to provide teachers with information regarding students' level of understanding prior to beginning a unit of instruction. Examples include pretests, KWL charts, anticipation guides, and brainstorming activities. Digital resources, such as online polls, surveys, and quizzes are also valuable resources for gathering diagnostic feedback.
- **Formative:** These assessments occur throughout instruction to provide the teacher with feedback regarding student understanding. Examples include warm-up and closure activities, checking frequently for understanding, student reflection activities, and providing students with color-coded cards to indicate their level of understanding. Short quizzes and total participation activities, such as four corners, are also valuable formative assessments. Numerous digital resources, including polls, surveys, and review games, are also beneficial in providing teachers with formative feedback to indicate instructional effectiveness.
- **Summative:** Summative assessments are intended to indicate students' levels of mastery and progress toward reaching academic learning standards. These assessments may take the form of written or digital exams and include multiple choice, short answer, or long answer questions. Examples also include projects, final essays, presentations, or portfolios to demonstrate student progress over time.
- **Benchmark:** Benchmark assessments measure students' progress in achieving academic standards. These assessments are typically standardized to ensure uniformity, objectivity, and accuracy. Benchmark assessments are typically given as a written multiple choice or short answer exam, or as a digital exam in which students answer questions on the computer.

> **Review Video: Formative and Summative Assessments**
> Visit mometrix.com/academy and enter code: 804991

Determining Appropriate Assessment Strategies

As varying assessment methods provide different information regarding student performance and achievement, the teacher must consider the most applicable and effective assessment strategy in each stage of instruction. This includes determining the **desired outcomes** of assessment as well as the information the teacher intends to ascertain and how they will apply the results to further instruction. **Age-** and **grade-level-**appropriateness must be considered when selecting which assessment strategies will enable students to successfully demonstrate their learning. Additionally, the teacher must be cognizant of students' individual differences and learning needs to determine which assessment model is most **accommodating** and reflective of their progress. It is also important that teachers consider the practicality of assessment strategies and methods they will use to implement the assessment for maximized feedback regarding individual and whole-class progress in achieving learning goals.

Assessments That Reflect Real-World Applications

Assessments that reflect **real-world applications** enhance relevancy and students' ability to establish personal connections to learning that deepen understanding. Implementing such assessments provides authenticity and enhances engagement by defining a clear and practical purpose for learning. These assessments often allow for hands-on opportunities for demonstrating learning and can be adjusted to accommodate students' varying learning styles and needs while measuring individual progress; however, assessments that focus on real-world applications can be subjective, thus making it difficult to extract concrete data and quantify student progress to guide future instructional decisions. In addition, teachers may have difficulty analyzing assessment results on a large scale and comparing student performance with other schools and districts, as individual assessments may vary.

Diagnostic Tests

Diagnostic tests are integral to planning and delivering effective instruction. These tests are typically administered prior to beginning a unit or lesson and provide valuable feedback for guiding and planning instruction. Diagnostic tests provide **preliminary information** regarding students' levels of understanding and prior knowledge. This serves as a baseline for instructional planning that connects and builds upon students' background knowledge and experiences to enhance success in learning. Diagnostic tests allow the teacher to identify and clarify areas of student misconception prior to engaging in instruction to ensure continued comprehension and avoid the need for remediation. They indicate areas of student strength and need as well as individual instructional aids that may need to be incorporated into lessons to support student achievement. In addition, these tests enable the teacher to determine which instructional strategies, activities, groupings, and materials will be most valuable in maximizing engagement and learning. Diagnostic tests can be **formal** or **informal** and include pre-tests, pre-reading activities, surveys, vocabulary inventories, and graphic organizers (such as KWL charts). These tests are used to assess student understanding prior to engaging in learning. Diagnostic tests are generally not graded, as there is little expectation that all students in a class possess the same baseline of proficiency at the start of a unit.

Formative Assessments

Formative assessments are any assessments that take place in the **middle of a unit of instruction**. The goals of formative assessments are to help teachers understand where a student is in his or her progress toward **mastering** the current unit's content and to provide the students with **ongoing feedback** throughout the unit. The advantage of relying heavily on formative assessments in instruction is that it allows the teacher to continuously **check for comprehension** and adjust instruction as needed to ensure that the whole class is adequately prepared to proceed at the end of the unit. To understand formative assessments well, teachers need to understand that any interaction that can provide information about the student's comprehension is a type of formative assessment which can be used to inform future instruction.

Formative assessments are often a mixture of formal and informal assessments. **Formal formative assessments** often include classwork, homework, and quizzes. Examples of **informal formative assessments** include simple comprehension checks during instruction, class-wide discussions of the current topic, and exit slips, which are written questions posed by teachers at the end of class, which helps the teacher quickly review which students are struggling with the concepts.

SUMMATIVE ASSESSMENTS

Summative assessment refers to an evaluation at the end of a discrete unit of instruction, such as the end of a course, unit, or semester. Classic examples of summative assessments include end-of-course assessments, final exams, or even qualifying standardized tests such as the SAT or ACT. Most summative assessments are created to measure student mastery of particular **academic standards**. Whereas formative assessment generally informs current instruction, summative assessments are used to objectively demonstrate that each individual has achieved adequate mastery of the standards in question. If a student has not met the benchmark, he or she may need extra instruction or may need to repeat the course.

These assessments usually take the form of **tests** or formal portfolios with rubrics and clearly defined goals. Summative assessments are usually high-stakes, heavily-weighted, and they should always be formally graded. These types of assessments often feature a narrower range of question types, such as multiple choice, short answer, and essay questions to help with systematic grading.

Project-based assessments are beneficial in evaluating achievement, as they incorporate several elements of instruction and highlight real-world applications of learning. This allows students to demonstrate understanding through a hands-on, individualized approach that reinforces connections to learning and increases retainment. **Portfolios** of student work over time serve as a valuable method for assessing individual progress toward reaching learning targets. Summative assessments provide insight regarding overall instructional effectiveness and are necessary for guiding future instruction in subsequent years but are not usually used to modify current instruction.

> **Review Video: Assessment Reliability and Validity**
> Visit mometrix.com/academy and enter code: 424680

BENCHMARK ASSESSMENTS

Benchmark assessments are intended to quantify, evaluate, and compare individual and groups of students' achievement of school-wide, district, and state **academic standards.** They are typically administered in specific intervals throughout the school year and encompass entire or large units of curriculum to determine student mastery and readiness for academic advancement. Benchmark assessments provide data that enable the teacher to determine students' progress toward reaching academic goals to guide current and continued instruction. This data can be utilized by the school and individual teachers to create learning goals and objectives aligned with academic standards. It can also be used to plan instructional strategies, activities, and assessments to support students in achieving these academic standards. In addition, benchmark assessments provide feedback regarding understanding and the potential need for remediation to allow the teacher to instill necessary supports in future instruction that prepare students for success in achieving learning targets.

Alignment of Assessments with Instructional Goals and Objectives

To effectively monitor student progress, assessments must align with **instructional goals** and **objectives**. This allows the teacher to determine whether students are advancing at an appropriate pace to achieve state and district academic standards. When assessments are aligned with specific learning targets, the teacher ensures that students are learning relevant material to establish a foundation of knowledge necessary for growth and academic achievement. To achieve this, teachers must determine which instructional goals and objectives their students must achieve and derive instruction, content, and activities from these specifications. Instruction must reflect and reinforce learning targets, and the teacher must select the most effective strategies for addressing students' needs as they work to achieve them. Assessments must be reflective of content instruction to ensure they are aligned with learning goals and objectives, as well as to enable the teacher to evaluate student progress in mastering them. The teacher must clearly communicate learning goals and objectives throughout all stages of instruction to provide students with clarity on expectations. This establishes a clear purpose and focus for learning that enhances relevancy and strengthens connections to support student achievement.

Clearly Communicating Assessment Criteria and Standards

Students must be clear on the purpose of learning throughout all stages of instruction to enhance understanding and facilitate success. When assessment **criteria** and **standards** are clearly communicated, the purpose of learning is established, and students are able to effectively connect instructional activities to learning goals and criteria for assessment. Communicating assessment criteria and standards provides students with clarity on tasks and learning goals they are expected to accomplish as they prepare themselves for assessment. This allows for more **focused instruction** and engagement in learning, as it enhances relevancy and student motivation. Utilizing appropriate forms of **rubrics** is an effective strategy in specifying assessment criteria and standards, as it informs students about learning goals they are working toward, the quality of work they are expected to achieve, and skills they must master to succeed on the assessment. Rubrics indicate to students exactly how they will be evaluated, thus supporting their understanding and focus as they engage in learning to promote academic success.

Rubrics for Communicating Standards

The following are varying styles of rubrics that can be used to communicate criteria and standards:

- **Analytic:** Analytic rubrics break down criteria for an assignment into several categories and provide an explanation of the varying levels of performance in each one. This style of rubric is beneficial for detailing the characteristics of quality work as well as providing students with feedback regarding specific components of their performance. Analytic rubrics are most effective when used for summative assessments, such as long-term projects or essays.
- **Holistic:** Holistic rubrics evaluate the quality of the student's assignment as a whole rather than scoring individual components. Students' scores are determined based upon their performance across multiple performance indicators. This style of rubric is beneficial for providing a comprehensive evaluation but limits the amount of feedback that students receive regarding their performance in specific areas.

- **Single-point:** Single-point rubrics outline criteria for assignments into several categories. Rather than providing a numeric score to each category, however, the teacher provides written feedback regarding the students' strengths and ways in which they can improve their performance. This style of rubric is beneficial in providing student-centered feedback that focuses on their overall progress.
- **Checklist:** Checklists typically outline a set of criteria that is scored using a binary approach based upon completion of each component. This style increases the efficiency of grading assignments and is often easy for students to comprehend but does not provide detailed feedback. This method of grading should generally be reserved for shorter assignments.

COMMUNICATING HIGH ACADEMIC EXPECTATIONS IN ASSESSMENTS

The attitudes and behaviors exhibited by the teacher are highly influential on students' attitudes toward learning. Teachers demonstrate belief in students' abilities to be successful in learning when they communicate **high academic expectations**. This promotes students' **self-concept** and establishes a **growth mindset** to create confident, empowered learners that are motivated to achieve. High expectations for assessments and reaching academic standards communicates to students the quality of work that is expected of them and encourages them to overcome obstacles as they engage in learning. When communicating expectations for student achievement, it is important that the teacher is aware of students' individual learning needs to provide the necessary support that establishes equitable opportunities for success in meeting assessment criteria and standards. Setting high expectations through assessment criteria and standards while supporting students in their learning enhances overall achievement and establishes a foundation for continuous academic success.

EFFECTIVE COMMUNICATION AND IMPACT ON STUDENT LEARNING

Communicating high academic expectations enhances students' self-concept and increases personal motivation for success in learning. To maximize student achievement, it is important that the teacher set high academic expectations that are **clearly** communicated through **age-appropriate** terms and consistently reinforced. Expectations must be reflected through learning goals and objectives and must be **visible** at all times to ensure student awareness. Teachers must be **specific** in communicating what they want students to accomplish and clearly detail necessary steps for achievement while assuming the role of facilitator to guide learning and provide support. Providing constructive **feedback** throughout instruction is integral in reminding students of academic expectations and ensuring they are making adequate progress toward reaching learning goals. When high academic expectations are communicated and reinforced, students are empowered with a sense of confidence and self-responsibility for their own learning that promotes their desire to learn. This ultimately enhances achievement and equips them with the tools necessary for future academic success.

ANALYZING AND INTERPRETING ASSESSMENT DATA

Teachers can utilize multiple techniques to effectively analyze and interpret assessment data. This typically involves creating charts and graphs outlining different data subsets. They can list each learning standard that was assessed, determine how many students overall demonstrated proficiency on the standard, and identify individual students who did not demonstrate proficiency on each standard. This information can be used to differentiate instruction. Additionally, they can track individual student performance and progress on each standard over time.

Teachers can take note of overall patterns and trends in assessment data. For example, they can determine if any subgroups of students did not meet expectations. They can consider whether the data confirms or challenges any existing beliefs, implications this may have on instructional planning and what, if any, conclusions can be drawn from this data.

Analyzing and interpreting assessment data may raise new questions for educators, so they can also determine if additional data collection is needed.

USING ASSESSMENT DATA TO DIFFERENTIATE INSTRUCTION FOR INDIVIDUAL LEARNERS

By analyzing and interpreting assessment data, teachers can determine if there are any specific learning standards that need to be retaught to their entire classes. This may be necessary if the data shows that all students struggled in these specific areas. Teachers may consider reteaching these standards using different methods if the initial methods were unsuccessful.

Teachers can also form groups of students who did not demonstrate proficiency on the same learning standards. Targeted instruction can be planned for these groups to help them make progress in these areas. Interventions can also be planned for individual students who did not show proficiency in certain areas. If interventions have already been in place and have not led to increased learning outcomes, the interventions may be redesigned. If interventions have been in place and assessment data now shows proficiency, the interventions may be discontinued.

If assessment data shows that certain students have met or exceeded expectations in certain areas, enrichment activities can be planned to challenge these students and meet their learning needs.

ALIGNING ASSESSMENTS WITH INSTRUCTIONAL GOALS AND OBJECTIVES

Assessments that are congruent to instructional goals and objectives provide a **clear purpose** for learning that enhances student understanding and motivation. When learning targets are reflected in assessments, instructional activities and materials become more **relevant**, as they are derived from these specifications. Such clarity in purpose allows for more focus and productivity as students engage in instruction and fosters connections that strengthen overall understanding for maximized success in learning. Aligning assessments with instructional goals and objectives ensures that students are learning material that is relevant to the curriculum and academic standards to ensure **preparedness** as they advance in their academic careers. In addition, it enables the teacher to evaluate and monitor student progress to determine whether they are progressing at an ideal pace for achieving academic standards. With this information, the teacher can effectively modify instruction as necessary to support students' needs in reaching desired learning outcomes.

NORM-REFERENCED TESTS

On **norm-referenced tests**, students' performances are compared to the performances of sample groups of similar students. Norm-referenced tests identify students who score above and below the average. To ensure reliability, the tests must be given in a standardized manner to all students.

Norm-referenced tests usually cover a broad range of skills, such as the entire grade-level curriculum for a subject. They typically contain a few questions per skill. Whereas scores in component areas of the tests may be calculated, usually overall test scores are reported. Scores are often reported using percentile ranks, which indicate what percentage of test takers scored lower than the student being assessed. For example, a student's score in the 75th percentile means the student scored better than 75% of other test takers. Other times, scores may be reported using grade-level equivalency.

One advantage of norm-referenced tests is their objectivity. They also allow educators to compare large groups of students at once. This may be helpful for making decisions regarding class placements and groupings. A disadvantage of norm-referenced tests is that they only indicate how well students perform in comparison to one another. They do not indicate whether or not students have mastered certain skills.

Criterion-Referenced Tests

Criterion-referenced tests measure how well students perform on certain skills or standards. The goal of these tests is to indicate whether or not students have mastered certain skills and which skills require additional instruction. Scores are typically reported using the percentage of questions answered correctly or students' performance levels. Performance levels are outlined using terms such as *below expectations*, *met expectations*, and *exceeded expectations*.

One advantage of criterion-referenced tests is that they provide teachers with useful information to guide instruction. They can identify which specific skills students have mastered and which skills need additional practice. Teachers can use this information to plan whole-class, small-group, and individualized instruction. Analyzing results of criterion-referenced tests over time can also help teachers track student progress on certain skills. A disadvantage of criterion-referenced tests is that they do not allow educators to compare students' performances to samples of their peers.

Ways That Standardized Test Results Are Reported

- **Raw scores** are sometimes reported and indicate how many questions students answered correctly on a test. By themselves, they do not provide much useful information. They do not indicate how students performed in comparison to other students or to grade-level expectations.
- **Grade-level equivalents** are also sometimes reported. A grade-level equivalent score of 3.4 indicates that a student performed as well as an average third grader in the fourth month of school. It can indicate whether a student is performing above or below grade-level expectations, but it does not indicate that the student should be moved to a different grade level.
- **Standard scores** are used to compare students' performances on tests to standardized samples of their peers. Standard deviation refers to the amount that a set of scores differs from the mean score on a test.
- **Percentile ranks** are used on criterion-referenced tests to indicate what percentage of test takers scored lower than the student whose score is being reported.
- **Cutoff scores** refer to predetermined scores students must obtain in order to be considered proficient in certain areas. Scores below the cutoff level indicate improvement is needed and may result in interventions or instructional changes.

Formal and Informal Assessments

Assessments are any method a teacher uses to gather information about student comprehension of curriculum, including improvised questions for the class and highly-structured tests. **Formal assessments** are assessments that have **clearly defined standards and methodology** and which are applied consistently to all students. Formal tests should be objective and scrutinized for validity and reliability since they tend to carry higher weight for the student. Summative assessments, such as end-of-unit tests, lend themselves to being formal tests because it is necessary that a teacher test the comprehension of all students in a consistent and thorough way.

Although formal assessments can provide useful data about student performance and progress, they can be costly and time-consuming to implement. Administering formal assessments often interrupts classroom instruction and may cause testing anxiety.

Informal assessments are assessments that do not adhere to formal objectives, and they do not have to be administered consistently to all students. As a result, they do not have to be scored or recorded as a grade and generally act as a **subjective measure** of class comprehension. Informal assessments can be as simple as asking the students to raise their hands if they are ready to proceed to the next step or asking a particular question of an individual student.

Informal assessments do not provide objective data for analysis, but they can be implemented quickly and inexpensively. Informal assessments can also be incorporated into regular classroom instruction and activities, making them more authentic and less stressful for students.

Using Various Assessments

The goal of **assessment** in education is to gather data that, when evaluated, can be used to further student learning and achievement. **Standardized tests** are helpful for placement purposes and to reflect student progress toward goals set by a school district or state. If a textbook is chosen to align with district learning standards, the textbook assessments can provide teachers with convenient, small-scale, regular checks of student knowledge against the target standard.

In order be effective, teachers must know where their students are in the learning process. Teachers use a multitude of **formal and informal assessment methods** to do this. Posing differentiated discussion questions is an example of an informal assessment method that allows teachers to gauge individual student progress rather than their standing in relation to a universal benchmark.

Effective teachers employ a variety of assessments, as different formats assess different skills, promote different learning experiences, and appeal to different learners. A portfolio is an example of an assessment that gauges student progress in multiple skills and through multiple media. Teachers can use authentic or performance-based assessments to stimulate student interest and provide visible connections between language-learning and the real world.

Assessment Reliability

Assessment reliability refers to how well an assessment is constructed and is made up of a variety of measures. An assessment is generally considered **reliable** if it yields similar results across multiple administrations of the assessment. A test should perform similarly with different test administrators, graders, test-takers, and over multiple iterations. Factors that affect reliability include the day-to-day wellbeing of the student (students can sometimes underperform), the physical environment of the test, the way it is administered, and the subjectivity of the scorer (with written-response assessments).

Perhaps the most important threat to assessment reliability is the nature of the **exam questions** themselves. An assessment question is designed to test knowledge of a certain construct. A question is reliable in this sense if students who understand the content answer the question correctly. Statisticians look for patterns in student marks, both within the single test and over multiple tests, as a way of measuring reliability. Teachers should watch out for circumstances in which a student or students answer correctly a series of questions about a given concept (demonstrating their understanding) but then answer a related question incorrectly. The latter question may be an unreliable indicator of concept knowledge.

Measures of Assessment Reliability

- **Test-retest reliability** refers to an assessment's consistency of results with the same test-taker over multiple retests. If one student shows inconsistent results over time, the test is not considered to have test-retest reliability.

- **Intertester reliability** refers to an assessment's consistency of results between multiple test-takers at the same level. Students at similar levels of proficiency should show similar results.
- **Inter-rater reliability** refers to an assessment's consistency of results between different administrators of the test. This plays an especially critical role in tests with interactive or subjective responses, such as Likert-scales, cloze tests, and short answer tests. Different raters of the same test need to have a consistent means of evaluating the test-takers' performance. Clear rubrics can help keep two or more raters consistent in scoring.
- **Intra-rater reliability** refers to an assessment's consistency of results with one rater over time. One test rater should be able to score different students objectively to rate subjective test formats fairly.
- **Parallel-forms reliability** refers to an assessment's consistency between multiple different forms. For instance, end-of-course assessments may have many distinctive test forms, with different questions or question orders. If the different forms of a test do not provide the same results, the test is said to be lacking in parallel-forms reliability.
- **Internal consistency reliability** refers to the consistency of results of similar questions on a particular assessment. If there are two or more questions targeted at the same standard and at the same level, they should show the same results across each question.

Assessment Validity

Assessment validity is a measure of the relevancy that an assessment has to the skill or ability being evaluated and the degree to which students' performance is representative of their mastery of the topic of assessment. In other words, a teacher should ask how well an assessment's results correlate to what it is looking to assess. Assessments should be evaluated for validity on both the **individual question** level and as a **test overall**. This can be especially helpful in refining tests for future classes. The overall validity of an assessment is determined by several types of validity measures.

An assessment is considered **valid** if it measures what it is intended to measure. One common error that can reduce the validity of a test (or a question on a test) occurs if the instructions are written at a reading level the students can't understand. In this case, it is not valid to take the student's failed answer as a true indication of his or her knowledge of the subject. Factors internal to the student might also affect exam validity: anxiety and a lack of self-esteem often lower assessments results, reducing their validity as a measure of student knowledge.

An assessment has content validity if it includes all the **relevant aspects** of the subject being tested—if it is comprehensive, in other words. An assessment has **predictive validity** if a score on the test is an accurate predictor of future success in the same domain. For example, SAT exams purport to have validity in predicting student success in a college. An assessment has construct validity if it accurately measures student knowledge of the subject being tested.

Measures of Assessment Validity

- **Face validity** refers to the initial impression of whether an assessment seems to be fit for the task. As this method is subjective to interpretation and unquantifiable, it should not be used singularly as a measurement of validity.

- **Construct validity** asks if an assessment actually assesses what it is intended to assess. Some topics are more straightforward, such as assessing if a student can perform two-digit multiplication. This can be directly tested, which gives the assessment a strong content validity. Other measures, such as a person's overall happiness, must be measured indirectly. If an assessment asserted that a person is generally happy if he or she smiles frequently, it would be fair to question the construct validity of that assessment because smiling is unlikely to be a consistent measure of all peoples' general happiness.
- **Content validity** indicates whether the assessment is comprehensive of all aspects of the content being assessed. If a test leaves out an important topic, then the teacher will not have a full picture as a result of the assessment.
- **Criterion validity** refers to whether the results of an assessment can be used to **predict** a related value, known as **criterion**. An example of this is the hypothesis that IQ tests would predict a person's success later in life, but many critics believe that IQ tests are not valid predictors of success because intelligence is not the only predictor of success in life. IQ tests have shown validity toward predicting academic success, however. The measure of an assessment's criterion validity depends on how closely related the criterion is.
- **Discriminant validity** refers to how well an assessment tests only that which it is intended to test and successfully discriminates one piece of information from another. For instance, a student who is exceptional in mathematics should not be able to put that information into use on a science test and gain an unfair advantage. If the student is able to score well due to his or her mathematics knowledge, the science test did not adequately discriminate science knowledge from mathematics knowledge.
- **Convergent validity** is related to discriminant validity, but takes into account that two measures may be distinct but correlated. For instance, a personality test should distinguish self-esteem from extraversion so that they can be measured independently, but if an assessment has convergent validity, it should show a correlation between related measures.

PRACTICALITY

An assessment is **practical** if it uses an appropriate amount of human and budgetary resources. A practical exam doesn't take very long to design or score, nor does it take students very long to complete in relation to other learning objectives and priorities. Teachers often need to balance a desire to construct comprehensive or content-valid tests with a need for practicality: lengthy exams consume large amounts of instruction time and may return unreliable results if students become tired and lose focus.

ASSESSMENT BIAS

An assessment is considered biased if it disadvantages a certain group of students, such as students of a certain gender, race, cultural background, or socioeconomic class. A **content bias** exists when the subject matter of a question or assessment is familiar to one group and not another. For example, a reading comprehension passage that discusses an event in American history would be biased against students new to the country. An **attitudinal bias** exists when a teacher has a preconceived idea about the likely success of an assessment of a particular individual or group. A **method bias** arises when the format of an assessment is unfamiliar to a given group of students. **Language bias** occurs when an assessment utilizes idioms, collocations, or cultural references unfamiliar to a group of students. Finally, **translation bias** may arise when educators attempt to translate content-area assessments into a student's native language—rough or hurried translations often result in a loss of nuance important for accurate assessment.

AUTHENTIC ASSESSMENTS

An authentic assessment is an assessment designed to closely resemble something that a student does, or will do, in the real world. For example, students will never encounter a multiple-choice test requiring them to choose the right tense of a verb, but they will encounter contexts in which they have to write a narration of an event that has antecedents and consequents spread out in time—like narrating their version of what caused a traffic accident. The latter is an example of a potential **authentic assessment**.

Well-designed authentic assessments require a student to exercise **advanced cognitive skills** (e.g., solving problems, integrating information, performing deductions), integrate **background knowledge**, and confront **ambiguity**. Research has demonstrated that mere language proficiency is not predictive of future language success—learning how to utilize knowledge in a complex context is an essential additional skill.

The terms "authentic" and "performance-based" are often used interchangeably when describing assessments; however, a performance-based assessment doesn't necessarily have to be grounded in a possible authentic experience.

PERFORMANCE-BASED ASSESSMENTS

A performance-based assessment is one in which students demonstrate their learning by performing a **task** rather than by answering questions in a traditional test format. Proponents of **performance-based assessments** argue that they lead students to use **high-level cognitive skills** since they focus on how to put their knowledge to use and plan a sequence of stages in an activity or presentation. They also allow students more opportunities to individualize their presentations or responses based on preferred learning styles. Research suggests that students welcome the chance to put their knowledge to use in real-world scenarios.

Advocates of performance-based assessments suggest that they avoid many of the problems of language or cultural bias present in traditional assessments, allowing more accurate assessment of how well students learned the underlying concepts. In discussions regarding English as a second language, they argue that performance assessments come closer to replicating what should be the true goal of language learning—the effective use of language in real contexts—than do more traditional exams. Critics point out that performance assessments are difficult and time-consuming for teachers to construct and for students to perform. Finally, performative assessments are difficult to grade in the absence of a well-constructed and detailed rubric.

TECHNOLOGY-BASED ASSESSMENTS

Technology-based assessments provide teachers with multiple resources for evaluating student progress to guide instruction. They are applicable in most formal and informal instructional settings and can be utilized as formative and summative assessments. Technology-based assessments simplify and enhance the efficiency of determining comprehension and instructional effectiveness, as they quickly present the teacher with information regarding student progress. This data enables the teacher to make necessary adjustments to facilitate student learning and growth. Implementing this assessment format simplifies the process of aligning them to school and district academic standards. This establishes objectivity and uniformity for comparing results and progress among students. It also helps ensure that all students are held to the same academic expectations. While technology-based assessments are beneficial, there are some shortcomings to consider. This format may not be entirely effective for all learning styles in demonstrating understanding, as individualization in technology-based assessment can be limited. These assessments may not illustrate individual students' growth over time but rather their mastery of an academic standard, thus hindering the ability to evaluate overall achievement. As technology-based evaluation limits hands-on opportunities, the real-world application and relevancy of the assessment may be unapparent to students.

ADVANTAGES AND DISADVANTAGES OF TECHNOLOGY-BASED ASSESSMENTS

Technology-based assessments can have many advantages. They can be given to large numbers of students at once, limited only by the amounts of technological equipment schools possess. Many types of technology-based assessments are instantly scored, and feedback is provided quickly. Students are sometimes able to view their results and feedback at the conclusion of their testing sessions. Data can be quickly compiled and reported in easy-to-understand formats. Technology-based assessments can also often track student progress over time.

Technology-based assessments can have some disadvantages as well. Glitches and system errors can interfere with the assessment process or score reporting. Students must also have the necessary prerequisite technological skills to take the assessments, or the results may not measure the content they are designed to measure. For example, if students take timed, computer-based writing tests, they should have proficient typing skills. Otherwise, they may perform poorly on the tests despite strong writing abilities. Other prerequisite skills include knowing how to use a keyboard and mouse and understanding how to locate necessary information on the screen.

PORTFOLIO ASSESSMENTS

A **portfolio** is a collection of student work in multiple forms and media gathered over time. Teachers may assess the portfolio both for evidence of progress over time or in its end state as a demonstration of the achievement of certain proficiency levels.

One advantage of **portfolio assessments** is their breadth. Unlike traditional assessments, which focus on one or two language skills, portfolios may contain work in multiple forms, such as writing samples, pictures, and graphs designed for content courses, video and audio clips, student reflections, teacher observations, and student exams. A second advantage is that they allow a student to develop work in authentic contexts, including in other classrooms and at home.

In order for portfolios to function as an objective assessment tool, teachers should negotiate with students in advance of what genres of work will be included and outline a grading rubric that makes clear what will be assessed, such as linguistic proficiency, use of English in academic contexts, and demonstrated use of target cognitive skills.

CURRICULUM-BASED ASSESSMENTS

Curriculum-based assessments, also known as **curriculum-based measurements (CBM)**, are short, frequent assessments designed to measure student progress toward meeting curriculum **benchmarks**.

Teachers implement CBMs by designing **probes**, or short assessments that target specific skills. For example, a teacher might design a spelling probe, administered weekly, that requires students to spell 10 unfamiliar but level-appropriate words. The data from these assessments can be tracked over time to measure student progress toward defined grade-level goals.

CBM has several clear advantages. If structured well, the probes have high reliability and validity. Furthermore, they provide clear and objective evidence of student progress—a welcome outcome for students and parents who often grapple with less-clear and subjective evidence. Used correctly, CBMs also motivate students and provide them with evidence of their own progress; however, while CBMs are helpful in identifying areas of student weaknesses, they do not identify the causes of those weaknesses or provide teachers with strategies for improving instruction.

TEXTBOOK ASSESSMENTS

Textbook assessments are the assessments provided at the end of a chapter or unit in an approved textbook. **Textbook assessments** present several advantages for a teacher: they are already made; they are likely to be accurate representations of the chapter or unit materials; and, if the textbook has been prescribed or recommended by the state, it is likely to correspond closely to Common Core or other tested standards.

Textbook assessments can be limiting for students who lag in the comprehension of academic English or whose preferred learning style is not verbal. While textbooks may come with DVDs or recommended audio links, ESOL teachers will likely need to supplement these assessment materials with some of their own findings. Finally, textbook assessments are unlikely to represent the range of assessment types used in the modern classroom, such as a portfolio or performance-based assessments.

PEER ASSESSMENT

A peer assessment is when students grade one another's work based on a teacher-provided framework. **Peer assessments** are promoted as a means of saving teacher time and building student metacognitive skills. They are typically used as **formative** rather than summative assessments, given concerns about the reliability of student scoring and the tensions that can result if student scores contribute to overall grades. Peer assessments are used most often to grade essay-type written work or presentations. Proponents point out that peer assessments require students to apply metacognition, build cooperative work and interpersonal skills, and broaden the sense that the student is accountable to peers and not just the teacher. Even advocates of the practice agree that students need detailed rubrics in order to succeed. Critics often argue that low-performing students have little to offer high-performing students in terms of valuable feedback—and this disparity may be more pronounced in ESOL classrooms or special education environments than in mainstream ones. One way to overcome this weakness is for the teacher to lead the evaluation exercise, guiding the students through a point-by-point framework of evaluation.

Developmental Screening

TYPES OF DEVELOPMENTAL ASSESSMENTS

Developmental assessments measure the development of infants, toddlers, and preschoolers. These **norm-referenced tests** measure fine and gross motor skills; communication and language; and social, cognitive, and self-help milestones that young children should achieve at certain ages. When a child is suspected of having a **developmental delay**, a developmental assessment is useful in identifying the child's strengths and weaknesses. These assessments map out the **progress** of a child compared to the progress of similar-aged children. Developmental assessments are also useful in identifying if the delay is significant or can be overcome with time. These assessments can be used to determine what **educational placement** is most appropriate for a child with a developmental delay. Developmental assessments are administered via observations and questionnaires. Parents, legal guardians, caregivers, and instructors who are most familiar with the child provide the most insight on developmental strengths and weaknesses.

> **Review Video: Identifying Appropriate Evaluation Strategies**
> Visit mometrix.com/academy and enter code: 100353

SCREENING TESTS FOR IDENTIFYING STUDENTS WHO NEED SPECIAL EDUCATION

When determining if a child needs special education, **screening tests** are the first step. The Individuals with Disabilities Education Act offers guidance for schools to implement screening tests. Districts and schools often have school-wide processes in place for screening students for **special education**. Screening tests can also be used to identify students who are falling behind in class. The advantage of screening tests is that they are easily administered. They require few materials and little time and planning in order to administer. Additionally, they can be used to quickly assess students' strengths and weaknesses, they do not have to be administered one-on-one, and they can be used for everyone in the class. Screening tests can be as simple as paper-and-pencil quizzes assessing what students know. They are used for measuring visual acuity, auditory skills, physical health, development, basic academic skills, behavioral problems, risk of behavioral problems, language skills, and verbal and nonverbal intelligence.

INDIVIDUAL INTELLIGENCE TESTS VS. INDIVIDUAL ACADEMIC ACHIEVEMENT TESTS

Intelligence tests measure a student's capacity for abstract thinking, mental reasoning, judgment, and decision-making. These **norm-referenced tests** help determine a student's **overall intelligence**, which correlates with **potential academic performance**. Intelligence tests can be used to determine if a student's deficits are due to intellectual disabilities or related to specific learning disabilities or emotional disorders. They can also measure verbal skills, motor performance, and visual reasoning. Intelligence tests are also known as **intelligence quotient tests (IQ tests)**. IQ tests should be administered by trained professionals to ensure the tests are administered accurately. Unlike intelligence tests, individual academic achievement tests measure a student's strengths and weaknesses in individual skills. They are also norm referenced and used to determine if a student needs **special education services**. Results from individual academic tests help determine areas of concern or possible deficits for an individual student. Unlike intelligence tests, individual academic tests can be administered by teachers.

ADAPTIVE BEHAVIOR SCALE ASSESSMENTS

Adaptive behavior scales are useful for diagnosing a student with an **intellectual disability** that affects the development or progression of adaptive behavior. They are used in preschools and for determining eligibility for **special education** in grade schools. They are also used in planning the **curriculum** for students with intellectual disabilities. Adaptive behavior scales are standardized but not always norm referenced because of difficulties comparing expectations for some adaptive and maladaptive skills exhibited by similar-aged peers. In terms of curriculum planning, these assessments can determine the type and quantity of assistance a student may need. Adaptive behavior scale assessments identify a student's level of **independence**. Adaptive behavior scales can be used to determine **skill abilities** associated with daily living, community functioning, social skills, communication, motor functions, and basic academic skills. Teachers and other professionals can administer adaptive behavior scales to students with intellectual disabilities to determine starting points for improving their adaptive behavior deficits.

CURRICULUM-BASED MEASUREMENT OF STUDENT ACADEMIC PROGRESS

Curriculum-based measurement (**CBM**) is a way for teachers to track how students are **progressing** in mathematics, language arts, social studies, science, and other skills. It is also useful for communicating progress to parents or legal guardians. CBM results can determine whether or not current **instructional strategies** are effective for particular students. In the same respect, CBM can determine if students are meeting the **standards** laid out in their Individualized Education Program goals. If CBM results show that instructional strategies are not effective or goals are not being met, teachers should change instructional strategies. CBM can be revisited to determine whether or not the newly implemented strategies are effective. Progress can sometimes be charted to present a visual for how a student is progressing in a particular content area or with a specific skill.

WOODCOCK-JOHNSON TESTS
HIGH-INCIDENCE DISABILITIES
Woodcock-Johnson tests can be used as diagnostic tools for identifying children with **high-incidence disabilities**. The Woodcock-Johnson Tests of Achievement, the Woodcock-Johnson Tests of Cognitive Abilities, and the Woodcock-Johnson Tests of Oral Language are comprehensively useful for assessing children's:

- Intellectual abilities
- Cognitive abilities
- Aptitude
- Oral language
- Academic achievements

These norm-referenced tests are valuable in understanding children's strengths and weaknesses and how they compare to cohorts of normally progressing, similar-aged peers. For example, **Woodcock-Johnson tests (WJ tests)** are useful in identifying children with language disorders because children with language disorders typically score lower on the listening comprehension and fluid reasoning test sections. The WJ tests are useful diagnostic tools for identifying children with attention-deficit/hyperactivity disorder (ADHD) as well. While children with ADHD may perform similarly to children with learning disabilities, their key deficits are in the cognitive efficiency, processing speed, academic fluency, short-term memory, and long-term retrieval test sections.

PRENATAL, PERINATAL, AND NEONATAL DISABILITIES
Prenatal, perinatal, and neonatal risk factors can be genetic or environmental. These factors put infants at risk for developing **intellectual disabilities** that affect their day-to-day lives. An intellectual disability is a disability that significantly limits a child's overall cognitive abilities. **Prenatal** risk factors include genetic syndromes (e.g., Down syndrome), brain malformation, maternal diseases, and environmental influences. Drugs, alcohol, or poison exposure can all affect an unborn child. **Perinatal** (during delivery) risk factors include labor and delivery trauma or anoxia at birth. **Neonatal** (post-birth) risk factors include hypoxic ischemic brain injury, traumatic brain injury, infections, seizure disorders, and toxic metabolic syndromes. Early screening and applicable assessments are tools used to identify young children with intellectual disabilities and can assist with providing special education services under the Individuals with Disabilities Education Act. These tools can also help assess the severity of deficits and the need for special services, such as occupational therapy.

LEARNING DISABILITIES IN READING AND MATHEMATICS
The Woodcock-Johnson tests (WJ tests) include tests of achievement, cognitive abilities, and oral language. Together, these assessments are useful in the diagnostic process of identifying a student with a **disability**. Additionally, they are helpful for identifying specific **deficits** in a student's reading or math skills. WJ tests are norm-referenced and compare the results of a child's performance to that of a cohort of children of similar age and average intellectual abilities. These assessments provide information about **reading disorders**, such as dyslexia, because they measure phonological awareness, rapid automatized naming, processing speed, and working memory. WJ tests report on a child's cognitive functioning in these test areas. These assessments also provide useful information for students with learning deficits in **mathematics**. Performance on the math

calculation skills and math reasoning test sections provides information on specific deficits in general comprehension, fluid reasoning, and processing speed. Deficits in these areas are correlated with learning disabilities in mathematics.

THE WECHSLER INTELLIGENCE SCALES

The Wechsler Intelligence Scales are assessments that measure the cognitive abilities of children and adults. The **Wechsler Intelligence Scale for Children (WISC)**, now in its fifth edition (WISC-V), is used for children ages 6–16 and measures the child's intellectual ability through 10 primary subtests and 6 secondary subtests. The result is an overall composite score, the Full-Scale Intelligence Quotient (FSIQ), as well as index scores in subcategories such as verbal comprehension, fluid reasoning, and quantitative reasoning. WISC-V results are useful tools for evaluating a student with a disability. Test results can be used to measure and report on a student's general intelligence and provide insight into the student's cognitive abilities in order to determine an appropriate educational pathway. Results can be reported in a student's Evaluation Team Report (ETR) and Individualized Education Program (IEP) in order to justify special education services or have a starting point for IEP goals. WISC-V results are especially important in an ETR, and they are generally completed at least once every three years, because they contribute to describing the **overall performance profile** of a student with a disability.

KAUFMAN ASSESSMENT BATTERY FOR CHILDREN

The Kaufman Assessment Battery for Children (KABC), updated to a second edition in 2008 with a normative update in 2014 (**KABC-II NU**) is a unique standardized test because it is used to evaluate preschoolers, minority groups, and children with learning disabilities. The KABC-II NU can be used to assess children ages 3–18 and is meant to be used with children who are nonverbal, bilingual, or English-speaking. However, it is especially useful in assessing the abilities of students who are **nonverbal**. The KABC-II NU can be used to help determine students' educational placements and assist with their educational planning. This assessment consists of subtests that may be combined and interpreted according to one of two different models depending on the child's language background. The subtests lead to both individual scaled scores and a global score. The scales are:

- Simultaneous
- Sequential
- Planning
- Learning
- Knowledge

The KABC-II NU is also unique because it includes a **nonverbal scale** that can be administered to children with hearing or speech impairments and children who do not speak English.

VINELAND ADAPTIVE BEHAVIOR SCALES

The Vineland Adaptive Behavior Scales, Third Edition (**Vineland-3**), assesses the personal and social skills of children and adults. **Adaptive behavior** refers to the skills needed for day-to-day activities and independent living. Children with disabilities sometimes have deficits in adaptive behavior, and the Vineland-3 is useful for planning their **educational pathways**. It is an especially useful tool for developing **transition plans and goals** for students of appropriate ages on Individualized Education Programs. The Vineland-3 is a process that involves people who know the students best, like parents and teachers. The teacher version and parent version of this assessment can be delivered via interview or survey. The parent version focuses on a student's adaptive behavior at home, while the teacher version focuses on adaptive behavior in the school setting. Vineland-3 assesses four **domains**: communication, activities of daily living, social relationships, and motor skills. A student's parents or caregivers fill out a form pertaining to home life, and a teacher fills out a form pertaining to school settings. The comprehensive score from both the teacher and parent version are used to report abilities in the four domains.

TYPES OF COGNITIVE ASSESSMENTS

Cognitive tests assess the **cognitive functioning abilities** of children and adults. They are useful tools for diagnosing or identifying children with disabilities who are eligible for **special education services** under the Individuals with Disabilities Education Act. Examples of cognitive tests used in diagnosing or identifying children with disabilities include aptitude tests and intelligence quotient (IQ) tests. There are also cognitive assessments that measure verbal reasoning, numerical reasoning, abstract reasoning, spatial ability, verbal ability, and more. Children's cognitive abilities are related to how quickly they **process** information. Assessment results can be good measurements of how quickly children may learn new information or tasks. Cognitive assessments provide specific information about children's cognitive functioning by providing measurements of their intelligence, attention, concentration, processing speed, language and communication, visual-spatial abilities, and short- and long-term memory capabilities. Results can also be used on a child's Evaluation Team Report or to develop goals for an Individualized Education Program.

ADVANTAGES AND DISADVANTAGES OF CURRICULUM-BASED ASSESSMENTS

Curriculum-based assessments (**CBAs**) determine if students are making adequate progress through the curriculum. They can be administered by a teacher, special educator, or school psychologist. CBAs have advantages over norm-referenced assessments, like developmental assessments, because they are not used to compare performance between students. Other types of assessments measure a student's cumulative abilities across multiple skills instead of assessing individual skills. CBAs measure student progress in more **individualized** ways. They are especially useful for measuring IEP goal progress. Since CBAs are **teacher-created assessments**, they provide opportunities to assess students informally and formally on IEP goals. For example, a teacher may verbally quiz a student on ten addition problems to determine if the student is making progress on math IEP goals. CBAs are also used in the "response to intervention" process to identify students with special needs by measuring the effectiveness of interventions provided to them.

Individualized Education Programs

DEVELOPING AND WRITING MEASURABLE IEP GOALS

According to the Individuals with Disabilities Education Act, students eligible for special education receive Individualized Education Program (IEP) goals, which must contain specific **components**. Components of a **measurable IEP goal** include condition, performance, criteria, assessment, and standard. Measurable goals also include how skill mastery will be **assessed**, such as through observations or work samples. In the provided example below, the criterion is clearly measurable, as Jacob will either succeed or fail at multiple trials, and the ratio of successes to numbers of attempts should be recorded and dated throughout the IEP year to show his progress. Goals should also be **standards-based** whenever possible and may be required.

For example, an IEP goal may state, "By the end of this IEP, Jacob will use appropriate skills to communicate his needs in four out of five trials."

- **Condition** refers to when, where, and how the disability will be addressed. "By the end of this IEP" is the condition of the goal.
- **Performance** is what the student is expected to accomplish during the condition of the goal. In this case, that is "Jacob will use appropriate skills to communicate his needs."
- The last part of the goal stating "in four out of five trials" is the **criterion** that outlines how well the goal will be performed.

> **Review Video: IEPs**
> Visit mometrix.com/academy and enter code: 153484

ROLE OF LOCAL EDUCATION AGENCY REPRESENTATIVES IN IEP MEETINGS

A local education agency (**LEA**) representative is a member of the IEP team who is trained in special education curriculum, general education curriculum, and community resources. In many cases, a school building leader or principal may fulfill the role of LEA representative. An LEA rep must be a licensed professional who knows the student and is familiar with the IEP process. The role of LEA representatives in IEP meetings is to make sure the information presented is compliant with the Individuals with Disabilities Education Act (IDEA) standards. LEA representatives are also responsible for ensuring that the school district is **compliant** with procedural components of IDEA and that eligible students are receiving free and appropriate public educations. This role is necessary on the IEP team because whereas the whole IEP team should have the students' best interests in mind, they may not understand the doctrines of IDEA and be able to consider compliance. As a result, the LEA representative must act as the primary advocate for effective implementation of the IEP.

INVOLVEMENT OF STUDENTS WITH IEPS IN THE TRANSITION PROCESS IN HIGH SCHOOL

Most states require **transition statements** to be made when students reach age 14 during the IEP year. Federal law requires students 16 years of age or older to have transition statements; postsecondary goals for independent living, employment, and education; and summaries of performance that include the results of the most recent transition assessments. Per federal law, students of transition age must be invited to their **IEP meetings**. It is important for students on IEPs to **participate** in the transition process because it helps them figure out what they want to do after they graduate from high school. Participation in the process gets them thinking about living independently, postsecondary education options, and employment options. Students usually have opportunities to participate in formal and informal assessments like interest inventories that help them define their interests. Transition goals for independent living, employment, and education should be based on the results of these assessments and any other interests the students have expressed. The students participate in the **implementation** of the transition goals by completing activities associated with their indicated interests.

STUDENT SUPPORT TEAMS

A **student support team (SST)** is a team made up of parents and educational professionals who work to support students in the general education classroom who are struggling with academics, discipline, health problems, or any other anticipated or actual problem that does not qualify the student for special education or supports from an Individualized Education Program. In this support team model, a group of educators works to identify and provide early intervention services for any student exhibiting academic or behavioral problems. The purpose of this kind of SST is to offer different supports, such as monitoring student progress, developing intervention plans, and referring students for intervention services. While the primary goal of this kind of SST is to provide support for students **struggling with school**, it can also shift focus to supporting students at risk of **dropping out of school**. Another primary objective of an SST is to identify students who are likely to have disabilities or who may need 504 Plans to succeed in school and to recommend them for referrals so they are not left without necessary supports.

AMENDMENTS TO AN INDIVIDUALIZED EDUCATION PROGRAM

A student's IEP is in effect for one year. Academic goals, objectives, benchmarks, transition goals, and any accommodations and modifications are to be in place for the student for the duration of the IEP. An **amendment** to the IEP can be made when a change is needed before the year is over. An amendment is an agreement between the student, parents or legal guardians, and the IEP team. IEP meetings for amendments can be requested at any time. IEP amendments can be requested if a student is not making adequate progress toward the goals, if the goals become inappropriate in some way for the student, or when the student has met all IEP goals and requires new ones. If new information about the student becomes available, the IEP can be amended. Students, parents, and other team members may also request amendment meetings if they think that other accommodations and modifications are needed or should be removed.

HOW THE NEEDS OF STUDENTS WITH IEPS ARE MET IN THE SCHOOL ENVIRONMENT

IEPs communicate what **services** are to be provided for children with disabilities in the school setting, the children's **present levels of performance**, and how their disabilities affect **academic performance**. IEPs also specify **annual goals** appropriate to the students' specific needs and any accommodations or modifications that need to be provided. Schools and teachers have the responsibility to implement these IEP components when working with students with disabilities. Additionally, schools and teachers working with students with disabilities must ensure that students' individualized annual goals are met within a year of the students' IEP effective dates. It is up to the IEP teams to determine what classroom settings would most benefit the students while also appropriately meeting their IEP goals with the fewest barriers. Special educators must determine how data is collected and then obtain and record data on how the students are meeting their IEP goals. Special educators are responsible for providing intervention services based on the data results. They must also ensure that any accommodations or modifications listed on the IEPs are implemented in both general education and self-contained classrooms.

ACCOMMODATION VS. MODIFICATION IN IEPS

Formal accommodations, adaptations, and modifications for a student with a disability are listed on the Individualized Education Program. **Accommodations** change *how* a student learns the material, while an **adaptation** or **modification** changes *what* a student is taught or expected to learn.

- **Accommodations** are changes to the instruction or assessment that do *not* alter the curricular requirements. For instance, a student with accommodations may be allowed to answer a test orally instead of writing the answers or might be given pre-structured notes to help organize thoughts during instruction. These types of changes do not fundamentally change the information taught or the requirements for passing.
- **Adaptations** or **modifications** are changes to the instruction or assessment that fundamentally change the curricular requirements, but which enable a student with a disability to participate. Examples of adaptations include substitution of activities for related materials, exemption from answering particular types of questions on assessments, and removing or reducing time limits when taking tests.

For state standardized tests, accommodations like extra time and frequent breaks can be provided. Students that need modifications to state tests may complete alternate assessments that may not cover the same material as the standard exams.

> **Review Video: Adapting and Modifying Lessons or Activities**
> Visit mometrix.com/academy and enter code: 834946

DETERMINING THE PLACEMENT OF A STUDENT WITH A DISABILITY

With every student, the ideal goal is placement in the **general education classroom** as much as possible while still meeting the student's educational needs and ensuring a successful educational experience. The Individuals with Disabilities Education Act does not require that students be placed in the regular education classroom, but it does require that students be placed in their **least restrictive environment** as defined by the student's IEP team. Ultimately, the IEP team determines what **environment** best suits the student based on the student's specific needs. The IEP team is responsible for determining what educational environment would provide the student with the maximum appropriate educational benefit. While justification for removing a student from the regular education classroom is common and appropriate, as occurs when a student is placed in a resource room, the IEP team must explain the reasoning in the student's IEP. **Justification** must specifically state why the student cannot be educated with accommodations and services in the regular education classroom during any part of the school day. Justification for removal cannot be the perceived instructional limitations of the regular education teacher or concerns over extra instructional time needed to educate a student with a disability.

CREATING A SMART ANNUAL GOAL IN AN IEP

A good IEP goal describes how far the student is expected to **progress** toward the goal by the next IEP. Since IEPs should be revised once a year, a good annual IEP goal should describe what the student is capable of doing in a one-year time frame. Creating **SMART** IEP goals can help the student determine realistic expectations of what can be achieved in a year. SMART IEP goals are specific, measurable, attainable, relevant, and time-bound. Goals are **specific** when they list the targeted result in the skill or subject area. Goals should also be specific to the student's needs. Goals that are **measurable** state the way a student's progress will be measured. Measurable goals list how accurately a student should meet the goal. **Attainable** goals are realistic for the student to achieve in one year. **Relevant** goals outline what a student needs to do to accomplish the goal. For example, a SMART goal may state, "During the school week, Robert will use his device to communicate greetings 80 percent of the time in four out of five trials." **Time-bound** goals include a time frame for the student to achieve the goal. They also list when and how often progress will be measured.

> **Review Video: SMART Goals**
> Visit mometrix.com/academy and enter code: 100378

ROLE OF AN INITIAL EVALUATION ASSESSMENT IN QUALIFYING FOR SPECIAL EDUCATION

When a student is determined to need special education, it means the student has a disability or disabilities adversely affecting educational performance. It may also mean the student's needs cannot be addressed in the general education classroom with or without accommodations and that **specially designed instruction** is required. An **initial evaluation** of the student is required for special education eligibility. The evaluation is comprehensive and includes existing data collected on the student and additional assessments needed to determine eligibility. Individual school districts decide what assessments should be completed for the student's initial evaluation. Each district is responsible for and should provide assessments that measure functional, developmental, and academic information. The student's parents or legal guardians are responsible for providing outside information relevant to the student's education, such as medical needs assessed outside of the school district by qualified providers.

PURPOSE OF AN IEP

The purpose of an IEP is to guide the learning of a student with a **disability** in the educational environment. An IEP is a written statement for a student eligible for **special education**. An initial IEP is **implemented** once the child has been evaluated and determined to be in need of special education. After the initial IEP, **IEP meetings** are conducted annually (or more often) in order to update the plan to meet the needs of the student. IEPs are created, reviewed, and revised according to individual state and federal laws. These plans include the amount of time the student will spend in the special education classroom based on the level of need. They also include any related services the student might need (such as speech-language therapy) as well as academic and behavioral goals for the year. As the student learns and changes, performance levels and goals change as well. A student's present levels of performance are included and updated yearly, as are the academic and behavioral goals.

MEMBERS OF AN INDIVIDUALIZED EDUCATION PROGRAM TEAM

IEPs are updated **annually** following the initial IEP. IEP team members meet at least once a year to discuss a student's progress and make changes to the IEP. The required members of a student's IEP team include the student's parents or legal guardians, one of the student's general education teachers, the special education teacher, a school representative, an individual who can interpret the instructional implications of evaluation results, and if appropriate, the student. Anyone else who has knowledge or expertise about the student may also attend. **Parents and legal guardians** contribute unique expertise about the student, typically having the benefit of knowing the child well. **General education teachers** can speak to how the student is performing in the general education classroom. The **special education teacher** can report on progress made toward academic and behavioral goals and present levels of performance. A **school representative** must be qualified to provide or supervise specially designed instruction, be knowledgeable of the general education curriculum, and be knowledgeable about school resources. The **individual who can interpret evaluation results** can be an existing team member or someone else who is qualified to report on evaluation results. **Advocates**, such as counselors or therapists who see the student outside the school day, can also attend the meeting to speak on the student's behalf.

LEGAL RIGHTS OF PARENTS OR LEGAL GUARDIANS

IEP meetings occur annually for each student. However, it is a **parent or legal guardian's right** to request a meeting at any point during the school year. The student's school is responsible for identifying and evaluating the child; developing, reviewing, or revising the IEP; and determining what placement setting best suits the needs of the student. It is within the parent or legal guardian's rights to have **input** in all processes related to the student. Under the Individuals with Disabilities Education Act, parents have the right to participate in IEP meetings, have an independent evaluation in addition to the one the school provides, give or deny consent for the IEP, contest a school's decision, and obtain private education paid for by the public school. In specific circumstances, if the student is determined to need services that the public school cannot provide, the public school district may need to pay for the student's tuition at a private school where the student's needs can be met.

COLLABORATIVE CONSULTATION BETWEEN EDUCATIONAL PROFESSIONALS

Collaborative consultation refers to the special educator or other professional providing advice to the general education teacher about a student on an IEP. Special educators and other IEP team members, such as school psychologists and related service professionals, serve as the **experts** and have knowledge about how individual students learn and behave. This is especially important when students with IEPs are included in the general education classroom. Special educators and general education teachers must work collaboratively to ensure that students are reaching their potential in the general education setting. Examples of **collaborative consultation** include the special educator serving as a consultant to the general education teacher by providing advice on a student's IEP, accommodations, modifications, and IEP goal tracking. Another way the special educator or other professional can assist the general educator is by providing skill and strategy instruction to students on IEPs outside the general education classroom. The idea behind this method is for students to generalize these skills and strategies to the general education classroom.

> **Review Video: Collaborating with Other Professionals**
> Visit mometrix.com/academy and enter code: 100351

PUBLIC SCHOOL RESPONSIBILITIES TO PARENTS OF STUDENTS ON IEPS

The school must invite the parents or legal guardians to any **IEP meetings** and provide advance notice of the meetings. Each meeting notice is required to include the purpose of the meeting, its time and location, and who will attend. The location of the meeting is likely the student's school, but legally it must be held at a mutually agreed-upon place and time. If the parent or legal guardian cannot attend the IEP meeting, the school must ensure participation in another way, such as video or telephone conference. The meeting can be conducted without the parent or legal guardian if the school district cannot get the parent or legal guardian to attend. A parent or legal guardian can request a meeting, and the school can refuse or deny the request. If denied, the school must provide a **prior written notice** explaining their refusal. A prior written notice is a document outlining important school district decisions about a student on an IEP.

Collaborating with IEP Team Members

It is important for Individualized Education Program (IEP) team members to **collaborate** with each other in order to ensure that students are receiving educational plans that are suitable to their needs in the least restrictive environments. **IEP team members** include special education teachers, general education teachers, parents or legal guardians, students, school district representatives, and others knowledgeable about the students' performances. Each member brings a valuable piece of information about the students for instructional planning and IEP planning meetings. It is important for special educators to establish good relationships and collaborate with the students and parents or legal guardians in order to gauge the students' strengths and weaknesses. Collaboration is essential between the general and special educators in order to ensure that students' IEP goals and needs are being met in the appropriate settings. Collaboration with district team members or others like school psychologists is helpful for gaining insight on special education procedures or assessment results.

> **Review Video: Collaborating with Other Professionals**
> Visit mometrix.com/academy and enter code: 100351

COMMUNICATING WITH SERVICE MEMBERS ACROSS ALL SPECIAL EDUCATION SETTINGS

In order to provide the best educations possible for students with disabilities, it is important for special educators and related service members to **communicate** effectively. Communication is important due to the degree of collaboration required between the special educators and the related service members. Related service members are often IEP team members and help students meet their IEP goals and objectives. **Related service members**, like speech pathologists and

occupational therapists, also work on a consultation basis with special educators. They may also consult with general education teachers to ensure that students receive required related services in the general education or inclusive classroom settings. Special educators and related service members must collaborate in order to ensure the needs of the students are met, especially when IEP goals or objectives are out of the scope of the special educators' knowledge bases. For example, a speech pathologist might help a teacher address a student's fluency goal.

COMMUNICATING WITH PARENTS OF STUDENTS WITH DISABILITIES

It is good practice to communicate with parents outside of progress reporting times and Individualized Education Program meetings. This is especially important for students with **communication deficits** who may not be able to communicate with their parents or legal guardians. Communication also helps prevent potential crises or problem behaviors and alerts parents or legal guardians before any major issues arise. Special educators should find methods of communication that work best for parents or legal guardians, such as phone calls, emails, or writing in daily communication logs. Email is beneficial for creating paper trails, especially for any discussions about educating students. However, email lacks tone and body language and can sometimes be misunderstood. Phone calls fulfill an immediate need to speak with a parent or legal guardian. However, there are no paper trails with phone calls, and they can also lead to misunderstanding. Phone calls may be time consuming, but they can be conducted on special occasions or when behavioral issues need to be discussed. Written communication logs are useful for writing brief summaries about students' days. With any mode of communication, it is essential to **document** what is communicated between the parents or legal guardians and the educators.

THE ROLES AND RIGHTS FAMILIES HAVE IN THE EDUCATION OF CHILDREN WITH DISABILITIES

Under the Individuals with Disabilities Education Act, parents and legal guardians of children with disabilities have **procedural safeguards** that protect their rights. The safeguards also provide parents and legal guardians with the means to resolve any disputes with school systems. **Parents and legal guardians** may underestimate their importance to IEP teams. However, they are important members of IEP teams and integral parts of the decision-making processes for their children's educational journeys. Parents and legal guardians often work more closely with their children than other adults. Therefore, as part of IEP teams, they serve as **advocates** and can often provide insight regarding the children's backgrounds, educational and developmental histories, strengths, and weaknesses. Parents and legal guardians are also important decision-makers in transition meetings, when students with disabilities move from one level of school to another. Their input in transition meetings helps ensure that appropriate services and supports are in place at the next levels of school so that students can succeed.

ROLES OF PARENTS/LEGAL GUARDIANS AND THE SCHOOL DISTRICT DURING EVALUATION

If parents or legal guardians suspect their children have disabilities, they can request that the school districts **evaluate** the children for special education. A parent or legal guardian can send a **written evaluation request** to the child's school, principal, and the school district's director or director of special education services. In some states, parents and legal guardians may be required to sign a school district form requesting the evaluation. Parents should follow up on the request and/or set a time frame for the school district to respond. The school district may choose to implement the **Response to Intervention (RTI) pre-referral process**. RTI is a process by which the school gives the student special academic support before determining whether or not to move forward with the evaluation process. Not all states or school districts have the same method for applying RTI. Under the Individuals with Disabilities Education Act, the time frame for completion of RTI is 60 days. However, some states can set their own timelines. RTI should not be the only means by which the school district collects data on the student and should be part of a comprehensive evaluation conducted by the student's school.

Speech Language Pathologist

Speech language pathologists (**SLPs**) provide interventions for children with communication disorders. They can assist, evaluate, prevent, and diagnose a variety of **speech issues**, from fluency to voice disorders. Before children reach grade school age, it is important that they receive early interventions for suspected communication disorders. SLPs are helpful with targeting speech or language issues, identifying at-risk students, or providing interventions for children and adults. SLPs also play a role in helping children develop good reading and writing skills, especially when deficits are evident. SLPs work collaboratively with special educators to deliver **interventions** to children with speech and language disorders in grade school. In schools, SLPs play a role in prevention, assessment, intervention, program design, data collection and analysis, and Individualized Education Program compliance. SLPs work with special educators, parents, students, reading specialists, occupational therapists, school psychologists, and others in order to provide effective services to students who require them.

Occupational Therapist

Students with special needs may need **occupational therapy services**. The number of services students receive is defined on their IEPs. **Occupational therapists (OTs)** may help students on IEPs refine their fine motor skills, improve sensory processing deficits, improve visual skills, and improve self-care skills. OTs can also assist with behavior management, social skills, and improving attention and focus. When a student is identified as possibly needing occupational therapy, the OT spends time observing the student in a variety of settings where the skill or skill deficit will be demonstrated. Prior to the student's IEP meeting, the OT typically meets with the student's teachers, parents, and other professionals in order to discuss observations, assessment results, and determinations. **Determinations** are then put into the IEP and implemented as related services. Fine motor skill instruction begins with the OT instructing the student on a particular skill. OTs can set up regimens for teachers and parents to generalize using the fine motor skills in the classroom and home environments.

Paraprofessional

The US Department of Education requires paraprofessionals to have high school diplomas or the equivalent under Title I law. Paraprofessionals (paras), sometimes called **paraeducators**, assist classroom teachers with classroom activities and help students with special needs. In a special education setting, a para works with a certified teacher to help deliver **instruction** and help students meet **Individualized Education Program goals and objectives**. Paras are not responsible for teaching new skills or introducing new goals and objectives to students. In this respect, special educators generally work alongside the paras and students to introduce new skills, goals, or objectives. At times, paras may be responsible for helping students maintain behavior plans, working with students who may be aggressive or violent, and providing physical assistance if necessary. Training is usually provided by the school district for situations when physical assistance is a possible necessity. Paras can also help take notes on students' progress toward meeting their goals or objectives. They can also discuss how students are progressing with behavior plans.

Behavior Assessment and Intervention

COGNITIVE BEHAVIORAL THEORY

The cognitive behavioral theory states that people form their own negative or positive concepts that affect their behaviors. The cognitive behavioral theory involves a **cognitive triad** of thoughts and behaviors. This triad refers to thoughts about the **self**, the **world and environment**, and the **future**. In times of stress, people's thoughts can become distressed or dysfunctional. Sometimes cognitive behavioral therapy, based on the cognitive behavioral theory model, is used to help people address and manage their thoughts. This process involves people examining their thoughts more closely in order to bring them back to more realistic, grounded ways of thinking. People's thoughts and perceptions can often affect their lives negatively and lead to unhealthy emotions and behaviors. **Cognitive behavioral therapy** helps people to adjust their thinking, learn ways to access healthy thoughts, and learn healthier or safer behaviors.

ANTECEDENTS, BEHAVIOR, AND CONSEQUENCES AS STIMULI USED IN BEHAVIOR ANALYSIS

Antecedents and consequences play a role in behavioral analysis, which is important for evaluating the behaviors of students. The purpose of behavior analysis is to gather information about a specific behavior demonstrated by a student. **Antecedents** are the actions or events that occur before the behavior occurs. It is important to recognize antecedents for behaviors to better understand under what circumstances the behavior is occurring. The **behavior** is the undesirable action that occurs as a result of the antecedent. **Consequences** are what happens immediately after the behavior occurs. These can be natural or enforced. A student might desire a certain consequence when engaging in the behavior. Understanding the relationships between antecedents, behavior, and consequences allows a professional to determine how to minimize or eliminate the behavior. In some circumstances, antecedents and consequences can be manipulated, changed, or removed in order to avoid reinforcing the undesired behavior.

BEHAVIOR RATING SCALE ASSESSMENTS

Behavior rating scales address the needs of students with emotional disorders who are referred to special education. Problems with behavior are often the reason a student has been referred for special education. These scales are used in determining a student's **eligibility** for special education, and in addressing **undesirable behaviors** demonstrated by students already in special education for reasons other than behavior problems. They are similar to adaptive behavior scales in that teachers or other professionals can administer the scales with little training as long as they are familiar with the students. Behavior rating scales help measure the frequency and intensity of the behaviors for a particular student often by assigning numbered ratings. They serve as a starting point for learning more about a student's behavior so that behavior interventions and management can take place. These scales are **norm-referenced**, so the outcomes of the behavior rating scales are compared to the behaviors of others.

NEGATIVE AND POSITIVE REINFORCEMENT RELATED TO APPLIED BEHAVIOR ANALYSIS

Part of applied behavior analysis (**ABA**) is applying negative and positive reinforcement strategies, which are forms of conditioning strategies. In behavioral conditioning, the term **reinforcement** refers to trying to increase the frequency of a desired behavior, whereas the term **punishment** refers to trying to decrease the frequency of an undesired behavior. Similarly, when discussing behavioral conditioning methods, the word **positive** refers to the *addition* of a stimulus, whereas

the word **negative** refers to the *removal* of a stimulus. These four terms tend to be confused but are very specifically used to denote particular types of behavioral conditioning.

Positive reinforcement works by providing a desired **reward** for a desired behavior. For example, parents may give a child an allowance (the positive reinforcement) for doing chores (the behavior). In contrast, **negative reinforcement** removes an aversive stimulus to encourage a desired behavior. An example of this might be that a parent rewards a child's behavior by taking away some of his chores. Negative reinforcement is different from a punishment because the goal of punishment is to *discourage* an unwanted behavior while the goal of negative reinforcement is to *encourage* a desirable behavior. Although it is not commonly discussed, positive and negative stimuli may be used at the same time in conditioning to effect a greater change.

Term:	Example:
Positive Reinforcement	A teacher *gives* the high-scorers on a test a sticker.
Negative Reinforcement	A teacher *takes away* an assignment if the class performs well on a test.
Positive Punishment	A police officer *gives* a driver a speeding ticket.
Negative Punishment	A parent grounds a student, *taking away* video games for two weeks.
Combination Reinforcement	A physical education teacher *replaces* a workout (negative) with a game (positive) because the class was well-behaved.
Combination Punishment	A student gets low grades and is required to complete extra schoolwork (positive) and is not allowed to participate in sports for a week (negative).

DEVELOPING POSITIVE BEHAVIORAL INTERVENTIONS AND SUPPORTS

Positive behavioral intervention and support (**PBIS**) plans can be implemented in classrooms or schoolwide to encourage specific, positive outcomes in groups of students with and without disabilities. A PBIS plan, such as an anti-bullying campaign, is put in place to encourage **good behavior** and **school safety** and to remove **environmental triggers** of undesirable behavior. The goal of a PBIS plan is for students to learn appropriate behavior just as they would learn an academic subject. Effective PBIS plans are based on research and analysis of data collected on targeted, large-scale behaviors. As with any behavioral plan, the success of PBIS plans is determined by monitoring student progress. PBIS plans should change if they do not work or if they stop working.

DEVELOPING A FUNCTIONAL BEHAVIOR ASSESSMENT

A functional behavior assessment (**FBA**) is a formal process used to examine student behavior. The goal of an FBA is to identify what is causing a specific behavior and evaluate how the behavior is affecting the student's educational performance. Once these factors are determined, the FBA is useful in implementing **interventions** for the behavior. When an FBA is developed, a student's behavior must be specifically defined; then the teacher or other professional devises a plan for collecting data on the behavior. These points of data are helpful in determining possible causes of the behavior, such as environmental triggers. The teacher or other professional can then implement the most appropriate plan for addressing the student's behavior. Often, this means implementing a **behavior intervention plan**, which includes introducing the student to actions or processes that are incompatible with the problem behavior. It is important to monitor the plan to ensure its effectiveness or remediate certain steps.

> **Review Video: Functional Behavior Assessments**
> Visit mometrix.com/academy and enter code: 783262

DEVELOPING BEHAVIOR INTERVENTION PLANS

A behavior intervention plan (**BIP**) is based on a functional behavior assessment. The purpose of the BIP is to teach the student actions, behaviors, or processes that are incompatible with the problem behavior. The BIP may be included in an Individualized Education Program (IEP) or 504 Plan, or components of the BIP may be written out as IEP goals. Once an FBA is conducted, a BIP is put in place that describes the target behavior, lists factors that trigger the behavior, and lists any interventions that help the student avoid the behavior. The interventions include problem-solving skills for the student to use instead of demonstrating the target behavior. If the interventions fail to target the problem behavior or are no longer effective for targeting the behavior, then the FBA must be revisited and a new BIP developed.

POSITIVE CLASSROOM DISCIPLINE STRATEGIES

A core element of effective classroom management, positive classroom discipline is a means of holding students accountable for their actions, and it starts with establishing clear and consistent **consequences** for poor choices. Students learn to predict consequences and self-correct their behaviors. It is helpful to give students **reminders** about behavior and rules instead of immediately resorting to consequences. **Pre-reminders** about expectations can be given before starting a lesson. **Nonverbal reminders** such as looks, touches, silence, or removal are possible ways to discourage students from engaging in poor choices. Removal as a consequence involves sending the student out of the classroom either to protect the other students from harm or to prevent a student from impeding the course of instruction. Removal laws vary between states and local districts, but removal is generally mandatory whenever a student is being violent. **Spoken reminders** can be used to further encourage self-management skills and should be used as precursors for reminding students about expectations instead of delivering immediate consequences.

PROMOTING APPROPRIATE BEHAVIOR IN INCLUSIVE LEARNING ENVIRONMENTS

Effective classrooms have good management strategies in place that promote good learning environments and minimize disruptions. Teachers with effective classroom management strategies demonstrate good leadership and organization skills. They also promote positive classroom experiences, establish clear expectations for behavior, and reinforce positive behaviors. In **inclusive learning environments**, it is important for teachers to keep all students on track with their learning. When it comes to students with disabilities, planning classroom management strategies presents different challenges. Effective teachers understand how students' special needs come into play with expected classroom behaviors. General and special educators can demonstrate effective classroom management strategies by figuring out what is causing students to act out or misbehave. They should collaborate with other professionals and students' parents to ensure the success of students with special needs in their classrooms. Lastly, effective classroom management includes setting goals for inclusive classrooms to achieve. Clear goals help establish good rapport with students with special needs because they know what is expected of them.

Chapter Quiz

Ready to see how well you retained what you just read? Scan the QR code to go directly to the chapter quiz interface for this study guide. If you're using a computer, simply visit the online resources page at **mometrix.com/resources719/westeearchsped** and click the Chapter Quizzes link.

Delivering Specially Designed Instruction to Promote Development and Learning

Transform passive reading into active learning! After immersing yourself in this chapter, put your comprehension to the test by taking a quiz. The insights you gained will stay with you longer this way. Scan the QR code to go directly to the chapter quiz interface for this study guide. If you're using a computer, simply visit the online resources page at **mometrix.com/resources719/westeearchsped** and click the Chapter Quizzes link.

Adapting Instruction to Individual Needs

EVALUATING ACTIVITIES AND MATERIALS TO MEET LEARNING NEEDS

The careful selection of instructional activities and materials is integral to accommodating students' varying characteristics and needs. When evaluating the appropriateness of activities and materials, several considerations must be made. Teachers must consider whether activities and materials align with state and district **academic standards**. Teachers must also evaluate the quality and effectiveness of the activities and materials in supporting students' unique differences as they achieve learning goals and objectives. All materials and activities must be **developmentally appropriate** across domains yet adaptable to individual students' learning needs. In addition, they must be challenging yet feasible for student achievement relative to students' grade levels and abilities to promote engagement and the development of critical and **higher-order thinking** skills. Teachers must evaluate activities and materials for versatility to allow for student choice and differentiation in order to address varying characteristics and needs. Teachers must also ensure that activities and materials are accurate, **culturally sensitive**, and reflective of students' diversities to foster an inclusive learning environment that promotes engagement.

INSTRUCTIONAL RESOURCES AND TECHNOLOGIES

The implementation of varied instructional resources and technologies is highly valuable in supporting student engagement and achievement. Effective use of resources and technologies requires teachers to evaluate their appropriateness in addressing students' individual characteristics and learning needs for academic success. Teachers must be attuned to students' unique differences in order to seek high quality technologies and resources that address their students' needs and support the achievement of learning goals and objectives. Technologies and resources must be **accurate**, **comprehensible**, easily **accessible** to students, and **relevant** to the curriculum and the development of particular skills. Teachers must also consider the grade-level and **developmental appropriateness** of technologies and resources as well as their adaptability to allow for differentiation. Effective technologies and resources are interactive, engaging, and multifaceted to allow for varying levels of complexity based on students' abilities. This allows teachers to provide appropriate challenges while diversifying instruction to appeal to varied characteristics and learning needs, thus fostering an engaging environment that supports success in learning for all students.

Adapting Activities and Materials to Meet Individual Characteristics and Needs

In effective instruction, activities and materials are adapted to accommodate students' individual characteristics and needs. Teachers must be attuned to students' unique differences and understand how to adjust activities and materials accordingly to facilitate academic success and growth. To achieve this, teachers must incorporate a **variety** of activities and materials that appeal to all styles of learners. Activities and materials should provide **student choice** for engagement in learning and demonstration of understanding. By differentiating instruction, teachers can effectively scaffold activities and materials to provide supports as necessary as well as include extensions or alternate activities for enrichment. **Chunking** instruction, allowing extra time as necessary, and accompanying activities and materials with aids such as graphic organizers, visual representations, and anticipation guides further differentiates learning to accommodate students' learning characteristics and needs. Conducting **formative assessments** provides teachers with valuable feedback regarding student understanding and engagement, thus allowing them to modify and adjust the complexity of activities and materials as necessary to adapt to varied characteristics and learning differences.

Instructional Resources and Technologies

When teachers understand students' individual characteristics and needs, they can adapt instructional resources and technologies accordingly to maximize learning. To do so effectively, the teacher must incorporate a diverse array of **multifaceted** resources and technologies that support and enhance learning through a variety of methods. This ensures that varying learning needs are met, as students of all learning styles are provided with several avenues for building and strengthening understanding. Additionally, the teacher can adapt resources and technologies to accommodate individual students by **varying the complexity** to provide challenges, support, and opportunities for enrichment based on ability level. Supplementing technologies and resources with **scaffolds**, such as extra time, visual representations, or opportunities for collaborative learning, further enables the teacher to adapt to individual learning needs. When effectively implemented and adapted to students' characteristics and needs, instructional technologies and resources serve as valuable tools for differentiating curriculum to enhance the learning experience.

Modifications, Accommodations, and Adaptations

Accommodations and Modifications

Accommodations and modifications are different types of educational supports put in place to help a student participate effectively in school. An **accommodation** changes *how* a student is taught or assessed by providing more time or other supports that remove barriers to the material. Students who receive accommodations are taught and assessed to the same standards as students without accommodations. A **modification** changes *what* is taught or assessed by changing or omitting parts of the materials. Students with modifications may receive fewer problems to solve or lower-rigor versions of the materials compared to other students.

Modifications

Modifications are changes to *what* students are taught or expected to learn. Students with disabilities can receive modifications as determined by their specific needs and as written out in their Individualized Education Programs.

- **Curriculum modifications** allow students to learn material that is different from what their general education peers learn. For example, students with classroom modifications may receive assignments with fewer math problems or with reading samples appropriate for their reading levels. Students with curriculum modifications may receive different grading tiers than their peers. The ways teachers grade their assignments may be different from how the teachers grade their peers' assignments. Students may also be excused from particular projects or given project guidelines that are different and better suited to their individual needs.
- **Assignment modifications** include completing fewer or different homework problems than peers, writing shorter papers, answering fewer questions on classwork and tests, and creating alternate projects or assignments.

Environmental Modifications

Students with disabilities may need environmental modifications in order to be successful in their classrooms, homes, and communities. **Environmental modifications** are adaptations that allow people with disabilities to maneuver through their environments with as little resistance as possible. They allow for more **independent living experiences**, especially for those with limited mobility. Environmental modifications ensure the health, safety, and welfare of the people who need them. Examples of environmental modifications in the home, community, or school include ramps, hydraulic lifts, widened doorways and hallways, automatic doors, handrails, and grab bars. Roll-in showers, water faucet controls, worktable or work surface adaptations, and cabinet and shelving adaptations are also environmental modifications that can be provided if necessary. Other adaptations include heating and cooling adaptations and electrical adaptations to accommodate devices or equipment. Environmental modifications in the home are typically provided by qualified agencies or providers. The Americans with Disabilities Act ensures that environmental modifications are provided in the **community** to help avoid discrimination against people with disabilities.

Accommodations

Accommodations are flexible classroom tools because they can be used to provide **interventions** without time or location boundaries. They remove **barriers** to learning for students with disabilities, and they change how students learn. Accommodations do not change what students are learning or expected to know. Classroom accommodations may be outlined in students' Individualized Education Programs (IEPs) and 504 Plans or simply provided as needed by special educators or general educators. Accommodations are put into place to ensure that students with disabilities are accessing the learning process with the fewest barriers, putting them on the same levels as their peers without disabilities. **Presentation accommodations** include allowing students to listen to oral instructions, providing written lists of instructions, and allowing students to use readers to assist with comprehension. **Response accommodations** include allowing students to provide oral responses, capture responses via audio recording, and use spelling dictionaries or spell-checkers when writing. **Accommodations to setting** include special seating (wherever the students learn best), use of sensory tools, and special lighting.

Types of Accommodations

Timing, schedule, and organizational accommodations change the ways students with disabilities have access to classrooms with the fewest barriers to learning. Students who need these accommodations receive them as written statements in their IEPs, 504 Plans, or as teachers see fit during classroom time.

- **Timing accommodations** allow students more time to complete tasks or tests and/or process instructions. They also allow students to access frequent breaks during assignments or tests.
- **Schedule accommodations** include taking tests in chunks over periods of time or several days, taking test sections in different orders, and/or taking tests during specific times of day.
- **Organizational skill accommodations** include assistance with time management, marking texts with highlighters, maintaining daily assignment or work schedules, and/or receiving study skills instruction.

When accommodations are written in a student's IEP, the student has access to them for state standardized tests. When and how accommodations are put into place is left to the discretion of the teacher unless specifically written in the student's IEP or 504 Plan.

OBTAINING ACCOMMODATIONS

When parents or legal guardians of children with disabilities believe that **accommodations** may help their children, they can arrange to speak with teachers about informal supports. **Informal supports** are strategies teachers can put into place to assist students with their learning processes. These changes do not require paperwork and can be implemented during classroom instruction. Teachers can experiment with informal supports to determine what will be most helpful for removing the barriers to learning students might be experiencing. If it is determined that students need bigger changes to how they learn, **formal evaluations** can take place. Students who do not already have IEPs or 504 Plans may be evaluated to collect data on their needs. For students with IEPs or 504 Plans, accommodations can be included the next time these plans are updated. The IEPs or 504 Plans can also be **amended** if the need for the accommodations is immediate, such as when they need to be put in place before standardized testing time. **Data** supporting the need for the accommodations must be provided and listed in the comprehensive initial evaluations and all versions of IEPs and 504 Plans.

PARENTS AND LEGAL GUARDIANS ENSURING ACCOMMODATIONS ARE BEING PROVIDED

Accommodations are changes to the ways children with disabilities learn, not changes to what the children are learning. While parents and legal guardians may only receive **formal updates** on how accommodations are being provided or helping the students during specified reporting times (unless students' IEPs or 504 Plans specifically state otherwise), they can ask for **reports** on goal progress or accommodations for their students at any time. Parents and legal guardians can ensure that accommodations are successfully implemented by using the progress reports and asking the right questions. Parents and legal guardians can ensure that accommodations are being provided in a number of ways. They can **advocate** for their students by making sure the accommodations are being implemented on a regular basis. Parents and legal guardians also have the right to ask if their students are using the accommodations on a **regular basis**. If they are being used on a regular basis, parents and legal guardians can explore additional options that might help their students. Parents and legal guardians can work with special education teachers and the IEP teams to ensure that their students' accommodations are being received and are effective.

INFORMAL SUPPORTS VS. FORMAL ACCOMMODATIONS

Informal supports are generally easier to implement in the classroom setting. They do not necessarily have to be implemented only for students with Individualized Education Programs or students with disabilities. Students who have not been evaluated for special education services can receive **informal supports** to ensure classroom success. Teachers may use informal supports to help students who are struggling with the ways they are learning. They may demonstrate that the students are able to learn with the accommodations in place. Informal supports are often the first step to indicating that students are in need of **special education services**.

Formal accommodations are put in place when students become eligible for IEPs or 504 Plans. Formal supports are written into the IEPs or 504 Plans and then required by law to be provided. Examples of informal supports include frequent breaks, special seating, quiet areas for test taking or studying, teacher cues, and help with basic organizational skills. These informal supports may eventually turn into formal supports if students become eligible for special education services.

REASONABLE ACCOMMODATIONS ACCORDING TO ADA

According to the Americans with Disabilities Act (ADA), a **reasonable accommodation** is a change to workplace conditions, equipment, or environment that allows an individual to effectively perform a job. Title I under the ADA requires businesses with more than 15 employees to abide by certain regulations, ensuring that their needs are reasonably met. Any change to the work environment or the way a job is performed that gives a person with a disability access to **equal employment** is considered a reasonable accommodation. Reasonable accommodations fall into **three categories**: changes to a job application process, changes to the work environment or to the way a job is usually done, and changes that enable employee access to equal benefits and privileges that employees without disabilities receive. These effectively level the playing field for people with disabilities to receive the same benefits as their peers. It also allows for the fewest barriers to success in the workplace. Many communities have resources available to help people with disabilities find jobs. They also have resources that help employers make their workplaces accessible for people with disabilities.

TYPES OF ASSISTIVE TECHNOLOGY

Assistive technology (AT) tools can be physical objects and devices or online resources that assist students with disabilities in their learning. The purpose of AT tools is to provide students with disabilities **equal access to the curriculum** by accommodating their individual needs to promote positive outcomes. **Personal listening devices (PLDs)**, sometimes called FM systems, are devices that clarify teachers' words. With a PLD, a teacher speaks into a small microphone and the words transmit clearly into a student's headphone or earpiece. **Sound field systems** amplify teachers' voices to eliminate sound issues in classroom environments. **Noise-cancelling headphones** are useful for students who need to work independently and limit distractions or behavioral triggers. **Audio recorders** allow students to record lectures or lessons and refer to the recordings later at their own pace. Some note-taking applications will transcribe audio into written words. Captioning is available to pair visual words with spoken words. **Text-to-speech (TTS) software** lets students see and hear words at the same time. TTS and audiobook technology can help students with fluency, decoding, and comprehension skills.

VOICE RECOGNITION SOFTWARE

Voice recognition software and communication software can assist students who struggle with speaking or communicating. **Voice recognition software** allows people to speak commands into microphones to interact with the computer instead of using a keyboard. This feature helps create a **least restrictive environment** for a student with a disability because it removes the sometimes challenging aspect of using a keyboard while working on a computer. Voice recognition software allows users to carry out actions such as opening documents, saving documents, and moving the cursor. It also allows users to "write" sentences and paragraphs by speaking into the microphones in word processing programs. In order for voice recognition software to be effective, the user must learn to dictate words distinctly into a microphone. This ensures that the correct word is heard and dictated by the voice-to-text software. Some programs collect information and familiarize themselves with people's particular voice qualities. Over time, the systems adapt to people's voices and become more efficient.

Effectively Instructing Students Using Assistive Technology

Assistive technology (**AT**) refers to tools that are effective for teaching students with learning disabilities, as they address a number of potential special needs. The purpose of AT is to level the playing field for students with **learning disabilities**, particularly when they are participating in general education classrooms. AT can address learning difficulties in math, listening, organization, memory, reading, and writing. **AT for listening** can assist students who have difficulties processing language. For example, a personal listening device can help a student hear a teacher's voice more clearly. **AT for organization and memory** can help students with self-management tasks, such as keeping assignment calendars or retrieving information using handheld devices. **AT for reading** often includes text-to-speech devices that assist with students' reading fluency, decoding, comprehension, and other skill deficits. **AT for writing** assists students who struggle with handwriting or writing development. Some AT writing devices help with actual handwriting, while others assist with spelling, punctuation, grammar, word usage, or text organization.

Augmentative and Alternative Communication Systems

Students with communication disorders may require the use of augmentative or alternative communication systems. Communication systems are used to help the students effectively demonstrate **expressive and receptive language** and engage in **social skills**. Teaching appropriate communication skills is a collaborative effort between the students' caretakers, teachers, and other professionals. Typically, **speech services** are written into students' IEPs, and the services are delivered by **speech language pathologists (SLPs)**. Depending on the requirements in the IEPs, the SLPs may work one-on-one with students or work with the teachers to incorporate speech and language skills throughout students' school days. In order for communication systems to work for nonverbal students, measures must be taken to ensure that the particular systems are appropriate for what the students need. It is important for the caretakers, teachers, other professionals, and even classmates to model using the devices so the students can learn how to "talk" appropriately. Students must also have constant access to the systems and receive consistent opportunities to communicate using the systems at home and at school.

Use of Visual Representation Systems with Students with Autism

Assistive technology (AT) helps increase learning opportunities for students with autism by eliminating barriers to learning. AT can help improve students' expressive communication skills, attention skills, motivation skills, academic skills, and more. **Visual representation systems** in the form of objects, photographs, drawings, or written words provide concrete representations of words for students with autism. Visual representations, such as simple pictures paired with words, can be used to create visual schedules for students with autism. Photographs can be used to help students learn vocabulary words and the names of people and places. Written words should be paired with the visual representations in order to create links between the concrete objects and the actual words. The goal is for students to eventually recognize the words without the pictures. Visual representation systems can also help facilitate easier transitions between activities or places, which can be difficult for students with autism.

Communication Systems

Students who are nonverbal may have access to **communication systems** implemented by trained professionals. Teachers, caretakers, and other professionals work with the students to use the communication systems effectively. The goal of a communication system is to teach a nonverbal student how to "talk" and engage in **age-appropriate social skills**. In order for nonverbal students to learn appropriate social interactions, they must spend time learning communication skills, just as they learn academic content. Communication skills can be taught in isolation or as part of students' daily activities. Giving nonverbal students opportunities to foster communication skills in **familiar environments** makes it easier for them to learn appropriate social interactions. Teachers, caregivers, and other professionals must demonstrate how to use communication systems to engage in conversations, make requests, and answer questions. Most importantly, nonverbal students must be instructed to **access** their "words" (communication systems) at all times throughout the school and home environments.

ACCESSIBILITY COMPONENTS OF A PICTURE EXCHANGE COMMUNICATION SYSTEM

A Picture Exchange Communication System (**PECS**) is a communication system for people with little or no **communicative abilities**. This system is a way for the students to access their environments using **picture symbols** to communicate meaning, wants, and needs. For example, a child may point to a picture symbol to request a book. A PECS provides a way for students with communication disorders to develop their **verbal communication** without actually speaking. It reduces frustration and problem behaviors by providing students with an avenue to express what they want to say. It is commonly used for students with autism spectrum disorder in the form of augmentative communication devices. It can also be used for students with other impairments whose communicative abilities are affected. A PECS focuses on **functional communication skills** and can be practiced in home, school, and community environments.

SUPPORTING NONVERBAL STUDENTS

Nonverbal students have extra challenges in addition to learning content. These students may need extra instruction in academic areas as well as specialized instruction in the area of communication skills. Students with **nonverbal disabilities** may also need social skills instruction, struggle with abstract concepts, and dislike changes to their routines. Teachers can **facilitate learning** for nonverbal students by making changes to their classroom environments, by teaching strategies for comprehending concepts, and by providing materials to accommodate their needs. Teachers can also provide accommodations or modifications to classwork and tests to make the content accessible to nonverbal students. Using visuals to represent actions, words, or concepts is a helpful instructional strategy for teaching nonverbal students, especially when teaching new material. Additionally, teachers can assist nonverbal students by taking measures to prevent undesirable behaviors from occurring.

STRATEGIES AND ACCOMMODATIONS FOR STUDENTS WITH WORKING MEMORY DEFICITS

Working memory is critical for remembering letters and numbers, listening to short instructions, reading and understanding content, completing homework independently, and understanding social cues. When **working memory skills** are absent or slow to develop, learning may be difficult. This may get worse for children over time. As they fail to develop or retain working memory capabilities, their overall **cognitive abilities** begin to suffer. Working memory deficits vary among people with disabilities, but accommodations can make up for missing or underdeveloped skills. Educators can implement **strategies** like reducing the children's workload; being aware of when children might be reaching memory overload; and providing visual cues, positive feedback, testing alternatives, and extra time. **Accommodations** in an Individualized Education Program for a student with working memory deficits might include frequent breaks, small group instruction, and extended time for tests and assignments.

Social and Functional Living Skills

TARGETING AND IMPLEMENTING SOCIAL SKILLS INSTRUCTION

Developing good social skills is essential for lifelong success, and people with disabilities often struggle with these skills. Addressing social skill behavior is most effective when specific **social skill needs** are identified, and **social skills instruction** is implemented as a collaborative effort between parents and teachers.

Evaluating **developmental milestones** is helpful in targeting social skills that need to be addressed and taught. If a child with a disability is not demonstrating a milestone, such as back-and-forth communication, the skill can be evaluated to determine if it should be taught. However, meeting milestones is not a reliable way to measure a student's social skill ability, as some children naturally progress more slowly. **Social skill deficits** may be acquisition deficits, performance deficits, or fluency deficits. A student with an **acquisition deficit** demonstrates an absence of a skill or behavior. A student with a **performance deficit** does not implement a social skill consistently. A student with a **fluency deficit** needs assistance with demonstrating a social skill effectively or fluently. Once a student's social skill need is identified, teachers, parents, and other professionals can collaborate to address it by establishing a routine or a behavior contract or implementing applied behavior analysis.

USING INSTRUCTIONAL METHODS TO ADDRESS INDEPENDENT LIVING SKILLS

When applicable, goals for independent living skills are included in the **transition section** of students' Individualized Education Programs (IEPs). However, **independent living skills education** should begin well before students reach high school, regardless of whether these skills are addressed in their IEP goals. **Functional skills instruction** is necessary to teach students skills needed to gain independence. Instructional methods used to address independent living skills for students with disabilities include making life skills instruction part of the daily curriculum. An appropriate **task analysis** can be used to determine what skills need to be taught. **Functional academic skills**, especially in the areas of math and language arts, should also be included in the curriculum. Telling time, balancing a checkbook, and recognizing signs and symbols are just some examples of basic skills that students can generalize outside of the classroom environment. The goal of **community-based instruction** is to help students develop skills needed to succeed in the community, such as skills needed when riding a bus or shopping. This type of instruction may be harder to implement than basic social skills training, which should be part of the daily curriculum.

PURPOSES AND BENEFITS OF SOCIAL SKILLS GROUPS

Social skills groups are useful for helping students with social skill deficits learn and practice appropriate skills with their peers. Social skills groups are primarily composed of similarly aged peers with and without disabilities. An adult leads these groups and teaches students skills needed for making friends, succeeding in school and life, and sometimes obtaining and maintaining a job. Other professionals, such as school psychologists or speech language pathologists, may also lead social skills groups. Social skills groups work by facilitating **conversation** and focusing on **skill deficits**. These groups can help students learn to read facial cues, appropriately greet others, begin conversations, respond appropriately, maintain conversations, engage in turn-taking, and request help when needed.

EVIDENCE-BASED METHODS FOR PROMOTING SELF-DETERMINATION

Students with disabilities often need to be taught **self-determination** and **self-advocacy** skills. These skills may not come easily to students with specific disorders, like Autism Spectrum Disorder. Self-determination involves a comprehensive understanding of one's own **strengths and**

limitations. Self-determined people are **goal-oriented** and intrinsically motivated to **improve themselves**. Teachers can facilitate the development of these skills in a number of ways, starting in early elementary school. In early elementary school, teachers can promote self-determination by teaching choice-making skills and providing clear consequences for choices. Teachers can also promote problem-solving and self-management skills, like having students evaluate their own work. At the middle school and junior high school level, students can be taught to evaluate and analyze their choices. They can also learn academic and personal goal-setting skills and decision-making skills. At the high school level, teachers can promote decision-making skills, involvement in educational planning (e.g., students attending their Individualized Education Program meetings), and strategies like self-instruction, self-monitoring, and self-evaluation. Throughout the education process, teachers should establish and maintain high standards for learning, focus on students' strengths, and create positive learning environments that promote choice and problem-solving skills.

TEACHING SELF-AWARENESS SKILLS

Students engage in private self-awareness and public self-awareness. Some students with disabilities have the additional challenge of needing instruction in **self-awareness skills**. Special educators and other professionals can facilitate the instruction of self-awareness skills by teaching students to be **aware** of their thoughts, feelings, and actions; to recognize that other people have needs and feelings; and to recognize how their behaviors **affect other people**. Students can be taught self-awareness by identifying their own strengths and weaknesses and learning to self-monitor errors in assignments. They can also be taught to identify what materials or steps are needed to complete tasks and to advocate for accommodations or strategies that work for them. Special educators or other professionals should frequently talk with students about their performance and encourage them to discuss their mistakes without criticism.

IMPORTANCE OF LEARNING SELF-ADVOCACY SKILLS

Self-advocacy is an important skill to learn for people entering adulthood. For students with disabilities, **self-advocacy skills** are especially important for success in **postsecondary environments**. Teaching and learning self-advocacy skills should begin when students enter grade school and be reinforced in the upper grade levels. Students with disabilities who have the potential to enter postsecondary education or employment fields need to learn self-advocacy skills in order to **communicate** how their disabilities may affect their education or job performance and their need for supports and possible accommodations. Students with disabilities who graduate or age out of their Individualized Education Programs do not receive the **educational supports** they received at the grade school level. It is essential for students to advocate for themselves in the absence of teachers or caregivers advocating for them, especially when students independently enter postsecondary employment, training, or educational environments. Many colleges, universities, communities, and workplaces offer services to students with disabilities, but it is up to the students to advocate for themselves and seek them out.

TEACHING FUNCTIONAL LIVING SKILLS

Also known as life skills, functional living skills are skills that students need to live independently. Ideally, students leave high school having gained functional skills. For students with special needs, **functional living skills instruction** may be needed to gain independent living skills. Students with developmental or cognitive disabilities sometimes need to acquire basic living skills, such as self-feeding or toileting. **Applied behavior analysis** is a process by which these skills can be identified, modeled, and taught. Students must also learn functional math and language arts skills, such as managing money and reading bus schedules. Students may also participate in **community-based instruction** to learn skills while completing independent living tasks in the community. These skills include grocery shopping, reading restaurant menus, and riding public transportation. **Social skills instruction** is also important for these students, as learning appropriate social interactions is necessary to function with community members.

ADAPTIVE BEHAVIOR SKILLS INSTRUCTION

Adaptive behavior skills refer to age-appropriate behaviors that people need in order to live independently and function in daily life. **Adaptive behavior skills** include self-care, following rules, managing money, making friends, and more. For students with disabilities, especially severely limiting disabilities, adaptive behavior skills may need to be included in daily instruction. Adaptive behavior skills can be separated into conceptual skills, social skills, and practical life skills. **Conceptual skills** include academic concepts, such as reading, math, money, time, and communication skills. **Social skills** instruction focuses on teaching students to get along with others, communicate appropriately, and maintain appropriate behavior inside and outside the school environment. **Practical life skills** are skills needed to perform the daily living tasks, such as bathing, eating, sitting and standing, and using the bathroom. Adaptive behavior assessments are useful in assessing what adaptive behavior skills need to be addressed for each student. These assessments are usually conducted using observations and questionnaires completed by parents, teachers, or students.

SOCIAL SKILL DEFICITS

Social skills generally develop alongside language development and emotional development, as they are a major component of communication and awareness. Social skills need to be taught to some students with disabilities, such as students with autism. **Social skills instruction** involves the teaching of basic communication skills, empathy and rapport skills, interpersonal skills, problem-solving skills, and accountability. These are skills that do not come naturally to students with social skill deficits.

- **Basic communication skills** include listening, following directions, and taking turns in conversations.
- **Emotional communication skills** include demonstrating empathy and building rapport with others.
- **Interpersonal skills** include sharing, joining activities, and participating in turn-taking.
- **Problem-solving skills** include asking for help, apologizing to others, making decisions, and accepting consequences.
- **Accountability** includes following through on promises and accepting criticism appropriately.

INSTRUCTIONAL METHODS FOR TEACHING STUDENTS WITH SOCIAL SKILL DEFICITS

Students with social skill deficits may or may not require explicit social skills instruction. These deficits can be addressed in inclusive settings. **Social skills instruction** can be delivered to entire classes or individual students, depending on the needs of the students. Also, **one-on-one** or **small group social skills instruction** can be delivered by professionals like speech-language pathologists. In both settings, it is important to model appropriate manners, hold students responsible for their actions, and have clear and concise rules and consequences. This creates educational environments that are both predictable and safe. Social situations that produce undesired outcomes can be remediated by **role-playing** the situations and teaching students positive responses. **Social stories** are another way to foster social skills growth. Often, these social stories demonstrate appropriate responses to specific social situations. The goal is for the students to generalize learned concepts to their school and home environments.

Life Stage Transitions

SUPPORTING STUDENTS THROUGH TRANSITIONS

Transitioning to life after high school can be a difficult process, particularly for students with disabilities. It is important for teachers to facilitate and support these **transitions** before students exit their special education programs. **Structured learning environments** that include independent workstations and learning centers provide opportunities for independent learning to occur. **Independent workstations** give students chances to practice previously introduced concepts or perform previously introduced tasks. **Learning centers** provide small group settings where new skills can be taught. Students can also rotate through different learning centers that offer art lessons, focus on academic skills, or provide breaks or leisure activities. **Classroom layout** also plays an important role. Teachers should plan their classroom layouts based on individual student needs in order to create comfortable, predictable environments for students with disabilities. **Visual schedules** help students transition between centers by providing them with concrete schedule references.

BENEFITS OF VOCATIONAL EDUCATION

Students with disabilities often participate in vocational education in order to gain **independent living skills**. Often, schools and communities offer services that provide vocational training for people with disabilities. These programs offer students **job-specific skills training** and opportunities to earn certifications, diplomas, or certificates. They often involve **hands-on learning experiences** focused on building skills specific to certain occupations. These programs are beneficial to students with disabilities who may struggle with grasping abstract concepts learned in typical classroom environments. Hands-on training in vocational programs can be a meaningful way for students with disabilities to learn academic concepts and gain living skills needed to function in postgraduate life. Vocational education opportunities offer alternatives for students with disabilities who might otherwise drop out of high school. These programs also serve as a viable option for younger students to work towards, as most vocational education programs are offered to students in upper grade levels.

VOCATIONAL SKILLS NEEDED TO BE SUCCESSFUL IN WORK ENVIRONMENTS

Informal vocational training often begins before students even get to high school. Teachers include informal vocational training skills in their classrooms by teaching academic and communication skills. **Academic skills** can both spark and strengthen students' career interests and provide learning platforms to build upon. **Communication skills**, like giving and following instructions and processing information, generalize to work environments. **Social and interpersonal skills**, like problem-solving abilities and participating in phone conversations, are important for performance in workplaces. Students need to learn important **vocational and occupational skills** required by most jobs, such as interacting appropriately with coworkers and keeping track of worked hours. Students also need formal or informal training in completing resumes, cover letters, and tax forms. Training may also include interview practice and job search guidance.

RESOURCES TO PROMOTE SUCCESSFUL TRANSITIONS TO LIFE AFTER HIGH SCHOOL

In some states, **statements of transition** should be included in Individualized Education Programs (IEPs) at age 14 for students with disabilities. In most states, the Individuals with Disabilities Education Act mandates that transition plans be put in place for students with IEPs at age 16 and every year thereafter. Some schools and communities have programs and resources available to facilitate students' successful transitions to life after high school. Throughout the transition process, it is important that students and their caregivers participate in any decision-making processes.

Vocational education courses, sometimes called career and technical education courses, offer academic course alternatives. The courses usually specialize in specific trades or occupations. They can serve to spark or maintain students' interests in vocational fields. Some schools offer **postsecondary enrollment options**, where students can participate in college courses, earning both high school and college credits. **Career assessments**, including interest inventories and formal and informal vocational assessments, serve to gauge students' career interests. These can be worked into students' transitional goals in their IEPs and should be conducted frequently, as students' interests change.

COMPONENTS OF A TRANSITION PLAN

Transition plans are flexible but formal plans that help a student identify his or her goals for after school and act as a roadmap to help the support team advocate for the student's future. They generally include postsecondary goals and expected transition services. The four goal areas are vocational training, postsecondary education, employment, and independent living. **Transition goals** must be results oriented and measurable. Goals can be general, but the transition activities need to be quantified to reflect what the student can complete in the IEP year. It is common for interests to change from year to year; therefore, goals and plans may change as well. **Transition services** are determined once the goals are established. Transition services include types of instruction the student will receive in school, related services, community experiences, career or college counseling, and help with adaptive behavior skills. Goals and transition services must be reviewed and updated each year. Academic goals in the IEP can also support transition goals. For example, math goals can focus on money management skills as part of a transition plan.

FACTORS THAT INFLUENCE SUCCESSFUL TRANSITIONS TO POSTSECONDARY LIFE

Parents or legal guardians, teachers, school professionals, community members, and students themselves can all contribute to successful transitions to postsecondary life. Key **factors** that help students successfully transition include the following:

- Participation in standards-based education
- Work preparation and career-based learning experiences
- Leadership skills
- Access to and experience with community services, such as mental health and transportation services
- Family involvement and support

Standards-based education ensures that students receive consistent and clear expectations with a curriculum that is aligned to the universal design for learning standards. Exposure to work preparation and career-based learning experiences ensures that students receive opportunities to discover potential career interests or hobbies. Connections and experiences with community activities provide students with essential postsecondary independent living skills. Family involvement and support ensure that students have advocates for their needs and interests. Families can also help students connect with school and community-based supports that facilitate their career interests.

Instructional Design for Students with Disabilities

DEVELOPMENTALLY APPROPRIATE CURRICULUM

Choosing a developmentally appropriate curriculum is challenging for educators. Special educators have the additional challenge of finding a curriculum that meets the needs of the **individual students with disabilities**. The end result is not usually a one-size-fits-all curriculum because that goes against the intentions of Individualized Education Programs (IEPs) designed to meet the needs of students with special needs. Instead, special educators often pick and choose curriculum components that best meet the needs of differing abilities in the classroom. When selecting an appropriate curriculum, special educators should consider the following:

- Standards and goals that are appropriate to the needs of the students
- Best practices that have been found effective for students
- Curricula that are engaging and challenging
- Instruction and activities that are multimodal
- IEP goals
- Real-world experiences
- Different ways of learning that help teachers understand students' learning processes
- Collaboration with co-teachers to deliver appropriate instruction

In some special education settings, the curriculum is already chosen. In these settings, teachers can collaborate with co-teachers to find ways to provide instruction that meets standards and the individual needs of the students.

COMPONENTS OF DIFFERENTIATED INSTRUCTION

Differentiated instruction is different from individualized instruction. It targets the strengths of students and can work well in both special education and general education settings. **Differentiated instruction** is also useful for targeting the needs of students with **learning and attention deficits**. With differentiated instruction, teachers adjust their instructional processes to meet the needs of the individual students. Teaching strategies and classroom management skills are based largely on each particular class of students instead of on methods that may have been successful in the past. Teachers can differentiate content, classroom activities, student projects, and learning environments. For example, students may be encouraged to choose topics of personal interest to focus on for projects. Students are held to the same standards but have many choices in terms of project topics. **Differentiated content** provides access to a variety of resources to encourage student choice over what and how they learn. **Differentiated learning environments** are flexible to meet the ever-changing needs of the students.

> **Review Video: Differentiated Instruction**
> Visit mometrix.com/academy and enter code: 100342

EFFECTIVENESS OF DIFFERENTIATED INSTRUCTION

Differentiated instruction is effective in general education settings, team-teaching settings, and special education settings because it targets the **strengths** of students. Differentiated instruction is used to target the different ways that students learn instead of taking a one-size-fits-all approach. Differentiated instruction is used in lieu of individualized instruction because it uses a variety of instructional approaches and allows students to use a variety of materials to help them access the curriculum. **Effective differentiated instruction** includes small group work, reciprocal learning, and continual assessment.

Small group work allows for the individual learning styles and needs of students to be addressed. In small groups, students receive instruction by rotating through groups. Group work should be used sparingly or be well-regulated to ensure that all of the students in the group are learning for themselves and contributing to group work sufficiently. Groups may be shuffled or have assigned roles within the group to ensure a good division of labor. In **reciprocal learning**, students play the role of the teacher, instructing the class by sharing what they know and asking content questions of their peers. Teachers who practice **continual assessment** can determine if their differentiated instructional methods are effective or if they need to be changed. Assessments can determine what needs to be changed in order for students to participate in effective classroom environments.

DIFFERENT EDUCATIONAL LEVELS AND LEARNING STYLES

Learning styles of students differ, regardless of whether or not the students have disabilities. When addressing groups of students in inclusion settings, it is important for teachers to organize and implement teaching strategies that address learning at **different educational levels**. Students generally fall into one or more learning modes. Some are visual learners, some are auditory learners, some are kinesthetic or tactile learners, and some learn best using a combination of these approaches. Teachers can address students' educational levels by creating lessons that allow learning to take place visually, auditorily, and kinesthetically. **Visual learners** prefer information that has been visually organized, such as in graphic organizers or diagrams. **Auditory learners** prefer information presented in spoken words. Lessons that target auditory learners provide opportunities for students to engage in conversations and question material. **Kinesthetic learners** prefer a hands-on approach to learning. These learners prefer to try out new tasks and learn as they go. Lessons that include opportunities for these three types of learning to occur can successfully target different educational levels.

MULTIPLE MODALITY INSTRUCTION AND ACTIVITIES

The purpose of multiple modality instruction is to engage students by offering different ways to learn the same material. **Multiple modality teaching** also addresses students' unique learning styles. Learning modalities are generally separated into four categories: **visual** (seeing), **auditory** (hearing), **kinesthetic** (moving), and **tactile** (touch) modalities. This way of teaching targets students who may have deficits in one or more modalities. It is also helpful for students who struggle in one or more of the learning categories. If a student struggles with understanding content that is presented visually, a lesson that includes auditory, kinesthetic, and tactile components may engage learning. Additionally, presenting lesson material and activities in a multimodal approach helps improve student memory and retention by solidifying concepts through multiple means of engagement. This approach is also useful for students with **attention disorders** who may struggle in environments where one mode of teaching is used. The multiple modality approach ensures that activities, such as kinesthetic or tactile activities, keep more than one sense involved with the learning process.

> **Review Video: Teaching Through Multiple Modalities**
> Visit mometrix.com/academy and enter code: 100371

USING VISUAL SUPPORTS TO FACILITATE INSTRUCTION AND SELF-MONITORING STRATEGIES

Many students learn best when provided with instruction and activities that appeal to multiple senses. A **multimodal approach** is especially important for students with developmental disabilities, who may need supports that match their individual ways of learning. **Visual supports** are concrete representations of information used to convey meaning. Teachers can use visual supports to help students with developmental disabilities understand what is being taught and communicated to them. Visual supports can help students with understanding classroom rules, making decisions, communicating with others, staying organized, and reducing frustrations. **Visual schedules** show students visual representations of their daily schedules. This assists with transitions between activities, which can sometimes be difficult for students with disabilities. Visuals can be used to help students share information about themselves or their school days with their peers and parents. Visual supports can also be used with checklists to help facilitate independence. For example, behavior checklists can be used to help students monitor their own behaviors.

UNIVERSAL DESIGN FOR LEARNING

Universal design for learning (UDL) is a flexible approach to learning that keeps students' individual needs in mind. Teachers that utilize **UDL** offer different ways for students to access material and engage in content. This approach is helpful for many students but particularly those with learning and attention issues. The **principles of UDL** all center on varying instruction and assessment to appeal to the needs of students who think in various ways.

Principles of the Universal Design for Learning	
Multiple means of *representation*	*Instructional content* should be demonstrated in various ways so that students may learn in a mode that is effective for them.
Multiple means of *expression*	*Assessment* should be administered in a variety of ways to adequately allow students to demonstrate their knowledge. This includes quizzes, homework, presentations, classwork, etc.
Multiple means of *engagement*	Instruction should include a variety of *motivational factors* that help to interest and challenge students in exciting ways.

> **Review Video: Universal Design for Learning**
> Visit mometrix.com/academy and enter code: 523916

EVALUATING, MODIFYING, AND ADAPTING THE CLASSROOM SETTING USING THE UDL

The **universal design for learning (UDL)** is a framework that encourages teachers to design their instruction and assessment in ways that allow **multiple means** for the student to learn and express their knowledge. The UDL model is most successful when the teacher prepares a classroom setting that encourages the success of students with and without disabilities. Knowledge of the **characteristics** of students with different disabilities, as well as the unique **learning needs** of these students, enables the teacher to address these needs in the classroom setting. Setting clear short- and long-term goals for students is one way to meet the UDL standards. A traditional classroom may offer one assignment for all students to complete, but a UDL-compliant classroom may offer **different assignments** or **different ways** for students to complete assignments. UDL-compliant classrooms often offer **flexible workspaces** for students to complete their classwork and may offer quiet spaces for individual work or group tables for group work. UDL-compliant teachers recognize that students access information differently and provide different ways for students to gain **access** to the information, such as through audio text or physical models to work with. The universal design for learning assumes students learn in a variety of ways, even if those ways have not been clearly identified; it follows that all instruction and assessment can be improved by making it more varied and accessible.

MODIFYING CLASSROOM CURRICULUM AND MATERIALS FOR UDL

In order for a **universal design for learning (UDL) model classroom** to be successful, the teacher must evaluate, modify, and adapt the **curriculum** and **materials** to best suit the needs of the individual students. UDL contrasts with a one-size-fits-all concept of curriculum planning, where lesson plans are developed and implemented strictly based on how teachers expect students to learn. Instead, a successful UDL model addresses the many **specific needs** of the students. These needs vary depending on the unique abilities each classroom of students presents. UDL-compliant teachers can evaluate the success of lessons by checking for comprehension throughout lessons instead of only upon lesson completion. Evaluation methods used informally can provide a lot of information about whether students are grasping the concepts. Teachers use the results of the evaluations to modify and adapt classroom instruction to meet the needs of the students. Other means for diversifying the materials include using multiple assignment completion options and varied means of accessing the materials, such as both written, digital, and audio forms of a text. These means of instruction can take place simultaneously. For instance, a UDL-compliant teacher may choose to pair audio output and text for all students during a reading assignment in order to target students with listening or comprehension difficulties.

PRINCIPLES OF THE UNIVERSAL DESIGN FOR LEARNING MODEL

The universal design for learning (UDL) model contains three principles that aim to level the playing field for all learners. **Principle I** of the UDL model primarily focuses on what **representation or version** of information is being taught. This principle aims to target an audience of diverse learners. By providing multiple ways for students to approach content, teachers can ensure that the unique needs of all learners in their classrooms are met. **Principle II** examines how people learn. This principle focuses on the concept that students learn best when provided with **multiple ways** to demonstrate what they have learned. In classrooms compliant with Principle II, students are given more than one option for expressing themselves. **Principle III** focuses on providing multiple ways for students to engage in the learning process. Teachers compliant with Principle III provide options for keeping content **interesting and relevant** to all types of learners. Effective UDL-model classrooms provide multiple ways to present content, engage in learning, and express what was learned.

SPECIALLY DESIGNED INSTRUCTION

Specially designed instruction (**SDI**) in special education refers to specialized teaching given to students in a co-taught inclusion classroom. While a teacher teaches the class, the special education teacher provides specialized instruction in parallel to a student to help clarify the information. This is distinctive from adaptation and modification, as the content and its medium do not change for SDI. While the general education class engages in instruction, a special education teacher provides SDI to meet the specific needs of learners who may not be successful learning in the same ways as their similar-aged peers. The main purpose of SDI is to provide a student with access to the general education setting without substantially changing the content as it is aligned with state standards.

DIAGNOSTIC PRESCRIPTIVE METHOD

The diagnostic prescriptive approach to teaching is based on the fact that all students are unique learners. The **diagnostic prescriptive approach** examines factors that impede student learning and how to remedy specific issues. A successful approach begins with a **diagnosis** of what students are bringing to the classroom. This can be completed through careful observations and assessments. Once the skill deficits are clear, **prescriptive teaching** can be put into effect. In this process, teachers examine what will help students the most. It may be switching materials, changing to group settings, or recognizing the need for specialized interventions due to disabilities. In order to address multiple needs in the classroom, lesson plans should be **multimodal**. Developing strategies in advance to address students' needs is also a highlight of this method. Another important part of this method is evaluating results to determine what was effective or ineffective for entire classes and individual students.

GUIDED LEARNING

Guided learning is practice or instruction completed by the teacher and students together. The goal of **guided learning** is to help students engage in the learning process in order to learn more about how they think and acquire new information. **Guided practice** occurs when the teacher and students complete practice activities together. The advantage of guided practice is that students can learn ways to approach concepts they have just learned. It allows students to understand and ask questions about lesson-related activities before working independently. Guided practice is useful in classrooms for students with and without disabilities because it helps teachers gauge how students learn and what instructional methods work best for them. Additionally, guided practice allows teachers to understand how students are learning the material. It also allows teachers to revisit concepts that are unclear or fine tune any missed lesson objectives.

HOW COOPERATIVE LEARNING WORKS

Cooperative learning is an interpersonal group learning process where students learn concepts by working together in **small groups**. Cooperative learning involves collaboration among small groups to achieve common goals. With **formal cooperative learning**, an instructor oversees the learning of lesson material or completion of assignments for students in these small groups. With **informal cooperative learning**, the instructor supervises group activities by keeping students cognitively active but does not guide instruction or assignments. For example, a teacher might use a class period to show a movie but provide a list of questions for students to complete during the movie. In the special education classroom, cooperative learning is helpful when students need specific skills targeted or remediated. It is also helpful for separating students who are learning different content at different levels. For example, a cooperative learning activity may involve multiple groups of students with differing levels of mathematic abilities. Group work also promotes development of interpersonal skills as students interact with one another.

INTRINSIC MOTIVATION

Intrinsic motivation is a person's inner drive to engage in an activity or behavior. Students with special needs often struggle with intrinsic motivation as a skill. This requires special educators and other professionals to promote and teach intrinsic motivation to students. Teachers can **promote intrinsic motivation** by giving students opportunities to demonstrate **achievement**. This can be done by challenging students with intellectual risks and helping them focus on difficult classwork or tasks. Teachers can build upon students' strengths by providing daily opportunities in the classroom for students to demonstrate their **strengths** instead of focusing on their weaknesses. Offering choices throughout the day provides students with ownership of their decision-making and communicates that they have choices in the classroom environment. Teachers should allow students to **fail without criticism** and should promote self-reflection in order to build students' confidence. Teachers should promote self-management and organizational skills like instructing students on how to **break down tasks**.

PROMOTING CRITICAL THINKING SKILLS

Critical thinking is a self-directed thinking process that helps people make logical, reasonable judgments. This is an especially challenging skill for students with **developmental disabilities**, who often demonstrate deficits in logical thinking and reasoning abilities. In order to teach these students **critical thinking skills**, the focus should be on encouraging critical thinking across **home and school environments** and providing opportunities for students to practice this type of thinking. Teachers and parents can encourage critical thinking by implementing teaching strategies focused on fostering **creativity** in students. Instead of providing outlines or templates for lesson concepts, students can use their prior knowledge to figure out the boundaries of the lessons independently and explore new concepts. Parents and teachers should not always be quick to jump in and help students who are struggling. Sometimes the best way to help is by facilitating ways for students to solve problems without doing things for them. Opportunities for brainstorming, classifying and categorizing information, comparing and contrasting information, and making connections between topics are teaching strategies that also facilitate critical thinking skills.

CAREER-BASED EDUCATION

During their schooling years, students with disabilities have the additional challenge of determining possible **career options** for life after high school. Fortunately, instruction can be provided during the school day or within after-school programs that address career-based skills. Effective **career-based programs** for students with disabilities should work collaboratively with community and school resources. Students should receive information on career options, be exposed to a range of experiences, and learn how to self-advocate. Information regarding career options can be gathered via **career assessments** that explore students' possible career interests. Students should receive exposure to **postsecondary education** to determine if it is an option that aligns with their career interests. They should also learn about basic job requirements, such as entry requirements for different types of jobs and what it means to earn a living wage. Students should be given opportunities for job training, job shadowing, and community service. It is helpful to provide students with opportunities to learn and practice **work and occupational skills** that pertain to specific job interests. Students need to learn **self-advocacy skills**, such as communicating the implications of their disabilities to employers, in order to maintain success in postsecondary work environments.

Special Education Settings

LEAST RESTRICTIVE ENVIRONMENT

The Individuals with Disabilities Education Act (IDEA) requires a free and appropriate public education to be provided in a student's **least restrictive environment (LRE)**. This means that a student with a disability who qualifies for special education should be educated in a free, appropriate, and public setting and be placed in an instructional setting that meets the LRE principle. IDEA states that LRE means students with disabilities should participate in the general education classroom "to the maximum extent appropriate." **Mainstreaming** and **inclusion** are ways for students with disabilities to participate in general education classrooms while receiving appropriate accommodations, modifications, interventions, and related services. The amount of time students spend in an LRE suitable for their individual needs is stated in their Individualized Education Program (IEP). The accommodations, modifications, interventions, and related services the student should receive are also outlined in the IEP. Students who need special education services for more than 50% of the day may be placed in other instructional settings that meet their LRE needs, such as resource rooms or self-contained classrooms.

> **Review Video: Least Restrictive Environment**
> Visit mometrix.com/academy and enter code: 100354

CONTINUUM OF SPECIAL EDUCATION SERVICES

IDEA mandates that school systems educate students with disabilities with students who do not have disabilities to the maximum extent that is appropriate. IDEA also mandates that schools not take students out of regular education classes unless the classes are not benefiting the students. Supplementary aids and support services must be in place before students can be considered for removal. Schools must offer a **continuum of special education services** that range from restrictive to least restrictive. In a typical continuum of services, regular education classrooms offer the **least restrictive access** to students with disabilities. Next on the continuum are resource rooms, followed by special classes that target specific deficits. Special schools, homebound services, hospitals, and institutions are the most restrictive education environments. The number of students at each stage of the continuum decreases as restriction increases. Fewer students benefit more from being educated in hospitals or institutions than in resource rooms.

INCLUSION CLASSROOM SETTING

The principle of least restrictive environment (LRE) is a right guaranteed under IDEA to protect a student from unnecessary restriction or seclusion from the general population. IDEA does not expressly define an LRE for each specific disability, so it is the responsibility of the IEP team of professionals, including the student's parent or legal guardian, to determine the best **LRE setting** possible for an individual student. **Mainstreaming** or **inclusion** is the practice of keeping students with disabilities in the general education setting for the entire school day. The students may receive supports and services like aides, assistive technology, accommodations, and modifications that are appropriate for their individual needs. These supports and services are intended to help students with disabilities gain access to the general education curriculum with the fewest possible barriers. The principle of LRE also sits on a spectrum and allows for variable inclusion or separation throughout parts of the day depending on a student's particular needs. As this is a student right, any more restrictive setting must be **justified by necessity** in students' IEPs and cannot be determined by convenience or financial considerations of the school or staff.

COLLABORATIVE TEACHING IN AN INCLUSION CLASSROOM

If determined by an IEP, a student with a disability may participate in an **inclusive setting**. In some classrooms, students participate in **co-taught settings**. In this **collaborative teaching environment**, the general educator and special educator work together to meet the goals of the students with disabilities in the regular education classroom. Students in this setting are all taught to the same educational standards. However, accommodations and modifications may be implemented for students with disabilities. In a successful collaborative teaching model, the special educator and general educator may cooperatively implement the accommodations and modifications for these students. A two-teacher setting also gives students more opportunities to receive individualized instruction, work in small groups, or receive one-on-one attention. Collaborative teaching in the co-taught setting can facilitate differentiated instruction, help teachers follow the universal design for learning framework, and provide individualized learning opportunities.

IMPLEMENTING MODIFICATIONS AND ACCOMMODATIONS IN AN INCLUSION CLASSROOM

General educators can work with special educators to create an effective **co-teaching model**. In an effective co-teaching model, both general educators and special educators are guided by the **universal design for learning framework**. This helps ensure that the needs of the diverse group of learners are being met. Students' IEPs expressly document any required modifications, such as reduced work. In a co-teaching model, student modifications are communicated to the **general educator**. The **special educator** can work with the general educator to provide the modifications in an inclusive classroom setting. Students' IEPs also expressly document any required **accommodations**. These accommodations may or may not be used in an inclusive setting, depending on the relevancy of the accommodation. For example, the accommodation of using a calculator would be utilized in a math class but not a social studies class. In addition to expressly written accommodations, special educators and general educators can work together in an inclusive setting to provide appropriate accommodations during the learning process. These accommodations may be part of informal assessments used to adjust instruction.

ROLE OF PARAEDUCATORS

Paraeducators, sometimes referred to as aides or paraprofessionals, are part of students' education teams. **Paraeducators** work under the supervision of special educators or principals and are key contributors to the learning process for certain students. Their primary role, especially if their positions are funded by the Individuals with Disabilities Education Act, is to provide **educational support** for students. The use of paraeducators is noted in students' IEPs. Paraeducators can facilitate the learning process for students by removing learning barriers, keeping track of goal progress, and organizing goal-tracking activities. Paraeducators cannot introduce new concepts or take over the role of teachers. Paraeducators cannot make changes to what students are learning unless specific modifications are listed in students' IEPs. They cannot provide accommodations unless the accommodations are appropriate for what is written in students' IEPs. Paraeducators may also be instructed by supervising teachers or principals to facilitate and monitor accommodations or modifications for students and reinforce learned concepts.

SELF-CONTAINED CLASSROOM SETTING

According to the Individuals with Disabilities Education Act, LRE standards require students to spend as much time as possible with their nondisabled peers in the **general education setting**. This means students should receive general education "to the maximum extent appropriate," and special classes, special schools, or removal from the general education classroom should only be considered when students' needs are greater than what can be provided by supplementary aids and services. A **self-contained classroom setting** can be a separate class within a school or a separate school for students with disabilities whose needs are greater than what can be offered in the general education classroom even with educational supports. These settings may provide specialized instruction and support for students with similar needs. Placement in self-contained classrooms must be justified in students' IEPs.

PARTIAL MAINSTREAM/INCLUSION CLASSROOM SETTING

It is generally up to the IEP team of professionals and the parent or legal guardian to determine the LRE that best suits the needs of a student. In a partial mainstream/inclusion classroom setting, a student spends part of the day in the general education classroom and part of the day in a separate, special education classroom. This type of LRE is appropriate when a student's needs are greater than what can be provided in the general education classroom even with educational supports or services in place. For example, a student with severe deficits in mathematical skills may receive math instruction in a separate classroom or receive one-on-one or small group instruction. Placement in partial mainstream/inclusion classrooms must be justified in students' IEPs.

SPECIALIZED EDUCATION SETTINGS

School districts sometimes offer specialized education settings for students with disabilities, such as **special preschools**. Preschools for children with disabilities typically focus on children aged 3–5 years. They are important resources for teaching early learning, communication, and social skills that are essential for children with disabilities. In **life skills settings**, students with disabilities can receive specialized instruction in academic, social, behavioral, and daily-living skills. **Social behavior skills settings** are sometimes called "applied behavior skills settings" or "behavior skills settings." In this setting, the primary focus is on social and decision-making skills. **Transition settings** are available for students making the transition from high school to life after high school. Students with IEPs can stay in high school until the age of 21 or 22, depending on the calendar month they turn 22. Transition settings assist students with work experiences, postsecondary education experiences, and independent living skills.

Learning Environments for Students with Disabilities

DETERMINING THE SPECIAL EDUCATION SETTING PLACEMENT

Special education setting placement is determined in a student's Individualized Education Program (IEP), as specified by the Individuals with Disabilities Education Act (IDEA). IDEA requires that students be placed in **general education classrooms** to the maximum extent possible. Students should be placed in environments that are most appropriate for them, known as the **least restrictive environment**. If students can be educated in general education classrooms (**inclusion**) when provided with appropriate accommodations, they can be placed in general education classrooms. When students with disabilities need modifications to curriculum that are significantly below grade level or different than their peers, the students may be placed in **resource rooms** for remedial instruction. However, the students may also participate in the general education curriculum with modified work that meets their current abilities. For example, a student who struggles in math can use a calculator accommodation in the inclusion setting. A student whose math skills are two grade levels below the skills of same-aged peers may be placed in an inclusion setting with modifications or receive instruction in a resource room.

FULL OR PARTIAL INCLUSION SETTINGS VS. SELF-CONTAINED CLASSROOMS

Students with mild to moderate disabilities are often placed in **inclusion** or **partial inclusion classrooms**. The responsibilities of the special educator include assisting and collaborating with the general education teacher to create a curriculum with **modifications** that meets the learning styles and needs of the students with disabilities. The special educator may circulate during lessons or classwork to help students when needed and provide modifications to the general education curriculum to best meet the individual needs of each student.

The role of a special educator in a **self-contained classroom** is much different. Students in a self-contained classroom typically have disabilities that significantly limit their ability to receive quality education in inclusion or partial inclusion settings. Students with moderate disabilities in self-contained classrooms receive **modified instruction** with accommodations. The special educator is usually assisted by teaching assistants or paraprofessionals who help the educator meet the needs of individual students.

Special educators in inclusion, partial inclusion, and self-contained classrooms share some similar **responsibilities**. These responsibilities include monitoring IEP data on annual goals for each student, giving standardized pre-tests and post-tests, facilitating parent-teacher conferences, completing annual IEP reviews, and developing curriculum.

STRUCTURED LEARNING ENVIRONMENTS

A structured learning environment is an important component of good **classroom management**. Teachers that create environments that are conducive for teaching and learning create environments where students feel safe. In **effective structured learning environments**, teachers create solid relationships with students by getting to know them and their interests. Often, this information can be used to implement learning activities based on students' interests. Another way to promote effective structured learning environments is to consistently follow implemented rules and maintain **consistency** in procedures in order to communicate what to expect to students. Transitioning students appropriately between activities increases time spent learning. Additionally, teachers create solid environments for their students by spending time designing effective lesson plans that anticipate student behaviors. Teachers can also establish good learning environments by promoting target behaviors. This means promoting standards of behavior and clear consequences for breaking rules. Students that have clear expectations learn in effective structured learning environments.

Non-Traditional Classroom Seating Arrangements

Seating arrangements are part of good classroom management strategies, especially for students with disabilities. Special education settings and inclusion settings often require flexibility with instruction and versatility with **seating arrangements**. The traditional setting includes rows of desks facing the area where the teacher conducts instruction. More **student-centered arrangements** include a horseshoe seating arrangement, a group pod arrangement, or a paired arrangement. A **horseshoe seating arrangement** is conducive to student-centered instruction because it allows the students to face each other and the instructor to move around the classroom easily. This setup facilitates classroom discussions and encourages interactions between instructors and students and among peers. The **group pod** or **paired-pod arrangement** is useful for student-centered instruction like small group work. This arrangement is also helpful when students need to rotate through lesson stages or work in small groups on projects. Effective teachers do not use one seating arrangement for the entire year. Best practices indicate that seating arrangements should change and be tied to the intent of lesson objectives.

Inclusive Learning Environments That Meet Unique Needs

Effective inclusive environments abide by the **universal design for learning (UDL) framework**. Special educators and general educators can work together to create learning environments that are accessible to students with unique language or physical needs. This can be done by providing **multiple ways** for students to access lesson concepts, express learned concepts, and engage in the learning process. For students with language barriers, signs, symbols, pictures, and learning concepts may have different meanings than they do for students without language barriers. Keeping this in mind, teachers can address UDL guidelines for students with **language barriers** by providing diverse ways to activate prior knowledge, emphasizing key learning elements, and using visuals to guide the learning process. For students with **physical barriers**, teachers can level the learning process by making their physical classroom environments accessible and providing different ways for students to express what they have learned. In general, teachers abiding by the UDL framework would have these supports in place in order to ensure that the needs of diverse learners are met.

Positive and Inclusive Learning Environments

Whether in the general education classroom or special education classroom, the UDL model should foster **positive and inclusive learning environments**. General education and special education teachers can take measures to ensure the UDL concept is implemented to address the unique needs of students with **cognitive or behavioral needs**. Since each student presents different needs, a one-size-fits-all approach to learning is not suitable or UDL compliant for these students. Special educators and general educators should openly communicate about students' unique learning or cognitive needs. General strategies include receiving regular **input from special educators** on how to best meet the needs of the students in the classroom. This includes sharing information with any **paraprofessionals and aides** regarding how to assist the students in the general education classroom. UDL-based strategies include the general educators providing multiple means by which students can complete the assignments. Students with cognitive disabilities may also benefit from the use of concrete examples and instruction, especially when addressing abstract concepts.

Learning Environments that Support Students with Behavioral Needs

The **UDL concepts** can be implemented to reduce challenging behavior in the classroom. They can also be used to help students with behavioral needs find success in the general education classroom. **Lack of student engagement** is compatible with the presentation of **challenging behaviors**. When UDL concepts are demonstrated appropriately, engagement can improve. Providing **multiple means of representation** is one UDL strategy for improving engagement and challenging behavior. This means the classroom teacher provides multiple ways of presenting the teaching material in order to engage as many students as possible. Teachers that provide multiple means of representation look to activate prior knowledge and help students make sense of the current content. UDL-compliant strategies also include providing **multiple means of expression**. Teachers applying UDL principles recognize that differentiating activities and assignments addresses a variety of abilities and learning styles. UDL-compliant teachers should also provide **multiple means of engagement**. Successful engagement in learning can often offset challenging behaviors by helping students focus on lesson material. Offering both challenging and simplistic work options and making engaging, solid connections to past and/or future lesson content can minimize the possibility of problems arising in the classroom.

CLASSROOM STRATEGIES PROMOTING SOCIAL-EMOTIONAL DEVELOPMENT AND GROWTH

Classroom environments should emanate **positivity** and **growth**. Classrooms that promote **social-emotional development and growth** provide security for students and create environments where learning takes place. Teachers can promote social-emotional development and growth by creating predictable classroom routines with visual reminders, keeping classrooms free of dangerous objects and materials, and arranging for learning to take place in large and small groups. They can also rotate activities and materials to keep students engaged, provide appropriate materials for learning centers, and create opportunities for children to engage socially. Teachers can act as nurturing adults by encouraging social interactions and problem solving, modeling appropriate language and social skills, encouraging and validating children's thoughts and feelings, and using clear signals to indicate transitions between activities. Teachers should build community environments in their classrooms, build appropriate relationships with students by getting to know their strengths and weaknesses, and demonstrate good conflict resolution and problem-solving abilities.

EFFECT OF EMOTIONAL AND PSYCHOLOGICAL NEEDS OF STUDENTS WITH DISABILITIES

When a child is diagnosed with a disability, educators often primarily focus on the educational implications. However, students with disabilities also have **emotional needs** associated with their disabilities. These needs vary by student and disability. Generally, students with disabilities struggle emotionally. Symptoms may include low self-esteem, anxiety, acting out, reduced intrinsic motivation, and physical effects, like headaches. Educators, parents, and other professionals can manage the emotional needs of students with disabilities by talking with them about the disability diagnoses and educational implications. Educators can increase their **awareness** of how students might be feeling about the diagnoses and identify situations that may cause anxiety or acting out. Educators can also help by praising students consistently, even for small actions, which can help with confidence. Parents, educators, and other professionals can also work together to ensure that the students receive instruction in the most appropriate educational environments for their disabilities.

LIFTING GUIDELINES FOR STUDENTS WHO REQUIRE PHYSICAL LIFTING

Teachers and paraprofessionals may encounter students with physical disabilities who require **assisted transfers**. In some circumstances, students must be **lift-assisted** from their wheelchairs in order to participate in physical therapy or floor activities. While this practice is more common in low-incidence classrooms and not always a job requirement, it is important to know school guidelines for **lifting techniques** to keep staff and students safe. Knowing school guidelines for lifting can also help prevent back injuries from occurring. Physical therapists working with the students should be consulted before attempting student lifts. They are trained professionals who know specific procedures for lifting students in order to keep the students and staff members safe. Every school district has policies for lift-assisted student transfers. Each student should be evaluated to determine if a one-person lift or two-person lift is needed. Two-person lifts are for heavier students, and some school districts do not allow two-person lifts for safety reasons.

MANAGING DISTRACTIONS THAT MAY AFFECT LEARNING AND DEVELOPMENT

Managing distractions is a part of good teaching practices. Special educators demonstrate good **classroom management strategies** when they do the following:

- Create positive learning environments by getting to know students' individual emotional, intellectual, social, and physical needs.
- Remove or accommodate environmental triggers specific to students.
- Remove or accommodate behavioral triggers.
- Encourage students to help with classroom jobs and small tasks.
- Create lesson plans with anticipated behaviors in mind.
- Attempt verbal de-escalation first when behavioral issues arise.
- Set clear, consistent rules.
- Set and follow through with consequences for breaking the rules.
- Take time to get to know students and their triggers.
- Create seating arrangements that minimize distractions, such as placing distractible students closer to the teacher.
- Teach social, thinking, test-taking, problem-solving, and self-regulation skills alongside academic content.
- Use visual aids in lessons.
- Utilize peer-instruction opportunities.
- Provide opportunities for breaks.
- Incorporate computer-based programs, which can hold the attention of students with disabilities like autism.

EFFECT OF HOME LIFE FACTORS ON LEARNING AND DEVELOPMENT

Students' home lives are interconnected with their school lives. **Home life factors**, especially negative ones, are difficult for students to avoid generalizing to the school environment. **Home stressors** can often develop into dysfunction at school. Factors that affect the learning and development of students with disabilities include academic, environmental, intellectual, language, medical, perceptual, and psychological factors. **Academic factors** include developmental delays in core content areas, lack of basic skills, and apparent inconsistency of learning in certain stages of development. **Environmental factors** occur when children are exposed to home life trauma, such as divorce, drug abuse, alcoholism, parental fighting, or family illness. **Intellectual factors** include limited intellectual abilities or unnoticed gifted abilities. **Language factors** include issues with language barriers or language acquisition, such as aphasia, bilingualism, expressive language disorder, and pragmatic language disorder. **Medical factors** include attention-deficit/hyperactivity disorder, muscular problems, and hearing problems. **Perceptual factors** include any factors that affect or slow down students' processing of information. **Psychological factors** include depression, anxiety, and conduct disorders.

Behavioral Issues for Students with Disabilities

BEHAVIORAL ISSUES AND INTERVENTION STRATEGIES

Behavior issues occur with students with and without disabilities. However, they may occur more frequently or to a higher degree for some students with disabilities. Behavior issues are often a **manifestation** of a child's disability. For example, students with attention-deficit/hyperactivity disorder may present with attention and focus issues and impulsivity. **Common behavior issues** include the following:

- Emotional outbursts
- Inattention and inability to focus
- Impulsivity
- Aggression
- Abusive language
- Oppositional defiance
- Lying or stealing
- Threatening adults or peers

Other behavior issues may include inappropriate sexual behavior, inability to control sexual behavior, self-harm, or self-harm attempts. Behavior issues can be **avoided** or **remediated** with classroom management skills like setting clear and consistent classroom goals, setting time limits, and providing visuals to assist with transitions or concepts. When a student is in an aggressive state, it is important for the teacher to remain calm, provide choices for the student, and restate the consequences of any aggressive outbursts.

> **Review Video: Student Behavior Management Approaches**
> Visit mometrix.com/academy and enter code: 843846
>
> **Review Video: Promoting Appropriate Behavior**
> Visit mometrix.com/academy and enter code: 321015

MANAGING STUDENTS WITH EMOTIONAL DISORDERS

Managing a classroom of students with emotional disorders can be challenging and unpredictable. Students with emotional disorders have Individualized Education Program (IEP) goals that focus on **controlling** or **monitoring** their daily behavior choices. However, this does not always mean they will engage in meeting these goals. It is important for educators to know how to **manage** issues that students with emotional disorders may bring to the classroom. When creating resources and lesson plans, an educator should do the following:

- Establish a **safety plan**, which includes knowing how to implement a **crisis prevention plan**.
- Maintain an environment that reduces **stimulation** and provides **visual cues** for expected behavior.
- Implement **intervention-based strategies** for managing student behavior.
- Collect and use **data** to identify triggers, track behaviors, and recognize strategies that produce positive outcomes.
- Practice open **communication** about classroom expectations to students, parents, and other teachers.

Special education teachers can be helpful in implementing these guidelines, especially when students with emotional disorders are in inclusive settings.

Supporting Students with Mental Health Issues

Students with disabilities may also have mental health issues. These students may not necessarily be diagnosed with emotional disturbances, as mental health issues can occur concurrently with other disabilities. Students' mental health symptoms may fluctuate on an hourly, daily, or weekly basis. Intervention techniques and supports must be determined by the individual needs of each student. General and special educators across all special education settings can **support** these students by learning how to **recognize mental health issues** in schools. Teachers can use observations and research-based strategies for identifying issues. Training in working with students who have certain mental health disorders may also be useful. Occasionally, training in crisis prevention plans is required of teachers working with students who may become aggressive due to their disorders.

Crisis Prevention and Management

Crises and Crisis Prevention and Management Plans

Crises

A **crisis** is generally defined as a situation that is so emotionally impactful that an individual is not able to cope with the situation by normal means and is at risk of harming themselves or others. Crises can arise from either developmental changes that happen throughout life, such as going through puberty or graduating from school, or they can be situational and arise at any time. Examples of situational crises include sickness, losses, family deaths, and any other kind of unpredictable situation that comes up throughout life. Students with disabilities often have particular difficulty coping with stressful life situations and may need the help of a **crisis prevention plan** as a result. Crisis prevention and management goals generally focus on coping mechanisms and healthy anticipation of unavoidable situations to help the individual understand and safely navigate their way through a crisis.

Crisis Prevention Plans

Crisis prevention plans essentially serve to help with early identification of a crisis and to provide the necessary support to help the individual through a crisis to an effective resolution. These plans are often put together with the help of various members of an individual's support team, taking into account past behaviors, health, and other factors of his or her life. Some organizations, such as the Crisis Prevention Institute, specialize in crisis prevention and intervention training for professionals. Crisis prevention plans should take into account principles of least restrictive environment to support individuals in their normal environments, while also removing or being aware of any known **behavioral triggers** that may be problematic. In the event that the individual in crisis becomes physically violent or harmful to themselves, stronger emergent response may be warranted. The ultimate goal is to keep the individual and others safe until his or her emotional state has been normalized. There is no specific duration of time for a crisis, but any intervention should be treated as short-term to prevent restricting the individual's rights through unnecessary intervention. It is important to provide the individual with clear structures and expectations to help understand direct consequences for undesired choices prior to entering a crisis. Crisis prevention plans should also provide clear processes that professionals and family members can use when students do enter a crisis in order to de-escalate the situations.

> **Review Video: Crisis Management and Prevention**
> Visit mometrix.com/academy and enter code: 351872

Planning and Service Delivery

INDIVIDUALIZED FAMILY SERVICE PLAN (IFSP) - 0 TO 2 YEARS

When a child aged from birth through 2 years has been screened, referred for comprehensive evaluation to determine whether he or she has a disability eligible for early intervention services under the IDEA law Individualized Family Service Plan, and through the evaluation results, found eligible, the next step is to develop an IFSP. This is a written document that describes in detail what early intervention services the child will be receiving. The IFSP is guided by certain principles, including that the young child's needs are closely attached to his or her family's needs and that the family is the child's most important resource. Therefore, supporting the family and building upon the family's particular strengths are the best ways to meet the needs of and support the child. The IFSP is created by a multidisciplinary team that includes the parents and is a plan for the whole family. Other interagency team members, depending on the child's needs, may include medical personnel, therapists, social workers, child development specialists, and so on.

INFORMATION INCLUDED IN AN IFSP - 0 TO 2 YEARS

An IFSP is developed for children 0 to 2 years determined eligible through evaluation results for early intervention services. It must include: the child's current levels of functioning and needs in physical, cognitive, communication, emotional, social, and adaptive development; with parental consent, family information including the parents' and other close family members' concerns, priorities, and resources; primary effects of the IFSP expected for the child and family; specific services to be delivered; where the child will receive services in natural environments, like at home, in the community, elsewhere, or a combination; if services will not be in the natural environment, a rationale justifying this; specific service times and locations; number of sessions or days for services and session durations; whether services will be 1:1 or in groups; who will pay for the services; the name of the service coordinator managing IFSP implementation; steps supporting future transition from early intervention to other programs and services; and optionally, other services of interest to the family, for example, finances, raising children with disabilities, and so on.

ASPECTS OF IFSPS - 0 TO 2 YEARS

When infants and toddlers are determined eligible for IDEA (the Individuals with Disabilities Education Act) services, parents and professionals from multiple, relevant disciplines develop an IFSP for services to family and child. Professionals must thoroughly explain the plan to parents, and parents must give informed, written consent before the child receives services. Every U.S. state has its own set of IFSP guidelines. The service coordinator can explain state guidelines to parents. Early intervention services range from simple to complex, including things such as prescribing eyeglasses, special instruction, home visits, counseling, and family training to help meet the child's special needs. Some services are provided in the family's home and some in hospitals, local health departments, community day care centers, clinics, or other settings. Natural environments, that is, settings where the child normally lives, plays, and learns are preferred. Personnel delivering services must be qualified. Both public and private agencies may be involved in service delivery.

FINANCIAL ASPECTS OF RECEIVING EARLY INTERVENTION SERVICES

The IDEA provides that, if a child has a qualifying disability, is at risk for developmental delay or disability, or is suspected of having an eligible disability, families must be given Child Find services, developmental screenings, assessment referrals, comprehensive evaluations, a developed and reviewed IFSP in which parents participate, and service coordination all at no cost to the family. Whether families pay for services other than those named above is determined by each U.S. state's individual policies. Some services can be covered by Medicaid, by private health insurance policies, or for Native American families, by Indian Health Services. Some service providers may charge fees to families on a sliding scale basis according to the family's earned income so that lower-income families can afford them. The law provides that an eligible child cannot be denied special services simply because his or her family cannot afford to pay for them; providers must make all efforts to deliver services to all babies and toddlers needing assistance and support.

SPECIAL EDUCATION SERVICES - 3 TO 5 YEARS

If parents observe that their preschooler is not attaining developmental milestones within the expected age ranges or does not seem to be developing in the same way as most other children, they should seek evaluation for possible developmental delay or disability. Although 3- to 5-year-olds are likely not in elementary school yet, the elementary school in a family's school district is still the best first contact because the IDEA law (the Individuals with Disabilities Education Act) specifies that school districts must provide special education services at no family cost to eligible children, including preschoolers. Another excellent source of more information about special education is the National Dissemination Center for Children with Disabilities (NICHCY) of the U.S. Department of Education's Office of Special Education Programs. They partner with nonprofit organizations like the Academy for Educational Development (AED) to produce useful documents for families with special needs children. NICHCY supplies state resource sheets listing main contacts regarding special education services in each U.S. state. Families can obtain these sheets at NICHCY's website or by telephone.

INFORMATION SOURCES USED IN THE EVALUATION - 3 TO 5 YEARS

Under the IDEA (the Individuals with Disabilities Education Act), evaluation information sources include: physicians' reports, the child's medical history, developmental test results, current classroom observations and assessments (when applicable), completed developmental and behavioral checklists, feedback and observations from parents and all other members of the evaluation team, and any other significant records, reports, and observations regarding the child. Under the IDEA, involved in the evaluation are parents, at least one regular education teacher and special education teacher if the child has these, and any special education service provider working with the child—for children receiving early intervention services from birth through age 2 and transitioning to preschool special education, it may be an early intervention service provider; a school administrator knowledgeable about children with disabilities, special education policies, regular education curriculum, and resources available; a psychologist or educator who can interpret evaluation results and discuss indicated instruction; individuals with special expertise or knowledge regarding the child (recruited by school or parents); when appropriate, the child; and other professionals, for example, physical or occupational therapists, speech therapists, medical specialists, and so on.

SPECIAL EDUCATION SERVICES - 3 TO 5 YEARS

Special education for preschoolers is education specifically designed to meet the individual needs of a child aged 3 to 5 years with a disability or developmental delay. The specialized design of this instruction can include adaptations to the content, to the teaching methods, and the way instruction is delivered to meet a disabled child's unique needs. Special education for preschoolers includes various settings, such as in the home, in classrooms, hospitals, institutions, and others. It also includes a range of related services, such as speech-language pathology services, specialized physical education instruction, early vocational training, and training in travel skills. The school district's special education system provides evaluation and services to eligible preschoolers free of charge. Evaluation's purposes are to determine whether a child has a disability under the IDEA's (the Individuals with Disabilities Education Act) definitions and determine that child's present educational needs.

Post-Evaluation - 3 to 5 Years

After a preschool child is evaluated, the parents and involved school personnel meet to discuss the evaluation results. Parents are included in the group that decides whether the child is eligible for special education services based on those results. For eligible children, the parents and school personnel will develop an IEP. Every child who will receive special education services must have an IEP. The main purposes of the IEP are:

- to establish reasonable educational goals for the individual child
- to indicate what services the school district will provide to the child

The IEP includes a statement of the child's present levels of functioning and performance. It also includes a list of more general instructional goals for the child to achieve through school and parental support along with more specific learning objectives reflecting those goals and specifying exactly what the child will be able to demonstrate, under what circumstances, how much of the time—for example, a percentage of recorded instances—and within what time period (e.g., 1 year).

Individualized Education Program (IEP) Goals and Objectives - 3 to 5 Year

In an IEP, the goals are more global, describing a skill for the child to acquire or a task to master. The objectives are more specific articulations of achievements that will demonstrate the child's mastery of the goal. For example, if a goal is for the child to increase his or her functional communicative vocabulary, a related objective might be for the child to acquire X number of new words in X length of time; another related objective could be for the child to use the words acquired in 90% of recorded relevant situations. If the goal is for the child to demonstrate knowledge and discrimination of colors, one objective might be for the child to identify correctly a red, yellow, and blue block 95% of the time when asked to point out each color within a group of blocks. Progress toward or achievement of some objectives may be measured via formal tests; with preschoolers, many others are measured via observational data collection.

TPBA2

Transdisciplinary Play-Based Assessment, Second Edition (TPBA2) is a method for assessing a child's development through play behaviors. Very young children have not developed the cognitive skills needed to respond to many formal assessment instruments. For example, you would not ask a 3-year-old to conjugate verbs, add several single-digit numbers, or count more than a few concrete objects. This is true even of normally developing young children and even more so of those with developmental disabilities whose cognitive development may not be at typical age levels. However, most young children naturally engage in and enjoy playing. TPBA2 takes advantage of this by having trained professionals observe a young child at play. Together with parents' input, the observers can determine the child's performance levels of many motor, cognitive, adaptive, emotional, and social skills. Typically, a TPBA2 team collaborating or consulting with parents would include personnel such as a speech-language pathologist, a psychologist, a teacher, and a physical or occupational therapist. These specialists are most familiar with child skills across all domains of development that can be directly observed during play.

School Multidisciplinary Team (MDT)

While the new school or preschool is waiting for records to arrive from a transferring child's previous program, if the MDT has been informed that the child has already had an IEP developed and in place, the team should not place the child in a special education class or group in the interim, which would be premature and inappropriate without first having the prior school's records and conducting a team meeting to ascertain the child's instructional needs. Federal regulations provide that making an interim placement that is, placing the child in a regular education class or program, is more appropriate until the child's records are received and further, more detailed information is available. If the child already has an IEP, then a comprehensive evaluation was conducted to determine his or her special education eligibility. Therefore, the team should not duplicate this by performing another complete evaluation, consuming unnecessary time and resources.

Progress Monitoring, Updating, and Revising IEPs

Once a child has been identified with a disability, determined eligible for special education and related services under the IDEA (the Individuals with Disabilities Education Act), and had an IEP developed and implemented, the child's progress must be monitored. Monitoring methods may be related to evaluation methods. For example, if a child identified with problem behaviors was initially evaluated using a behavioral checklist, school personnel can use the same checklist periodically, comparing its results to the baseline levels of frequency and severity originally obtained. If an affective disorder or disturbance was identified and instruments like the Beck Depression Inventory or Anxiety Inventory were used, these can be used again periodically; reduced symptoms would indicate progress. If progress with IEP goals and objectives is less or greater than expected, the IEP team meets and may revise the program. This can include specifying shorter or longer times to achieve some goals and objectives; lowering or raising requirements proving too difficult or easy; resetting successive objective criteria in smaller or larger increments; changing teaching methods, content, or materials used, and so on.

Tiered Service Delivery Models

Response to Intervention (RTI), Positive Behavior Support/Positive Behavioral Interventions and Supports (PBS/PBIS), and other service delivery models are very similar. They are generally implemented school-wide, program-wide, or classroom-wide depending on the educational program; many schools use these approaches on a school-wide basis based on the philosophy of proactively preventing learning problems by providing positive support. These models consist of tiers of gradually increasing support along a continuum. Numbers of tiers may vary, but a common feature is using three tiers. For example, the first tier is called primary intervention and implements systems that apply to all students, settings, and staff. This tier generally applies to around 80% of the students in a school, program, or classroom. The second tier is called secondary intervention and involves specialized group systems for students identified as at risk, generally involving about 15% of students. The third tier, tertiary intervention, uses specialized, individualized systems for students with intensive needs, usually about 5% of student populations.

Characteristics of Tier 2 Instruction Within 3-Tiered Service Delivery Models

While Tier 1 in 3-tier models addresses all students and is meant to meet typical student needs, Tier 2 is designed with additional instruction to help at-risk children to attain expected grade-level skills when they fall behind with Tier 1 instruction. Tier 2 interventions are generally supplemental instruction in small groups, with teacher-student ratios of up to 1:5, usually lasting 8 to 12 weeks and administered by special education teachers, specialists, or tutors. Programs, procedures, and teaching strategies in Tier 2 support Tier 1 instruction as well as supplementing and enhancing it. Tier 2 focuses on research evidence-based practices found effective for at-risk children. Students are introduced to Tier 2 as soon as possible after Tier 1 student progress monitoring determines they have fallen behind grade levels. This benefits many students, such as with specific learning disabilities, in bypassing lengthy referral and evaluation procedures otherwise required for special education. Monitoring showing sufficient progress dictates a return to general education classrooms; insufficient progress leads to another round of Tier 2 intervention.

4-STEP APPROACH TO RESPONSE TO INTERVENTION (RTI)-TYPE TIERED MODELS

RTI models (and Positive Behavioral Support [PBS] models, which are very similar) generally use three tiers of instructional intervention. Tier 1 applies to all students, meets most student needs, and can prevent problems through proactive support. Students failing to meet grade-level expectations in Tier 1 are placed in Tier 2 to receive specialized supplemental instruction in smaller groups from a qualified specialist, special education teacher, or tutor. If this is ineffective, Tier 3 provides more intensive support, individualized to each student, in even smaller groups. Some educators recommend a 4-step process in a protocol treatment approach to RTI:

1. Screening, involving Tier 1 or all students—responsibility is shared by general and special education teachers.
2. Implementing general education and monitoring responses to it involves Tier 1—general education departments and teachers are responsible for this.
3. Implementing supplementary, diagnostic instructional trials and monitoring responses involves Tier 2—responsibility is shared by general and special education teachers.
4. Designating and classifying disability, special intensive instructional placement, and monitoring thereof affect Tier 3—special education professionals are responsible.

FEATURES OF TIER 1 INSTRUCTION WITHIN 3-TIER SERVICE DELIVERY MODELS

In 3-tiered service delivery models, Tier 1 targets all students for support to meet the needs of the general student population and prevent problems before they occur. In Tier 1, general education teachers deliver core instructional programs that are based on solid research evidence to students. While this entails reading, writing, and mathematics for school-age students, for preschoolers it involves pre-academic skills like phonological awareness, alphabetic awareness, vocabulary development, counting skills using concrete objects, categorizing objects, and adaptive skills development for functioning independently in daily life. Student progress is monitored using measurements based on the given curriculum. The results of student progress monitoring are analyzed to identify students who are not making sufficient progress and are therefore at risk for developmental delays or learning problems. Students thus identified as at risk would qualify for Tier 2 intervention.

FEATURES OF TIER 3 INSTRUCTION WITHIN RESPONSE TO INTERVENTION (RTI)

Children who fall behind in general Tier 1 instruction designed to support all or most students are placed in Tier 2, where supplemental instruction is given, providing additional support to children at risk for developmental delays, disorders, or learning problems. When progress monitoring finds a student is not making adequate progress toward grade levels after two rounds of Tier 2 intervention, or whose progress is severely limited in 1 round of Tier 2, Tier 3 intervention is indicated. Tier 3 involves instruction customized for the individual child; provides much more intensive, sustained support; and depending on the student's needs, can have much longer durations than Tier 2 interventions. Typically, instruction is in smaller groups with teacher-student ratios of no more than 1:3. Progress monitoring is closer and more ongoing in Tier 3. If a child meets the program's established benchmarks as determined by monitoring or testing, he or she may be exited to Tier 1. However, if the student then fails without such intensive support, he or she may be returned to Tier 2 or Tier 3.

PREMACK PRINCIPLE

The Premack principle is a principle derived from behaviorism or learning theory. It involves encouraging a child to engage in a behavior less desirable to him or her by making a behavior more desirable or rewarding to the child contingent upon demonstrating the less desired behavior. Behaviorism has established that people (and animals) are more likely to repeat any behavior that

receives a reward, or reinforcement, immediately after it occurs. Adults are more likely to repeat work tasks when they are paid money for them; children are more likely to eat their vegetables when they receive dessert for doing so. For example, if Johnny loves to play with finger paints but will only tolerate wearing the headphones that are an important part of his educational programming (and do not cause discomfort) for 1 to 2 minutes at a time, contingent reinforcement could be used to increase this time by letting him have finger paints only after progressively longer periods wearing the headphones—2 minutes, then 3, then 5, and so on.

ACTIVITY-BASED INTERVENTION

Activity-based intervention is:

- child directed
- embeds intervention across varied activities
- utilizes naturally and logically occurring antecedents (events coming before a desired behavior) and consequences (events immediately following a desired behavior)
- focuses on developing functional skills

For example, if a young child demonstrates particular interest in balloons, activity-based intervention using balloons in activities fulfills component 1 of being child directed. The teacher might elicit the child's requests for balloons, give directions for the child to follow in painting or decorating balloons, teach words related to balloons and have the child use them, and offer the child games to play with balloons. This fulfills component 2 of embedding intervention across varied activities. Component 3 of natural and logical antecedents and consequences is met by using balloons, which are naturally motivating and rewarding to this child. The activities named all develop functional skills 4: requesting desired objects, following directions, fine motor skills, vocabulary development and application, and learning and following (game) rules.

CUMULATIVE AND DELAYED INFLUENCES

Both positive and negative experiences children have early in life exert significant accumulating effects on their development. For example, some children's preschool social interactions promote confidence and social skills, facilitating making friends later, improving both their social competencies and academic performance. When other children do not develop basic social skills early on, peers reject or ignore them, putting them at higher risk for dropout, delinquency, or mental health issues later. Children's early neurological development is enhanced by receiving ample, varied, rich environmental stimuli, furthering formation of more neural connections, which then promote additional development and learning. Children deprived of such early stimulation have less ability to develop and learn through future experiences, triggering cumulative disadvantages. The earlier the intervention and support, the more effective they are. For example, it is much easier and cheaper to prevent reading problems than remediate them. Research indicates a child's first three years are the optimal time for developing spoken language. Giving children necessary stimuli and supports at optimal times most consistently produces appropriate conditions for healthy development.

DEVELOPMENTAL PRINCIPLE OF MOVEMENT FROM SIMPLER TO MORE COMPLEX ABILITIES

Increasing complexity is a principle throughout child development observed in nearly all domains including motor and physical, linguistic, cognitive, and social skills. Neurological development enables growing children to use their expanding memories and organizational abilities to combine simpler routines they have learned into more complex strategies. Even preschoolers understand some abstract concepts, such as that addition creates more while subtraction creates fewer and the one-to-one principle in counting things. However, children proceed in general from more concrete to more abstract thought as they grow. Children also progress from infancy's complete dependence to learning control and internalizing it, and adults play important parts in helping them. When babies are aroused and adults soothe them, this helps them learn to self-soothe. When preschool teachers provide scaffolding and support for dramatic role-plays, help young children learn how to express their feelings, and involve them in planning and decision making, they help them develop emotional self-regulation, to maintain focused attention, and to manage strong feelings.

CONSTRUCTIVIST ORIENTATIONS INFORM MULTIPLE, VARIED TEACHING METHODS

Constructivism states that young children build their comprehension and knowledge of reality through their experiences with the environment and interactions with family, peers, older children, teachers, and media. Through manipulating concrete objects and learning abstract concepts, children form hypotheses regarding the world and test these via interacting with things, people, and their own thinking processes. They observe events, reflect on their discoveries, imagine possibilities, ask questions, and form answers. Such owning of knowledge by children affords deeper comprehension and superior generalization and application of learning to different contexts. Variation in children's learning needs dictates variation in teaching methods. In both play and structured activities, teachers having wide ranges of strategies can choose the best one for each particular situation, context, learning goal, and individual child needs at the moment. This includes providing greater support, even during play or exploration, to children needing it. It also encompasses teacher demonstration and modeling, providing challenges, specific instruction, and directions, and organizing classrooms and planning to further education goals through opportunities presented in child- and teacher-initiated activities.

VYGOTSKY'S ZONE OF PROXIMAL DEVELOPMENT (ZPD) AND BRUNER'S SCAFFOLDING

What Vygotsky termed the ZPD is the area wherein children best learn skills just beyond their current mastery levels and accomplish learning tasks which they could not achieve alone through guidance and support from adults and from other children with slightly higher skill levels. Scaffolding is Bruner's related term for support that adults provide to learning children as needed and gradually withdraw as the child's competence increases until the child can complete a task or skill independently. When achieving autonomy in this manner, children can also generalize, applying skills learned to various new contexts. An important consideration for educators to maintaining children's motivation and persistence is enabling their success at new tasks more often than not. Most children give up trying after repeatedly failing. Another educator consideration is repeatedly giving children opportunities for practicing and consolidating new concepts and skills. This allows the mastery children need to apply and generalize learning. Educators need knowledge of child developmental sequences, plus close observation of individual children's thought processes, to provide challenges without frustration.

CONTRIBUTING TO CREATING A CARING LEARNING COMMUNITY FOR YOUNG CHILDREN

Children learn about themselves and their environments through observation of and participation in the learning community. By demonstrating that each member of the community values and is valued by other members, educators help children learn to establish constructive relationships with others. They also help them learn to value each individual and to recognize and respect all individual and group differences. Because a significant context wherein children develop and learn is relationships with adults and peers, educators can give them various opportunities to play with others, have conversations and discussions with peers and adults, and collaborate on projects and investigations to promote development and learning. By assigning young children to small groups, educators can give them opportunities to learn and practice social interaction; cooperation in problem solving, sharing and building upon each other's ideas; and expanding their thinking. Such interactions support young children's construction of their understandings of reality through their interactions with other members of the learning community.

PLANNING ENVIRONMENTS, SCHEDULES, AND ACTIVITIES

By offering richly varied ideas, challenges, and materials, ECE teachers can provide young children with firsthand activities that give them creatively and intellectually stimulating experiences that invite children's ongoing, active engagement, exploration, and investigation. During periods of child-initiated or child-chosen activity, teachers can help and guide children not yet able to put such activities to good use or enjoy them. They can also support children more able to choose by giving them opportunities to make meaningful choices and decisions. Effective ECE teachers organize daily and weekly schedules to afford children substantial time periods for uninterrupted play, exploration, investigation, and social interaction with peers and adults. ECE teachers should also arrange experiences and interactions and provide materials for young children that allow them to fully push the boundaries of their imaginations and of their linguistic, self-regulatory, and interactional abilities to practice the skills that they have newly developed.

ASSURING THE FULL PARTICIPATION, DEVELOPMENT, AND LEARNING

ECE teachers can encourage young children to select and plan their own learning activities, which helps them develop initiative. Teachers can ask children questions, pose problems, and make suggestions and comments to stimulate their thinking and expand their learning. To expand the scope of children's interests and thoughts, teachers can introduce stimulating ideas, problems, hypotheses, or problems, and experiences novel to them. In adjusting activity complexity for children's knowledge and skill levels, teachers increase challenges commensurately with children's increasing understanding and competency. Providing experiences with genuine challenge and success is a way teachers can enhance children's motivation, persistence, risk taking, confidence, and competence as learners. Intensive interviews, extended conversation and discourse, and similar strategies encouraging children to revisit and reflect upon their experiences are ways teachers can further children's conceptual understanding. ECE teachers should also give specific feedback (e.g., "You got the same total both times you counted those buttons!") rather than generic praises (e.g., "Good job!").

MAKING THE LEARNING EXPERIENCES RESPONSIVE AND ACCESSIBLE

In making learning responsive and accessible to all children's needs, ECE teachers must include those learning English as a new language, those from diverse cultures, those having disabilities, and those in impoverished and otherwise difficult living situations. To do this, teachers use a wide range of materials, equipment, teaching strategies, and experiences to address individual differences in children's previous experiences, developmental levels, abilities, skills, interests, and needs. They include each child's home language and culture into the learning community, such that the child's home and family ties are supported and the community realizes and values each culture and language's unique contributions. They include all children in all activities and model and encourage children's behaviors and peer interactions to be inclusive. ECE teachers can meet the needs of children with disabilities using their own strategies, plus consulting as needed with family and indicated specialists, and ensure children receive necessary adaptations or modifications and specialized services to succeed in learning.

Chapter Quiz

Ready to see how well you retained what you just read? Scan the QR code to go directly to the chapter quiz interface for this study guide. If you're using a computer, simply visit the online resources page at **mometrix.com/resources719/westeearchsped** and click the Chapter Quizzes link.

Foundations and Professional Practice

Transform passive reading into active learning! After immersing yourself in this chapter, put your comprehension to the test by taking a quiz. The insights you gained will stay with you longer this way. Scan the QR code to go directly to the chapter quiz interface for this study guide. If you're using a computer, simply visit the online resources page at **mometrix.com/resources719/westeearchsped** and click the Chapter Quizzes link.

Roles and Responsibilities within the Local Education System

DEPARTMENT CHAIRPERSONS

Department chairpersons are appointed to act as **leaders** within their subject areas. These individuals are responsible for a variety of instructional and administrative duties to ensure the **efficacy** of their academic department in supporting the goals and mission of the school. This includes contributing to curriculum development, communicating instructional expectations from administration to their colleagues, and ensuring that daily instruction within the department aligns with campus and district academic standards. Department chairpersons also serve as **resources** for their teams, including collaborating with them to design instructional activities and assessments, offering support, and facilitating positive communication with administration. When working with administration, department chairpersons discuss the progress of their departments in meeting academic goals, collaborate to develop strategies for assisting faculty in supporting student learning, and ensure their colleagues have the support, materials, and resources necessary for effective instruction. In addition, department chairpersons are often responsible for coordinating department activities and programs that promote student achievement and contribute to creating a positive school community.

SCHOOL PRINCIPAL

The primary role of the **principal** is establishing and maintaining a **school culture** that supports students, teachers, staff, and families in the educational program. This role comprises a multifaceted array of responsibilities that extend to nearly every aspect of the school. The principal is responsible for supervising the **daily operations** of the school to ensure a safe, orderly environment in which teachers, staff, and students are working in alignment with the school's mission. To achieve this, the principal must communicate expectations for a positive, productive school community, ensure academic and behavioral policies are followed by staff and students, and assign staff members specific duties to facilitate an organized, efficient learning environment. In addition, it is important that the principal support staff, students, and families by engaging in frequent, open communication, addressing concerns, and providing resources necessary to promote growth and achievement. The principal is also responsible for ensuring that the school's educational program is effective in supporting teachers, staff, and students in the achievement of academic standards. This includes overseeing curriculum, monitoring instructional practices, measuring the school's performance in relation to district academic standards, as well as communicating the progress and needs of the school to the board of education.

BOARD OF TRUSTEES

Each school within a district is overseen by a **board of trustees** responsible for making decisions to ensure that the educational program supports students' learning needs for academic achievement. The board of trustees is composed of a group of **elected individuals** who are typically members of the community in which they serve. As such, they have an understanding of the educational needs of the students within the community and can apply this knowledge to make effective decisions regarding the learning program. Members within a board of trustees are responsible for creating an educational program in alignment with students' needs as well as setting goals and developing strategies that support students in achieving them. This includes determining a **budget plan, allocating resources**, and making **administrative decisions** that benefit the school. In addition, board members are responsible for analyzing assessment data to make informed decisions regarding strategies to best support individual schools within the district and ensuring that measures are being implemented to effectively meet students' learning needs.

CURRICULUM COORDINATORS

Curriculum coordinators are responsible for the **development** and **implementation** of curriculum that is aligned with campus and district academic goals. These individuals work closely with teachers and administrators to analyze student progress in relation to the educational program, primarily through **assessment scores**, to determine the overall effectiveness of the curriculum in supporting students' achievement. Analyzing student progress enables curriculum coordinators to identify strengths and areas for improvement within the curriculum to make adjustments that best meet students' learning needs as they work to achieve learning targets. Ensuring that curriculum aligns with academic standards and students' learning needs facilitates more effective teaching and learning. Doing so provides teachers with a clear understanding of how to adequately prepare students for success, thus allowing them to design focused instruction and implement necessary supports to promote the achievement of campus and district academic standards.

SCHOOL TECHNOLOGY COORDINATORS

Incorporating technology into the classroom is highly valuable in diversifying instructional strategies to promote student learning and engagement. School **technology coordinators** facilitate this integration to enhance teaching and learning, as they are responsible for the **organization, maintenance**, and **allocation** of available technology resources within the school building. This includes ensuring that all technology is functional, updated, properly stored, and accessible to teachers. These individuals are also responsible for **staying current** on developing digital resources that could be implemented to improve the learning experience as well as communicating with the board of education regarding **acquiring** technology resources for their schools. Doing so ensures that teachers have the materials necessary to best support students' learning. In addition, technology coordinators **educate** teachers and staff on the uses of technology resources as well as strategies to implement them in the classroom for more effective instruction.

SPECIAL EDUCATION PROFESSIONALS

Special education professionals work with students of various disabilities, their teachers, and families to provide an equitable, inclusive environment that supports learning and development. These individuals are responsible for creating an educational plan that is tailored to support the unique needs of disabled students and ensuring that this plan is followed in all areas of the school. Special educators develop **individualized education programs** (IEPs) according to students' areas of need, develop academic and behavioral goals, as well as provide supports and modifications to accommodate students in achieving them. Special education professionals work with teachers to educate them on the proper implementation of individualized accommodations to ensure all students have the support necessary to successfully engage in learning. This includes collaborating with teachers to adapt and modify curriculum, instructional activities, and assessments to meet the individual needs of students with disabilities. In addition, special educators may work alongside classroom teachers in a team-teaching setting or provide individualized instruction as necessary. Students' academic and behavioral progress is monitored over time, and special educators communicate this information to families in order to collaborate in developing future goals and strategies to support achievement.

ROLES AND RESPONSIBILITIES OF PROFESSIONALS WITHIN THE EDUCATION PROGRAM

The roles and responsibilities of various professionals within the educational program are described as follows:

- **Principal**—The principal is responsible for ensuring that the daily operations of the school function in a safe, orderly manner that aligns with the goals of the educational program. This includes delegating tasks to staff, enforcing academic and behavioral policies, ensuring instructional practices support student achievement, and communicating with students, staff, and families to establish a positive learning environment.
- **Vice principal**—The vice principal's role is to assist the principal in supervising the daily operations of the school to create a safe, orderly, and productive learning environment. The vice principal is responsible for working with teachers, staff, students, and families to support them in the educational program. This includes enforcing academic and behavioral policies, addressing concerns, facilitating communication, and ensuring instructional practices support student achievement of campus and district academic goals.
- **Board of trustees**—The board of trustees is responsible for developing an educational program that reflects the learning needs of students within the community. This includes developing educational goals, strategies to support students in achieving them, and ensuring that schools within the district are in alignment with the educational program. The board of trustees is also responsible for administrative decisions such as developing a budget plan and allocating resources to schools within the district according to students' needs.
- **Curriculum coordinator**—Curriculum coordinators are responsible for developing a curriculum that aligns with campus and district academic goals and ensuring it is implemented properly to support student achievement. This includes working with teachers and administrators to measure student progress within the curriculum and adjusting instructional strategies as necessary to support student success.
- **Assessment coordinator**—Assessment coordinators schedule, disperse, and collect standardized assessments and testing materials within the school building. They are responsible for educating teachers on proper assessment protocols to ensure that all practices align with district policies, collaborating with them to develop strategies that support student achievement, and ensuring all students are provided with necessary accommodations according to individual need.
- **Technology coordinator**—Technology coordinators facilitate the integration of digital resources into the curriculum. They are responsible for acquiring, organizing, maintaining, and allocating technology within the school. These individuals also work with teachers and staff to educate them on ways to utilize technology resources to enhance instruction.

- **Department chair**—Department chairpersons act as leaders among the teachers within their content areas. Their responsibilities include contributing to curriculum development, facilitating communication between administration and their colleagues, and ensuring instructional practices align with the educational program. They also collaborate with members of their team to develop instructional practices that best support student achievement of campus and district academic goals.
- **Teacher assistant**—The teacher assistant's role is to support the classroom teacher in both instructional and non-instructional duties. This includes assisting with the preparation, organization, and cleanup of lesson materials, working with small groups of students, managing student behavior, and ensuring the classroom functions in a safe, orderly manner.
- **Paraprofessional**—Paraprofessionals are licensed within the field of education and are responsible for assisting the teacher with daily classroom operations. This includes working with individual or small groups of students to provide instructional support, assisting with the preparation of lesson plans and materials, managing student behavior, and completing administrative duties.
- **Speech-language pathologist**—Speech-language pathologists are special education professionals who work with students who have varying degrees of language and communication difficulties. They are responsible for evaluating and diagnosing disabilities related to speech and language as well as developing individualized treatment programs. Speech-language pathologists then work with these students to remedy language and communication disabilities as well as collaborate with teachers, staff, and families regarding ways to support their progress.
- **ESL specialist**—ESL (English as a second language) specialists work with students for whom English is not their native language. They are responsible for evaluating students' levels of English language proficiency across the domains of reading, writing, speaking, and listening, determining necessary linguistic supports, and working with teachers to develop strategies that support English language acquisition. ESL specialists also work with individual or small groups of students to monitor progress and develop English language proficiency skills.
- **Guidance counselor**—The role of guidance counselors is to support students' social, emotional, academic, and behavioral needs. This includes providing counseling services, mediation, and, for upper grade level students, advice regarding course selection and career choices. These individuals communicate with teachers, staff, and families to develop and implement plans to support students' personal growth and academic achievement.
- **School nurse**—The school nurse is responsible for providing a range of healthcare to students and staff in the school building. This includes evaluating the physical, mental, and emotional health of students and staff as well as delivering general first-aid treatments. School nurses are also responsible for organizing and dispersing prescribed medications to students in accordance with their healthcare plan and educating teachers and staff regarding best practices for ensuring students' health and safety. School nurses may work with special education professionals to assess students' needs in the development of an individualized education program.
- **Building service worker**—Building service workers are responsible for the general maintenance of the school building and outside campus. This includes ensuring that all areas, equipment, and furniture are clean, functional, and safe for student and staff use. These individuals are also responsible for transporting heavy equipment and furniture throughout the school building.

- **Secretary**—The school secretary is responsible for assisting the principal, vice principal, and other office personnel in daily administrative duties. This individual assumes a variety of responsibilities to ensure the efficient function of daily operations within the school. Their responsibilities include communicating with students, families, and other office visitors, directing phone calls to the appropriate location, handling financial matters, and coordinating the school calendar.
- **Library/media specialist**—Library and media specialists coordinate the organization, maintenance, and allocation of all library and media resources within the school building. They are responsible for educating students regarding the proper use of library and media resources to locate information, including how to navigate the internet safely and appropriately for educational purposes. Library and media specialists also direct students toward reading material aligned with their literacy skills and provide teachers with learning materials to incorporate into instruction.
- **Instructional leadership team (ILT)**—An instructional leadership team is composed of individuals responsible for educating teachers regarding current and relevant instructional philosophies and practices to enhance student learning. These individuals collaborate with teachers to educate them regarding how to implement instructional strategies, activities, and assessments to effectively meet students' learning needs and support their achievement of campus and district academic goals.
- **School resource officer**—The role of the school resource officer is to maintain a safe, orderly environment for teachers, staff, and students. They are responsible for ensuring the physical security of the school, handling legal infractions within the school, and addressing conflicts among students. The school resource officer also works with administration and staff to develop emergency drill procedures.
- **Pupil personnel worker (PPW)**—Pupil personnel workers are responsible for addressing issues that hinder the academic achievement of at-risk students. These individuals communicate with teachers, administration, staff, and families to ensure these students are supported both within and outside of the school building. This includes addressing issues related to behavior, crisis intervention, attendance, and home lives. Pupil personnel workers direct families toward school and community support resources and collaborate with teachers to implement supports that facilitate success in learning.

Professional Development

AVAILABLE RESOURCES AND SUPPORT SYSTEMS

Effective educators continuously seek professional development opportunities to refine their teaching practice. There are multiple resources and support systems that teachers can utilize to develop their professional knowledge and skills. Within the school building, mentors are available to offer ideas, advice, and support in developing teaching practices and strategies to implement in the classroom for effective teaching and learning. The school's **instructional leadership team** (ILT) is also a valuable resource for educating teachers regarding current instructional practices to enhance student engagement and learning. Teachers can continue their professional education by enrolling in university courses or participating in state-initiated programs to stay informed on relevant pedagogical theories and practices. Service centers are also available that offer workshops, training, and conferences on a variety of topics related to education to support teachers' professional development. In addition, numerous digital support resources are available that allow teachers to enroll in courses, participate in informational webinars, and collaborate with other educators in professional learning communities to build and enhance their teaching practice.

Example Opportunities That Can Enhance Teaching Practice

Professional development opportunities are available to address a variety of needs for refining one's practice and developing pedagogical knowledge. Professional development trainings can serve to educate teachers on how to utilize and incorporate current technologies into the classroom as well as teach strategies for implementing relevant and engaging instructional techniques, materials, and resources into the classroom. These opportunities can also be beneficial in teaching educators how to demonstrate cultural competency and skills for productive collaboration with colleagues to enhance student learning. Teachers can also seek professional development opportunities to learn best practices for addressing a variety of student needs, such as intellectual, physical, social, or emotional disabilities, or linguistic needs of ELLs. Actively seeking and participating in professional development trainings helps to ensure teachers stay current on pedagogical theories that can serve as a framework for their instructional practice.

Effectively Utilizing Resources and Support Systems

The field of education is multifaceted and continuously evolving. As such, it is important that teachers of all experience levels engage in the vast array of **available resources** and **support systems** to develop and refine their professional skills. Doing so enhances students' learning, as teachers who actively seek professional development are more current on pedagogical theories and practices as well as instructional strategies, resources, and technologies to incorporate in the classroom. This allows teachers to design and implement more effective instruction, as it provides them with an increased range of knowledge and tools to enhance student engagement and understanding. In addition, as students' individual needs are diverse, participating in resources and support systems allows teachers to educate themselves on how to properly accommodate them to enhance the learning experience. Utilizing resources and support systems also enables teachers to learn from and collaborate with other educators in professional learning communities to continuously develop new skills, ideas, and instructional methods that enhance student learning.

Teacher Appraisals
Characteristics, Goals, and Procedures

Teacher appraisals are a method of evaluation intended to provide teachers with continuous feedback regarding their **performance** and areas in which they can improve their professional skills to enhance student learning. Feedback is provided periodically throughout the school year and derives from classroom **observations** typically conducted by the principal or grade-level administrator. Observations can either be **formally** scheduled and last the duration of a lesson or can be in the form of shorter, informal **walk-through** evaluations. In both instances, the observer watches and collects information as the teacher delivers instruction, directs learning activities, and interacts with students. The teacher's performance is then measured against **criteria** across several domains pertaining to planning, preparing, and delivering instruction. This score is used to provide the teacher with detailed feedback in post-observation meetings regarding their strengths and specific areas in which they can improve their practice to more effectively meet students' learning needs. Feedback is used to support the teacher in developing specific **professional goals** and strategies for improving their teaching skills.

Benefits of Appraisal Results in Improving Professional Skills

The results of teacher appraisals are beneficial in providing educators with **specific feedback** regarding areas in which they can improve their professional skills. Effective teachers understand the value of continuously **refining their practice** to enhance student learning and actively seek opportunities to do so; however, it may prove difficult for teachers to objectively assess their own efficacy in the classroom. Appraisal results communicate feedback from the outside perspective of the observer for a comprehensive evaluation of their performance, thus providing teachers with clarity regarding their strengths and areas for growth. This allows educators to effectively develop **professional goals** to improve their skills in targeted areas and **strategies** to achieve these goals successfully.

Working with Supervisors, Mentors, and Colleagues
Enhancing Professional Knowledge and Skills

When teachers collaborate with supervisors, mentors, and other colleagues, it facilitates a productive **professional learning community** that supports the continuous development of knowledge and skills related to education. Doing so provides teachers with the opportunity to work with educational professionals of varying backgrounds, experiences, and expertise. This exposes teachers to a wide range of **perspectives**, **approaches**, and **philosophies** that they can learn from to build and enhance their practice. In such a setting, teachers can interact with other professionals within the school community to share ideas, support one another, and collaborate productively in developing strategies to improve their efficacy in the classroom. Additionally, actively engaging with supervisors, mentors, and colleagues facilitates the open communication necessary for productive collaboration in effectively addressing issues to enhance the school community.

Addressing Issues and Building Professional Skills

Productive collaboration with supervisors, mentors, and colleagues is essential to addressing issues related to the educational program and continuously developing professional practices. There are multiple opportunities for such collaboration within the school community that accommodate varying purposes. By participating in **professional learning communities**, members of the educational program can collaborate and support one another in addressing concerns and building professional skills. In subject-area **department** or **team meetings**, educators can work together to share ideas, strategies, and resources related to their content areas for more effective instruction. Working with supervisors and mentors in **post-observation conferences** provides teachers with valuable feedback regarding their strengths and areas for improvement. Such collaboration is beneficial in creating specific goals and strategies for professional growth. Additionally, engaging in collaborative **professional development opportunities**, including workshops, conferences, programs, and courses, is beneficial in allowing educators to build upon one another's experiences, backgrounds, and expertise to enhance professional practices.

Professional Development Resources

The various professional development resources available to teachers and staff are discussed below:

- **Mentors/support systems**: Mentors and other dedicated support resources within the school system are intended to provide teachers with guidance to enhance their professional knowledge, skills, and expertise. These individuals are typically highly experienced and work with teachers to develop effective instructional strategies, classroom management techniques, and learning materials to improve their teaching skills.
- **Conferences**: Education conferences are multifaceted events in which teachers can learn about current developments in their field to improve their professional knowledge, pedagogical skills, and technical expertise. Conference events are composed of numerous professional development opportunities, including presentations on current pedagogical theories and practices, collaborative workshops, and training sessions regarding the implementation of new instructional strategies and technology resources. At these events, teachers can also network with one another to connect and share resources, ideas, and strategies that enhance their teaching practice.

- **Professional associations**: Education associations provide teachers with access to numerous professional development opportunities for improving knowledge, pedagogical skills, and technical expertise. These associations can be related to general education or be content specific, and they offer information regarding education conferences, workshops, training opportunities, and courses to enhance teaching practices. Professional education associations also allow teachers the opportunity to network with one another to build professional knowledge by sharing ideas, resources, and strategies to implement in the classroom.
- **Online resources**: Numerous online resources, including websites, blogs, webinar trainings, and discussion forums are available to support teachers in enhancing their professional knowledge, skills, and technical expertise on a variety of topics. Teachers can utilize these resources to learn current pedagogical theories and practices, instructional and classroom management strategies, and relevant technology resources to implement in the classroom for enhanced student learning. Online resources are also valuable for collaborating with other teachers in building professional knowledge and sharing ideas, learning materials, and resources that improve instructional practices.
- **Workshops**: Workshop training sessions provide teachers the opportunity to build professional knowledge, skills, and expertise by educating them on current instructional strategies, classroom management techniques, and digital resources in a hands-on setting. Workshops are typically dedicated to a specific pedagogical topic and allow teachers to collaborate with one another in learning how to implement it in their classroom.
- **Journals**: Education journals publish newly researched information regarding pedagogical theories and practices teachers can utilize to enhance their professional knowledge. These journals include scholarly articles and case studies regarding topics such as instructional strategies and practices, classroom management techniques, and the implementation of digital resources. Education journals allow teachers to stay current on pedagogical developments in order to continuously improve their teaching skills.
- **Coursework**: Engaging in coursework is beneficial in continuing formal professional education to enhance knowledge, pedagogical skills, and technical expertise. Doing so allows teachers to learn from other experienced educators regarding current educational theories, practices, instructional strategies, and technology resources. By participating in formal coursework, teachers can continuously build upon their teaching skills and stay current regarding developments in their field.

REFLECTION AND SELF-ASSESSMENT
IMPROVING TEACHING PERFORMANCE AND ACHIEVING PROFESSIONAL GOALS

Just as students are encouraged to reflect upon their academic performance, it is important that teachers **reflect** on and **self-assess** their own efficacy in the classroom. Doing so is integral for improving professional knowledge and skills to enhance student learning. Effective teachers continuously self-evaluate their performance to ensure they are providing engaging, relevant instruction that effectively meets students' learning needs for success. Frequently reflecting upon and assessing the effectiveness of their lesson plans, instructional strategies, assessments, and approaches to classroom management is beneficial in providing teachers with insight regarding their **professional strengths** as well as specific **areas for growth**. With this insight, teachers can identify the knowledge, skills, and strategies they need to improve upon to deliver more effective instruction. This ultimately allows teachers to set relevant professional goals to enhance their teaching practice and determine the steps they need to take in achieving them.

METHODS

Continuous reflection and self-assessment through a variety of methods is beneficial in providing teachers with insight into the effectiveness of their teaching practice. **Reflecting on lessons** after they are finished allows teachers to self-assess their instruction by identifying specific elements that were successful as well as components that can be improved in the future to enhance student learning. By eliciting **student feedback**, teachers can evaluate whether their instructional strategies, lesson activities, and assessments promote student engagement and understanding. Working with **mentors** and **colleagues** to discuss the effectiveness of lessons, instructional approaches, and classroom management techniques is also valuable in facilitating self-evaluation of teaching practices to seek areas for improvement. In addition, teachers are typically provided the opportunity to **respond to post-observation feedback** prior to attending an appraisal conference. This provides teachers with the opportunity to reflect on their overall performance and prepare to collaborate with the observer in developing professional goals.

Team Teaching and Professional Collaboration

TEAM TEACHING

Team teaching refers to the collaboration of two or more teachers, paraprofessionals, instructional aides, or special education workers in planning and delivering instruction and assessments. There are **several structures** to this approach to accommodate varying teaching styles and student needs. One teacher may provide direct instruction while another engages in lesson activities or monitors student progress. Similarly, one teacher may instruct while another observes and collects information to improve future planning. Students may be grouped with teachers according to their needs to provide differentiation, or teachers may participate simultaneously and equally in all aspects of the learning process. The intention of this approach is to create a **student-centered environment** focused on enhancing and deepening the learning experience. Team teaching is beneficial in allowing increased **individualized instruction** that more effectively meets students' learning needs. Additionally, when multiple teachers are present, students have access to varying **ideas** and **perspectives** that strengthen their understanding. Team teaching also benefits teachers, as it enables them to utilize one another's strengths for improved instruction. There are, however, limitations to this approach. Differences in **classroom management** styles, **teaching practices**, and **personalities**, when not addressed properly through respectful communication and flexibility, hinder the effectiveness of team teaching.

VERTICAL TEAMING

Communication and collaboration among teachers of varying grade levels is integral to effective instruction that supports students' learning and development. Through **vertical teaming**, content specific teachers **across grade levels** have the opportunity to work together in discussing and planning curriculum, instruction, assessments, and strategies that prepare students for achievement. Teachers of lower grade levels are often unsure of what students in upper grade levels are learning. As a result, these teachers may be uncertain of the skills and abilities their students need to be adequately prepared for success as they transition through grade levels. Likewise, teachers of upper grade levels are often unsure of what students have learned in previous grades, thus hindering their ability to adequately plan instruction and implement necessary learning supports. Vertical teaming facilitates the communication necessary for teachers across grade levels to collaborate in **establishing expectations for preparedness** at each grade level and developing a common curriculum path. This enhances teaching and learning, in that teachers are more effectively able to plan instruction that is aligned with learning targets and prepare students with the necessary knowledge, tools, and supports for continued academic success.

HORIZONTAL TEAMING

Horizontal teaming refers to the collaboration of **same grade level** teachers and staff that work with a common group of students. These teams may comprise teachers within a **single subject area** or **across disciplines** and may also include special education workers, grade-level administrators, paraprofessionals, and guidance counselors. Horizontal teaming is beneficial in facilitating the **coordinated planning** of curriculum, instruction, assessments, and discussion regarding students' progress in the educational program. In addition, this method of teaming provides teachers and staff the opportunity to work together in developing educational goals, addressing areas of need, and implementing strategies to support students' success in learning. Horizontal teaming is also beneficial in encouraging teachers and staff to cooperate with one another in alignment with the goals and mission of the school to create a positive learning community focused on promoting student achievement.

BENEFITS OF MENTORS IN ENHANCING PROFESSIONAL KNOWLEDGE AND SKILLS

Mentors within the school community are typically experienced teachers who are available to offer support, guidance, and expertise to new teachers. As these individuals typically have a great deal of experience as educators, they are highly valuable resources in increasing professional knowledge and improving teaching skills. Mentors can provide **strategies, tools**, and **advice** for planning and delivering instruction, classroom management, and meeting students' learning needs to promote achievement. This includes suggesting ideas and resources for lesson activities and assessments as well as techniques for differentiating instruction, enhancing student engagement, and promoting positive behavior. In addition, mentors can offer insight on how to effectively **navigate the school community**, including how to interact appropriately with colleagues and superiors, complete administrative duties, and communicate effectively with students' families. Regularly working with mentors in the school building ensures that new teachers are supported in developing the knowledge and skills necessary to become effective educators.

INTERACTION WITH PROFESSIONALS IN THE SCHOOL COMMUNITY

In order for an educational community to function effectively, professionals in the building must work together cohesively on a daily basis to support the school's mission and student learning. The nature of these interactions significantly determines the climate and culture of the school environment. Appropriate, professional interactions are important in facilitating the productive collaboration necessary to create a positive school community that promotes student success in learning. All interactions must therefore be **respectful**, **constructive**, and **sensitive** to the varying backgrounds, cultures, and beliefs among professionals in the school community. This includes using **appropriate language**, practicing **active listening**, and ensuring that discussions regarding colleagues, superiors, students, and other individuals in the building remain positive. When interacting in a team setting, it is important to maintain open dialogue and support one another's contributions to the educational program. All professionals in the school building must understand one another's roles and appreciate how these roles function together to support the educational program. Doing so ensures that collaboration is productive, purposeful, and aligned with enhancing students' learning experience.

SUPPORTIVE AND COOPERATIVE RELATIONSHIPS WITH PROFESSIONAL COLLEAGUES
SUPPORTS LEARNING AND ACHIEVEMENT OF CAMPUS AND DISTRICT GOALS

Effective collaboration among school staff and faculty members is reliant on establishing and maintaining supportive, cooperative professional relationships. Doing so facilitates a sense of **mutual respect** and **open communication** that allows colleagues to work together constructively in developing educational goals, plans to support students in achieving them, and strategies to address areas of need within the educational program. Mutual support and cooperation are also beneficial in fostering the **coordinated planning** of curriculum, learning activities, assessments, and accommodations to meet students' individual needs for academic achievement. Such professional relationships allow for more effective teaching and learning, as students are supported by a school community that works together cohesively to promote learning and the achievement of campus and district academic goals.

STRATEGIES FOR ESTABLISHING AND MAINTAINING RELATIONSHIPS

Building and maintaining professional relationships founded on mutual support and cooperation is integral in creating a positive, productive school community focused on student achievement. **Frequent communication** with colleagues in a variety of settings is an important factor in establishing and sustaining such professional relationships. Maintaining continuous and open communication allows professional colleagues in the school building to develop the respect for and understanding of one another necessary to establish a strong rapport. By participating together in **school activities**, **events**, and **programs**, teachers and staff members can build connections while contributing to enhancing the school community and climate. **Community building** strategies, such as participating in activities or games that require teamwork, are also valuable opportunities for developing supportive and cooperative professional relationships among colleagues. In addition, **collaborating** with one another in regard to curriculum, lesson planning, and promoting student achievement contributes significantly to developing positive professional relationships. There are multiple avenues for such collaboration, including participating in professional learning communities (PLC's), department meetings, vertical or horizontal teaming, or engaging in team teaching. Doing so provides teachers and staff the opportunity to communicate and develop mutual goals that support the educational program and student learning.

> **Review Video: Collaborating with Other Professionals**
> Visit mometrix.com/academy and enter code: 100351

Family Involvement and Collaboration

EFFECTIVELY WORKING AND COMMUNICATING WITH FAMILIES

Utilizing multiple means of communication when working with students' families ensures information is **accessible** to and **inclusive** of all involved family members. As students' home lives are dynamic, conveying information through several avenues allows families in various situations to participate in their child's education. This is invaluable in establishing and maintaining the positive relationships necessary between students' families and schools for effective teaching and learning. General classroom information, including concepts being taught, important dates, assignments, or suggestions for activities to do at home that reinforce learning in the classroom, can be communicated both digitally and in written form. Newsletters, calendars, or handouts can be both printed and included on a class website to ensure accessibility for all families. Updates regarding individual students can be communicated electronically, through writing, or in person. Email, digital communication apps, and the telephone allow for frequent communication to address students' progress, express concerns, or offer praise. Teachers and families can also communicate through handwritten notes, progress reports, or students' daily agendas. In-person communication, such as during a scheduled conference, is beneficial for discussing individual students' progress and goals related to the education program in depth as well as ways to support their success in learning.

Building Positive Relationships That Enhance Overall Learning

Students are more supported and learn more effectively when the relationships between their teachers and families are founded on **mutual respect**, **understanding**, and **cooperation**. Establishing this positive rapport requires the teacher to work and communicate frequently with students' families. Doing so creates an inviting learning atmosphere in which family members feel welcomed and included as **equal contributors** to the educational program. This sentiment empowers and encourages family members to take an active role in their children's education, thus strengthening students' support systems and enhancing the overall learning experience. In addition, family members who feel a strong connection to their children's school are more likely to model positive attitudes toward education and reinforce learning at home. When teachers and family members communicate frequently, they develop a mutual sense of trust for one another. This allows for **productive collaboration** and the exchange of valuable insight regarding how to best support students' learning needs both within and outside of the classroom.

Appropriate Collaboration and Communication with Families

To effectively collaborate and communicate with students' families, the teacher must carefully consider appropriate methods for doing so. Communication and collaboration must always be **positive**, **respectful**, and **inclusive** to all families to ensure they feel welcomed as equal participants in their children's education. As such, the teacher must be mindful and responsive to the fact that students come from a variety of backgrounds, family dynamics, and living situations. This includes demonstrating **cultural competency** when interacting with families from different backgrounds, providing multiple and varied opportunities for family involvement, and communicating through a variety of means. Doing so ensures that families of varying situations have access to pertinent information and feel equally included in the educational program. The teacher must also be mindful of the nature and purpose of communication in order to ensure that sensitive details about individual students are shared only with appropriate family members. General classroom information, such as important dates, events, or assignments, may be shared publicly among the classroom community, whereas things like individual student progress or behavior records must be reserved for private communication with the appropriate family members.

Involvement of Families, Parents, Guardians, and Legal Caregivers
Strategies to Encourage Engagement

As students' family dynamics are diverse, it is important that the teacher implement a variety of methods to engage parents, guardians, and legal caregivers into the educational program. Doing so creates an inviting atmosphere in which family members of all situations feel encouraged to participate in their children's education. Efforts to engage families must always be **positive**, **inclusive**, and **accommodating** to a variety of needs, schedules, and situations. This includes ensuring that all opportunities for involvement are culturally sensitive, meaningful, and accepting of all families. Utilizing a variety of **communication methods**, such as weekly newsletters, calendars, phone calls, and electronic communication, ensures that opportunities to engage in the educational program are accessible to all families. Providing **multiple** and **varied** opportunities for involvement, such as family nights, field trips, award ceremonies, or inviting families to participate in classroom activities, further encourages family engagement in the educational program. This enables families in various situations to become involved in their children's education in the way that best suits their needs and abilities.

Forms of Active Involvement

Active involvement in the educational program can take a variety of forms both within and outside of the classroom to accommodate differences in families' schedules, dynamics, and abilities. Providing multiple avenues for involvement engages families of various situations to actively participate in their children's education. Within the classroom, family members can **volunteer** their time to assist as teachers' aides, tutors, or chaperones. In addition, if a family member is skilled in an area related to instruction, the teacher can ask the family member to come in to speak or teach a lesson. Inviting family members to **visit the classroom** or participate in special class activities allows them to actively engage in the learning process and gain insight into the educational program. Outside of daily classroom activities, family members can be encouraged to participate by attending **family nights, school social events, fundraisers**, or **parent-teacher association meetings**. Active involvement in the educational program can also occur at home. By frequently communicating with teachers, assisting with projects or homework, and emphasizing the importance of learning at home, family members can be informed and actively involved in their children's education.

Importance in Children's Education

As students spend a great deal of time between school and home, the degree to which their family is involved in the educational program significantly influences the quality of the learning experience. When teachers take measures to engage families in their children's education, they establish a welcoming tone that facilitates relationships founded on mutual respect, understanding, and acceptance. These positive relationships are necessary for encouraging and empowering families to actively participate in the learning process. Such involvement contributes to establishing a **positive learning community** in which teachers and families can collaborate productively to enhance students' learning. When students' families are actively involved in their education, it strengthens the **support system** in both influential areas of their lives, thus establishing a sense of security that allows them to confidently engage in learning. Families that participate in the educational program are more likely to emphasize its value at home by extending and reinforcing learning outside of the classroom. This is highly beneficial in promoting positive attitudes toward learning, academic achievement, and social and emotional development.

Influence on Student Learning and Development

The degree of family involvement in the educational program significantly influences the quality of students' learning and development. Learning is more effective when parents, guardians, or legal caregivers are actively engaged in their child's education, as this promotes positive relationships between students' school and home lives that strengthen their **support system** and encourage the extension of learning beyond the classroom. Families that participate in the educational program are likely to emphasize and model its importance at home, thus influencing students to adopt the same positive attitudes toward learning. This facilitates **academic achievement, decreased absences** from school, and **positive learning habits**. In addition, when families are actively involved in the educational process, they are more effectively able to support students with resources at home that reinforce concepts learned in the classroom to strengthen connections and understanding. Students develop healthy **social and emotional skills** as well when their families are actively involved in the educational program. This facilitates positive self-esteem and interpersonal skills that contribute to academic success and fewer behavioral issues in the classroom.

Benefits for Parents, Families, Guardians, and Legal Caregivers

Families, parents, guardians, and legal caregivers that are actively involved in the educational program gain greater **insight, understanding**, and **resources** that enable them to support their children's learning more effectively both within and outside of the classroom. Active engagement in the educational program fosters a positive rapport founded on mutual respect and support among family members, teachers, and the school. This provides family members with a sense of **confidence** in the merits of the educational program while contributing to the sense that they are **equal participants** in the learning process. These family members are more informed regarding what is being taught in the classroom and beneficial resources to reinforce learning at home. This leaves family members feeling more **empowered** and willing to reinforce their students' learning. In addition, participating in the learning process provides family members with a greater understanding of the characteristics and capabilities of their children's developmental level, thus equipping them with the knowledge to effectively support learning and growth.

BENEFITS FOR EFFECTIVE TEACHING

The involvement of families, parents, guardians, and legal caregivers in the educational program is highly beneficial for effective teaching. Family members that actively participate in the learning process are likely to develop a greater sense of **understanding** and **appreciation** of the teacher's role within it. Such involvement also facilitates positive and frequent communication with families that fosters relationships founded on mutual respect and increases the teacher's **morale** and effectiveness in the classroom. Active engagement from family members also allows the teacher to gain a better understanding of how to support individual students' needs. Family members provide valuable insight regarding students' cultures, values, beliefs, educational goals, and learning needs to allow for more effective teaching. In addition, family members that are involved in their children's education are more likely to reinforce and extend learning at home, thus allowing for more effective teaching in the classroom.

POSITIVE RAPPORT

A positive rapport between teachers and families enhances the quality of the learning experience. Establishing these positive relationships requires that teachers frequently take measures to engage families in the educational program in ways that are **meaningful**, **relevant**, and **responsive** to varying situations, backgrounds, and needs. In doing so, teachers communicate the sentiment that all families are welcomed, valued, and considered equal participants in the learning process. This serves to create an open, inviting learning atmosphere in which family involvement is encouraged, thus fostering the **participation** and **communication** necessary for developing a mutual positive rapport. Working to build positive relationships strengthens the connection between schools and families that facilitates productive **collaboration** to best support and enhance students' learning.

INTERACTING WITH FAMILIES OF VARIOUS BACKGROUNDS
DIVERSITIES THAT MAY BE ENCOUNTERED

Appropriate interaction when working and communicating with students' families requires teachers to recognize the wide range of diversities in characteristics, backgrounds, and needs that they will inevitably encounter. With **culturally diverse** families, the teacher will likely experience variances in language, values, traditions, and customs, including differences in beliefs regarding best practices for raising and educating children. **Socioeconomic** differences may influence the degree to which families have the ability and access to resources to support their children in learning. In some instances, socioeconomic differences may also impact the level of education that family members have attained and potentially the value they place on the importance of education. The teacher must also be mindful of the diversities that exist among **family dynamics**. Some families may have a single caregiver, whereas others may have many. Students may be only children, have several siblings, or come from a blended family. Differences in dynamics also include varying work schedules, lifestyle demands, and living situations that the teacher must consider when working and communicating with families. By acknowledging the diverse characteristics, backgrounds, and needs of students' families, the teacher can take measures to ensure appropriate and inclusive interactions that enhance the learning experience.

APPROPRIATE AND PRODUCTIVE INTERACTIONS

Recognizing the diverse nature of students' cultures, backgrounds, and experiences provides teachers with insight regarding how to interact with their families appropriately and productively. By self-educating to become **culturally competent** and building relationships with students, teachers develop an understanding of the unique characteristics, values, beliefs, and needs of each family. This enables teachers to tailor their communication with individual families in a way that is respectful, **culturally sensitive**, and responsive to their concerns and needs. Doing so ensures that all families feel welcomed and supported in the school environment, thus establishing positive relationships that encourage families to actively engage in the educational program and collaborate productively with teachers to enhance students' learning.

POSSIBLE OBSTACLES

As teachers work and interact with families of diverse backgrounds and experiences, they likely will encounter obstacles that must be addressed to facilitate effective communication. **Cultural differences** in values, beliefs, language, and nonverbal communication may cause misinterpretations between teachers and families that make it difficult to understand one another. It is, therefore, important that teachers educate themselves regarding students' backgrounds to learn how to communicate in a culturally sensitive manner. When language barriers are present, learning common words and phrases in the language or utilizing an interpreter is beneficial in facilitating communication. Family members may have experienced **negative interactions** with teachers in the past that affect their willingness to engage in communication. Taking measures to establish an inviting, accepting atmosphere that promotes open communication is beneficial in encouraging these families to become involved. **Lifestyle differences**, including varying work schedules, living situations, and family dynamics, may make it difficult to establish effective communication. In addition, **accessibility issues**, including lack of access to transportation, technology devices, or the internet, may hinder family members' abilities to maintain frequent communication. To address these issues, teachers must utilize several communication methods that accommodate families' varying needs and situations.

CONSIDERATIONS TO ENSURE BENEFICIAL INTERACTIONS

The ultimate goal when working and communicating with families is to benefit students' learning and development. When teachers and families develop a positive rapport between one another, it fosters productive collaboration to support the students' educational and developmental goals. Doing so requires that teachers ensure all interactions with students' families are appropriate, respectful, and considerate. This includes demonstrating awareness of varying **backgrounds, characteristics**, and **needs** of each family and interacting in a way that is responsive and accepting of differences. Teachers must practice **cultural competency** when communicating with families, including recognizing differences in perspectives, values, beliefs, and nonverbal communication. Teachers must also consider families' unique situations, including differing **work schedules**, **living arrangements**, and **family dynamics** to ensure that all interactions are considerate of their time, accommodating to their needs, and supportive of their role in the educational program. When interacting with families, it is important that teachers practice active listening and respond appropriately, meaningfully, and constructively. This communicates to families that their opinions, goals, and concerns related to the educational program are respected, thus encouraging them to actively participate in supporting their children's progress and development.

REGULAR COMMUNICATION WITH FAMILIES
STUDENTS' PROGRESS AND IMPORTANT CLASSROOM INFORMATION

Frequent communication regarding individual student progress and important classroom information is essential to actively engaging family members as equal contributors to the educational program. Doing so creates an inviting atmosphere focused on open and productive dialogue to enhance students' learning and development. Regular communication with families through a variety of methods establishes a strong connection between students' school and home lives that supports their achievement. When families are consistently updated and informed regarding their children's progress in the educational program, they can more effectively collaborate with the teacher to **proactively** address concerns and **implement necessary supports** for successful learning. Frequently communicating important classroom information, including curriculum, assignments, events, and opportunities for involvement, ensures that families are always informed regarding their children's educational program and ways in which they can actively participate. This equips family members with the knowledge and resources necessary to effectively support and reinforce learning both in the classroom and at home.

> **Review Video: Collaborating with Families**
> Visit mometrix.com/academy and enter code: 679996

POSITIVE RAPPORT THAT ENHANCES TEACHING AND LEARNING

Regularly interacting and working with students' families facilitates the **continuous** and **open** line of communication necessary to establishing and sustaining a positive rapport. Building such positive relationships is integral to quality teaching and learning, as frequent communication allows families and teachers to develop a sense of mutual respect, trust, and understanding over time. By frequently communicating with families, teachers create a welcoming, inclusive learning environment in which family members feel encouraged and empowered to contribute as **equal participants** in their child's educational program. This facilitates productive collaboration between teachers and families that supports and enhances students' learning. Developing a positive rapport with family members is also valuable in providing teachers with insight regarding strategies to best support and accommodate students' learning styles, needs, and individual differences. When teachers and families have a positive relationship with one another, students feel more supported in their learning both within and outside of the classroom, thus promoting positive attitudes toward learning and academic achievement.

LISTENING AND RESPONDING TO FAMILIES' CONCERNS

Actively **listening** and **responding** to students' families when interacting with them is an important part of building positive relationships that enhance teaching and learning. By listening attentively to families' concerns, ideas, and information regarding their child and the educational program, teachers gain a greater awareness of their unique backgrounds, characteristics, and experiences. With this understanding in mind, teachers can ensure that they respond to family members in a **sensitive**, **accepting**, and **empathetic** manner to promote the development of a mutual positive rapport. Doing so conveys the sentiment that family members are valued and respected as equal participants in the educational program, thus encouraging them to engage in positive communication to support their children's learning. Families can provide valuable insight regarding their children's learning styles, needs, and behaviors. When teachers listen and respond constructively to this information, they foster positive relationships with families by validating and including them in the learning process. In addition, listening and responding appropriately to students' families indicates acknowledgement and appreciation for their participation in the educational program that contributes to building positive relationships and encourages continued communication.

Conferences

Building Positive Relationships Between Schools and Families

Frequently conducting conferences with parents, guardians, and legal caregivers facilitates the consistent **in-person communication** necessary for building positive relationships founded on mutual understanding and respect. The conference setting provides a space in which teachers, school staff, and families can discuss the educational program and the student's individual progress as well as address concerns and collaborate in developing goals. By conducting conferences regularly, teachers, school staff, and families can maintain a continuous, **open dialogue** that provides insight regarding one another's perspectives, intentions, and roles in the educational program. This allows for increased understanding and appreciation for one another that contributes to building positive relationships. Families that attend conferences regularly feel more included in the educational program as equal contributors to their children's learning, thus encouraging them to establish positive strong connections with the school.

Support of Students' Success in Learning

Effective conferences between teachers and families are focused on open communication, productive collaboration, and strengthening the connection between students' home and school lives. When families and teachers work together in conferences to benefit the student, it strengthens their **support system** in both influential areas of their lives. This is beneficial in enhancing students' **academic achievement**, promoting **healthy development**, and encouraging **positive attitudes toward learning**. Conducting conferences frequently ensures that family members are consistently **informed** and **involved** as equal participants in their child's progress and the educational program. This equips families with the information, understanding, and resources to more effectively support their child's learning both within and outside of the classroom. In addition, effective conferences provide teachers with insight from families regarding students' learning needs, behaviors, and individual situations. With this knowledge in mind, teachers can work with families to develop a plan and implement strategies that best support students' learning and development.

Guidelines for Effectiveness

Family conferences are a valuable opportunity to discuss students' individual progress, collaborate to develop educational goals, and address concerns. To ensure conferences are productive, teachers must take measures to make families feel welcomed, respected, and included in the process. Conferences must be scheduled at a **convenient time** for all attending family members in order to accommodate varying needs and situations. It is also important that conferences take place in a comfortable, **inviting atmosphere**, as this establishes a positive tone and facilitates discussion. Teachers must arrive **on time** and **prepared** with specific information to discuss regarding the student, including positive remarks that highlight his or her strengths. This demonstrates that teachers know the student well and want him or her to succeed, thus making family members feel comfortable in discussing their child. Asking **open-ended questions**, encouraging families to talk, and practicing active listening is important in facilitating productive discussion as well as ensuring families feel heard and respected in their concerns. **Direct criticism** of the student must always be avoided; rather, teachers should focus on discussing ways that student can apply their strengths to improve in other areas.

Family Support Resources that Enhance Family Involvement

Families that are supported through school, community, and interagency resources are equipped to effectively support their child's learning and development. Often, families may be hesitant to become actively involved in their children's education because they lack the skills and understanding of how to do so. These support systems are beneficial in providing family members with the **tools, knowledge**, and **resources** that prepare them to effectively participate in the educational program and extend learning outside of the classroom. Such resources are valuable in educating families on the characteristics, needs, and abilities of their children's developmental level as well as strategies for developing and engaging in age-appropriate activities that support learning at home. This instills a sense of confidence within families regarding their ability to successfully support their children's learning that empowers and encourages them to become actively involved.

When families are supported through **school**, **community**, and **interagency** resources, they are able to more effectively become involved in the educational program. Numerous resources dedicated to educating families on ways they can support their children's learning are available to accommodate varying situations, needs, and abilities. Within the school, **teachers, guidance counselors**, and other **staff members** can provide valuable information regarding students' developmental characteristics, needs, and abilities as well as ways families can become involved to enhance learning within and outside of the classroom. **Support groups** hosted by the school enable families to share experiences and discuss ways to become involved in the learning process. Community support resources are often tailored to address the specific needs of families within the community. These resources offer **family education services**, such as classes, meetings, or programs, designed to provide families with the training, strategies, and knowledge necessary to become actively involved in their children's education. Several **national family support agencies** are also available to educate families on ways to become involved in their children's learning. Such agencies often have multiple locations as well as an array of digitally printed information, discussion forums, and training opportunities to enhance family involvement in learning.

Disability Education Laws

Individuals with Disabilities Education Act

The Individuals with Disabilities Education Act **(IDEA)** includes six major principles that focus on students' rights and the responsibilities public schools have for educating children with **disabilities**. One of the main principles of IDEA is to provide a **free and appropriate public education** suited to the individual needs of a child with a disability. This requires schools to provide special education and related services to students identified as having disabilities. Another purpose of IDEA is to require schools to provide an appropriate **evaluation** of a child with a suspected disability and an **Individualized Education Program (IEP)** for a child with a disability who qualifies under IDEA. Students with IEPs are guaranteed **least restrictive environment**, or a guarantee that they are educated in the general education classroom as much as possible. IDEA also ensures **parent participation**, providing a role for parents as equal participants and decision makers. Lastly, **procedural safeguards** also serve to protect parents' rights to advocate for their children with disabilities.

> **Review Video: Development of the Individuals with Disabilities Education Act**
> Visit mometrix.com/academy and enter code: 100350

People Protected by Parts B and C of IDEA

Early intervention services are provided to children with special needs from birth to age three under **IDEA Part C**. Children from birth to age 3 who are identified as having disabilities and qualify under IDEA receive **Individualized Family Service Plans (IFSPs)**.

Special education and related services are provided to children with disabilities from ages 3 to 21 under **IDEA Part B**. Children ages 3 to 21 who are identified as having disabilities and qualify under IDEA receive educational documents **IEPs**.

Individualized Education Programs vs. Individualized Family Service Plans

IFSPs and IEPs are both educational documents provided under the Individuals with Disabilities Education Act to service the rights of children with disabilities and their families. The major differences between IEPs and IFSPs, aside from the ages they service, is that **IFSPs** cover **broader services** for children with disabilities and their families. IFSP services are often provided in the children's homes. **IEPs** focus on special education and related services within the children's **school settings**.

Purpose of IEPs and Function of the PLOPs

An IEP is a written statement for a child with a disability. Its primary purposes are to establish **measurable annual goals** and to list the **services** needed to help the child with a disability meet the annual goals.

The Individuals with Disabilities Education Act mandates that a statement of the child's academic achievement and functional performance be included within the IEP. This statement is called **Present Levels of Performance**. It provides a snapshot of the student's current performance in school. Present Levels of Performance should also report how a student's disability is affecting, or not affecting, progress in school.

IDEA mandates that an **Annual Goals section** be provided within the IEP. Annual goals outline what a student is expected to learn within a 12-month period. These goals are influenced by the student's PLOPs and are developed using objective, measurable data based on the student's previous academic performance.

> **Review Video: 504 Plans and IEPs**
> Visit mometrix.com/academy and enter code: 881103

Child Find Law

Child Find is part of the Individuals with Disabilities Education Act and states that schools are legally required to find children who have **disabilities** and need **special education** or other services. According to the **Child Find law**, all school districts must have processes for identifying students who need special education and related services. Children with disabilities from birth to age 21, children who are homeschooled, and children in private schools are all covered by the Child Find law. Infants and toddlers can be identified and provided with services so that parents have the right tools in place to meet their children's needs before they enter grade school. The Child Find law does not mean that public schools need to agree to evaluate students when evaluations are requested. Schools may still refuse evaluation if school professionals do not suspect the children of having disabilities.

Steps to Implementing IEPs

The five most important steps in the IEP process are the identification via "Child Find" or the referral for special education services; evaluation; determination of eligibility; the first IEP meeting at which the IEP is written; and the ongoing provision of services during which progress is measured and reported. The referral can be initiated by a teacher, a special team in the school district, the student's parent, or another professional. The evaluation provides a snapshot of a student's background history, strengths, weaknesses, and academic, behavioral, or social needs. An IEP team of professionals as well as the student's parents/guardians use the evaluation and any other reports regarding a student's progress to determine if the student is eligible for special education services. Once a student has been found eligible for special education, the first IEP meeting is held during which an IEP is written by a special education teacher or other specialist familiar with the student. The IEP meeting, either initial or annual, is held before the new IEP is implemented. Once the IEP meeting has occurred, services will be provided as detailed in the written IEP, during which the student's progress will continually be measured and reported. The IEP team includes the student, parents/guardians, special education teacher, general education teacher, school psychologist, school administrator, appropriate related service professionals, and any other professionals or members that can comment on the student's strengths.

Manifestation Determination

Manifestation determination is a process defined by IDEA. The **manifestation determination process** is put into effect when a student receiving special education needs to be removed from the educational setting due to a suspension, expulsion, or alternative placement. Manifestation determination is the process that determines if the **disciplinary action** resulted from a **manifestation of the student's disability**. This is important because if the action was a manifestation of the disability, the outcome of the disciplinary action may change. During the initial part of this process, relevant data is collected about the student and the circumstances of the offending behavior. The student's Individualized Education Program team determines whether or not the student's behavior was related to the disability. If they determine that the behavior was not related to the disability, the disciplinary action is carried out. If the behavior is determined to be related to the disability, the student is placed back into the original educational setting.

Provision of Title III of the Americans with Disabilities Act

Title III of the Americans with Disabilities Act (ADA) prohibits discrimination against people with disabilities in **public accommodations**. Title III seeks to level the playing field of access for people with disabilities participating in public activities. Businesses open to the public, such as schools, restaurants, movie theaters, day care facilities, recreation facilities, doctor's offices, and restaurants, are required to comply with **ADA standards**. Additionally, commercial facilities, such as privately-owned businesses, factories, warehouses, and office buildings, are required to provide access per ADA standards. Title III of the ADA outlines the general requirements of the **reasonable modifications** that businesses must provide. Title III also provides detailed, specific requirements for reasonable modifications within businesses and requires new construction and building alterations to abide by ADA regulations. Title III also outlines rules regarding **enforcement of ADA regulations**, such as the consequences for a person or persons participating in discrimination of a person with a disability. Title III provides for **certification of state laws or local building codes**. This means that a state's Assistant Attorney General may issue certification to a place of public accommodation or commercial facility that meets or exceeds the minimum requirements of Title III.

LARRY P. V. RILES

The *Larry P. v. Riles* (1977) court case examined possible **cultural discrimination** against African-American students. The court case questioned whether an intelligence quotient (IQ) test was an accurate measurement of a student's true intelligence. The case argued that a disproportionate number of African-American students identified as needing special education services; the term at the time was "educable mentally retarded" (EMR) program services. The court plaintiff, Larry P., argued that IQ tests were **biased** against African-American students, which resulted in their placements in limiting educational settings. The defendant, Riles, argued that the prevalence of African-American students in the EMR classes was due to genetics and social and environmental factors. The court ultimately ruled that the IQ tests were discriminatory and resulted in the disproportionate placement of African-American students in the EMR setting. It was determined that these particular assessments were **culturally biased**, and the students' performances would be more accurately measured using adaptive behavior assessments, diagnostic tests, observations, and other assessments.

DIANA V. STATE BOARD OF EDUCATION

Diana v. State Board of Education (1970) was a court case involving a student who was placed in special education after results of the Stanford-Binet intelligence test indicated she had a mild case of "mental retardation." This class-action lawsuit was developed on behalf of nine **Mexican-American children**, arguing that IQ scores were not an adequate measurement to determine special education placement. The case argued that Mexican-American children might be at a disadvantage because the IQ tests were written and administered in English. This might possibly constitute **discrimination**. The plaintiffs in the case argued that IQ scores were not a valid measurement because the children might have been unable to comprehend the test written in English. In the conclusive results of this case, the court ordered children to be tested in their primary language, if it was not English. As a result of this case, IQ tests were no longer used as the sole assessments for determining **special education placement**. There was also increased focus on **cultural and linguistic diversity** in students.

WINKELMAN V. PARMA CITY SCHOOL DISTRICT

This court case began as an argument against a **free and appropriate public education** (FAPE) as required by IDEA. The parents of Jacob Winkelman believed their son was not provided with a FAPE in his special education setting in Parma City Schools. The disagreement became about whether or not children can be **represented by their parents** per IDEA in federal court. The U.S Court of Appeals for the Sixth Circuit argued that IDEA protected the rights of the children and not the parents. In the end, the District Court ruled that parents could represent their children within disputes over a free and appropriate public education as constituted by IDEA. Ultimately, this settled the question of whether or not **parents have rights under IDEA**, in addition to their children. The court case determined that parents play a significant role in the education of their children on IEPs and are IEP team members. Therefore, parents are entitled to litigate *pro se* for their children.

HONIG V. DOE

Honig v. Doe (1988) was a Supreme Court case examining the violation of the **Education for All Handicapped Children Act** (EAHCA, an earlier version of the Individuals with Disabilities Education Act) by the California School Board. The offense occurred when a child was suspended for a violent behavior outburst that was related to his disability. The court case centered on two plaintiffs. Both were diagnosed with an emotional disturbance and qualified for special education under EAHCA. Following the violent incident, the school suspended the students and recommended them for expulsion. The plaintiff's case argued that the suspension/expulsion went against the **stay-put provision of the EAHCA**, which states that children with disabilities must remain in their current educational placements during review proceedings unless otherwise agreed upon by both parents and educational representatives. The defendant argued that the violence of the situation marked an exception to the law. The court determined that schools are able to justify the placement removal of a student when maintaining a **safe learning environment** outweighs a student's right to a free and appropriate public education.

PENNSYLVANIA ASSOCIATION FOR RETARDED CHILDREN V. COMMONWEALTH OF PENNSYLVANIA

The Commonwealth of Pennsylvania was accused by the Pennsylvania Association for Retarded Children (PARC 1971), now known as the Arc of Pennsylvania, of denying a **free and appropriate public education** to students with disabilities. The Commonwealth of Pennsylvania was accused of refusing to educate students who had not reached the "mental age of 5." The groups argued before the District Court of the Eastern District of Pennsylvania. This case was significant because PARC was one of the first institutions in the country to challenge the **placement of students with special needs**. The plaintiffs argued that all children should and would benefit from some sort of educational instruction and training. Ultimately, this was the beginning of instituting the state requirement of a free and appropriate public education (**FAPE**) for all children in public education from ages 6–21. The Commonwealth of Pennsylvania was tasked with providing a FAPE and sufficient education and training for all eligible children receiving special education. They could no longer deny students based on their mental ages. This triggered other state institutions to make similar decisions and led to the creation of similar federal policies in the **Education for All Handicapped Children Act** (1974).

1990 AMENDMENTS TO IDEA

The Individuals with Disabilities Education Act (IDEA) replaced the Education for All Handicapped Children Act in 1990. IDEA amendments changed the **age range** for children to receive special education services to ages 3–21. IDEA also changed the language of the law, changing the focus onto the **individuals with disabilities** rather than the **handicapped children**. Therefore, the focus shifted from the conditions or disabilities to the individual children and their needs. IDEA amendments also **categorized** different disabilities. IDEA 1997 increased the emphasis on IEPs for students with disabilities and increased parents' roles in the educational decision-making processes for their children with disabilities. Part B of the 1997 amendment provided services to children ages 3–5, mandating that their learning needs be outlined in **IEPs** or **Individualized Family Service Plans**. Part C of IDEA provided **financial assistance** to the families of infants and toddlers with disabilities. Part C states that educational agencies must provide **early intervention services** that focus on children's developmental and medical needs, as well as the needs of their families. Part C also gives states the option to provide services to children who are at risk for developmental disabilities.

DISABILITIES EDUCATION IMPROVEMENT ACT OF 2004

In 2004, the Individuals with Disabilities Education Act (IDEA) implemented the **Individuals with Disabilities Education Improvement Act**; IDEA was reauthorized to better meet the needs of children in special education programs and children with special needs. As a result of these changes:

- Special educators are required to achieve **Highly Qualified Teacher status** and be **certified in special education**.
- Individualized Education Programs must contain measurable **annual goals** and descriptions of how progress toward the goals will be **measured and reported**.
- Schools or agencies must provide science or research-based **interventions** as part of the evaluation process to determine if children have specific learning disabilities. This may be done in addition to assessments that measure achievement or intelligence.

The changes made to require science or research-based interventions resulted in many districts implementing **Response to Intervention procedures**. These procedures meet IDEA 2004 requirement of providing interventions in addition to achievement reports or intelligence tests on the Individualized Education Programs for children with disabilities.

DEVELOPMENT OF EDUCATIONAL LAWS LIKE GOALS 2000 AND NO CHILD LEFT BEHIND

President Bill Clinton signed the **National Educational Goals Act**, also known as Goals 2000: Educate America Act, into effect in the 1990s to trigger standardized educational reform. The act focused on **outcomes-based education** and was intended to be completed by the year 2000. The goals of this act included ensuring that children are ready to learn by the time they start school; increasing high school graduation rates; demonstration of competency by students in grades 4, 8, and 12 in core content areas; and positioning the United States as first in the world in mathematics and science achievement. Goals 2000 was withdrawn when President George W. Bush implemented the **No Child Left Behind Act (NCLB)** in 2001. The NCLB also supported standards-based reform, and it mandated that states develop more **skills-based assessments**. The act emphasized state testing, annual academic progress, report cards, and increased teacher qualification standards. It also outlined changes in state funding. The NCLB required schools to meet **Adequate Yearly Progress (AYP)**. AYP was measured by results of achievement tests taken by students in each school district, and consequences were implemented for school districts that missed AYP during consecutive years.

EVERY STUDENT SUCCEEDS ACT OF 2015

The NCLB was replaced in 2015 by the Every Student Succeeds Act (**ESSA**). The ESSA built upon the foundations of NCLB and emphasized **equal opportunity** for students. The ESSA currently serves as the main K–12 educational law in the United States. The ESSA affects students in public education, including students with disabilities. The purpose of the ESSA is to ensure a **quality education** for all students. It also aims to address the achievement of **disadvantaged students**, including students living in poverty, minority groups, students receiving special education services, and students with limited English language skills. The ESSA determined that states may decide educational plans as long as they follow the government's framework. The ESSA also allows states to develop their own educational standards and mandates that the curriculum focus on preparing students for postsecondary educations or careers. The act requires students to be tested annually in math and reading during grades 3–8 and once in high school. Students must also be tested in science once in elementary school, middle school, and high school. **School accountability** was also mandated by the ESSA. The act requires states to have plans in place for any schools that are underperforming.

ESL Rights for Students and Parents

As public schools experience an influx of English as a Second Language (ESL) students, knowledge of their **rights** becomes increasingly important. The **Every Student Succeeds Act (ESSA)** of 2015 addresses funding discrepancies for ESL students and families. The ESSA allocates funds to schools and districts where low-income families comprise 40 percent or more of the enrollment. This is intended to assist with ESL students who are underperforming or at risk for underperforming. The ESSA also provides funding for ESL students to become English proficient and find academic success. However, in order for schools and districts to receive this funding, they must avoid discrimination, track ESL student progress, assess ESL student English proficiency, and notify parents of their children's ESL status. Avoiding discrimination includes preventing the over-identification of ESL students for special education services. The referral and evaluation process must be carried out with caution to ensure that students' perceived disabilities are actual deficits and not related to their English language learning abilities.

Rehabilitation Act of 1973

The Rehabilitation Act of 1973 was the law that preceded the Individuals with Disabilities Education Act of 1975. The Rehabilitation Act protects the rights of people with disabilities in several ways.

- It protects people with disabilities against discrimination relating to **employment**.
- It provides students with disabilities equal access to the **general education curriculum** (Section 504).

Americans with Disabilities Act of 1990 (ADA)

The Americans with Disabilities Act (1990) also protects the rights of people with disabilities.

- The ADA provides **equal employment** for people with disabilities. This means employers must provide reasonable accommodations for people with disabilities in their job and work environments.
- It provides **access** for people with disabilities to both public and private places open to the public (e.g., access ramps and automatic doors).
- It provides **telecommunications access** to people with disabilities. This ensures people with hearing and speech disabilities can communicate over the telephone and Internet.

Elementary and Secondary Education Act (ESEA)

The Elementary and Secondary Education Act (ESEA) also protects the rights of people with disabilities.

- Passed by President Johnson in 1965, the ESEA was part of the president's "War on Poverty." The law sought to allow **equal access to a quality education**.
- The ESEA extended more funding to secondary and primary schools and emphasized high **standards and accountability**.
- This law was authorized as the **No Child Left Behind** (2001) under President Bush, then reauthorized as the **Every Student Succeeds Act** under President Obama.

Section 504

A Section 504 Plan comes from the civil rights law, Section 504 of the Rehabilitation Act of 1973, and protects the rights of individuals with disabilities. A 504 Plan is a formal plan or blueprint for how the school will provide services to a student with a disability. This essentially removes barriers for individuals with disabilities by ensuring that **appropriate services** are provided to meet their special needs. A 504 Plan includes:

- **Accommodations**: A 504 Plan includes accommodations a student with a disability may need to be successful in a regular education classroom. For example, a student with ADHD may need to sit near the front of the room to limit distractions.
- **Related Services**: A 504 Plan includes related services, such as speech therapy or occupational therapy, a student may need to be successful in the general education classroom.
- **Modifications**: Although it is rare for a 504 Plan to include modifications, sometimes they are included. Modifications change what the student is expected to do, such as being given fewer homework assignments.

504 Plans vs. Individualized Education Programs

- A 504 Plan and an IEP are similar in that they serve as a blueprint for a student with a disability. However, a 504 Plan serves as a blueprint for how the student will have **access to school**, whereas the IEP serves as a blueprint for a student's **special education experience**.
- A 504 Plan helps level the playing field for a student with a disability by providing services and changes to the **learning environment**. An IEP provides individualized special education and related services to meet the **unique needs of a student with a disability**. Both IEPs and 504 Plans are provided at no cost to parents.
- The 504 Plan was established under the **Rehabilitation Act of 1973** as a civil rights law. The Individualized Education Program was established under the **Individuals with Disabilities Education Act** (1975 and amended in 2004).
- Unlike an IEP, a 504 Plan does **not** have to be a planned, written document. An IEP is a **planned, written document** that includes unique annual learning goals and describes related services for the student with a disability.

Informed Parental Consent

IDEA requires that parents be **informed** before a student is evaluated for special education services. IDEA mandates that a school district receive **parental consent** to initiate an evaluation of a student for special education services. Consent means the school district has fully informed the parent of their intentions or potential reasons for evaluation of the student. Legally, the request must be written in the parent's native language. This consent does not mean the parent gives consent for a student's placement in special education. In order for a student to be initially placed in special education or receive special education services, parental consent must be given for this issue separately. At any time, parents can withdraw consent for special education placement or special education services. Schools are able to file **due process** if they disagree with the parental withdrawal of consent. Parents also have a right to consent to parts of a student's IEP, but not necessarily all of the IEP. Once parental consent is granted for all parts of the IEP, it can be implemented.

TIERS OF THE RESPONSE TO INTERVENTION MODEL

- **Tier 1: High Quality Classroom Instruction, Screening, and Group Interventions**: In Tier 1, **all students** are screened using universal screening and/or the results of statewide assessments. Students identified as at risk receive supplemental instruction. Students who make adequate progress are returned to their regular instruction. Students who do not make adequate progress move to Tier 2.
- **Tier 2: Targeted Interventions**: These interventions are designed to improve the progress of the students who did not make adequate progress in Tier 1. Targeted instruction is usually in the areas of reading and math and does not last longer than one grading period. This is applied generally to smaller groups and not the full classroom as in Tier 1.
- **Tier 3: Intensive Interventions and Comprehensive Evaluation**: Students who are not successful in Tier 2 move on to Tier 3. They receive intensive interventions that target their specific deficits. Students who do not meet progress goals during intensive interventions are referred to receive comprehensive evaluations and are considered to be eligible for special education under the Individuals with Disabilities Education Act.

STAKEHOLDERS IN SPECIAL EDUCATION

Stakeholders that play roles in educating students with disabilities include the students, parents, general educators, administrators, and community members. Students should receive an educational **curriculum** based on strict standards, such as the Common Core Content Standards. This ensures that they receive good educational foundations from which to grow and expand upon during their school careers. Parents, legal guardians, and sometimes agencies act in the best interests of their children. If they do not think the IEPs suit the needs of their children, they can request **due process hearings** in court. Requirements for a free and appropriate public education and least restrictive environment ensure that students are educated alongside peers in general education classrooms by general educators. General educators collaborate with special educators to create **successful inclusion classrooms**. When inclusion is done successfully, the students with disabilities meet their IEP goals.

MULTI-FACTORED EVALUATIONS OR EVALUATION TEAM REPORTS

Multi-Factored Evaluations (MFEs) are processes required by the Individuals with Disabilities Education Act to determine if a student is eligible for special education. When a student is suspected of having a disability, the parent or school district can initiate the evaluation process. **Student information** that is evaluated in an MFE includes background information, health information, vision testing, hearing testing, social and emotional development, general intelligence, past and current academic performance, communication needs, gross and fine motor abilities, results of aptitude or achievement tests, academic skills, and current progress toward IEP goals. Progress reporting on IEP goals is only appropriate during an annual MFE when a student has already qualified for special education services. The purpose of an MFE is to provide **comprehensive information** about a student for professionals working with the student. An MFE also helps determine what academic or behavioral **goals** or related services might be appropriate for a student with disabilities.

FREE AND APPROPRIATE PUBLIC EDUCATION COMPONENTS

IDEA defines free and appropriate public education (FAPE) as an educational right for children with disabilities in the United States. FAPE stands for:

- **Free**: All students found eligible for special education services must receive free services, expensed to the public instead of the parents.
- **Appropriate**: Students are eligible for educations that are appropriate for their specific needs, as stated in their IEPs.
- **Public**: Students with disabilities have the right to be educated in public schools.
- **Education**: An education must be provided to any school-aged child with a disability. Education and services are defined in a student's IEP.

Ideally, FAPE components are put in place in order to guarantee the best education possible that also suits the individual needs of a student with a disability. FAPE should take place in the least restrictive environment, or the environment with the fewest barriers to learning for the individual student with a disability.

> **Review Video: Legal and Ethical Issues in Special Education**
> Visit mometrix.com/academy and enter code: 934372

MULTI-FACTORED EVALUATION OR EVALUATION TEAM REPORT

A Multi-Factored Evaluation (**MFE**), sometimes referred to as an Evaluation Team Report (**ETR**), serves as a snapshot of a child's abilities, strengths, and weaknesses. An MFE is conducted to determine a student's eligibility for special education. Once a student with a disability qualifies for special education, an MFE is conducted at least every three years after the initial MFE date. MFEs are conducted for students ages 3 to 21 who are on IEPs. The purpose of the MFE is to influence a student's IEP. An MFE reports on a student's **current abilities** and how the disability may affect **educational performance**. MFEs can also determine if a student qualifies for related services, such as occupational therapy or speech-language therapy. An MFE can be requested by a parent or school district when a child is suspected of having a disability. The school district typically has 30 days or less to respond to a parental request to evaluate a student, giving consent or refusal for an evaluation. While initial MFEs are conducted as a means to determine special education qualification, annual MFEs are conducted to address any changes in the needs or services of a student already receiving special education services.

LEAST RESTRICTIVE ENVIRONMENTS TO DELIVER SPECIAL EDUCATION SERVICES

Special education services are delivered to students that qualify with a **disability** defined by IDEA. IDEA also requires that students who qualify for special education must receive special education services in **least restrictive environments** that provide the fewest barriers to their learning. A student's most appropriate instructional setting is written out in the **IEP**. Some special education instructional settings include:

- No instructional setting
- Mainstream setting
- Resource room
- Self-contained classroom
- Homebound instruction

With **no instructional setting**, students participate in the general education curriculum but may receive related services, such as speech-language therapy or occupational therapy. In the **mainstream setting**, students are instructed in the general education classroom for most or part of the day and provided with special education supports, accommodations, modifications, and related services. A **resource room** is an environment where students receive remedial instruction when they cannot participate in the general curriculum for one or more subject areas. A **self-contained classroom** is a setting for students who need special education and related services for more than 50 percent of the day. **Homebound instruction** is for students who are homebound or hospitalized for more than four consecutive weeks.

Due Process Rights Available to Parents and Legal Guardians

When parents or legal guardians and school districts cannot agree on components of IEPs for students with disabilities, parents and legal guardians have a right to **due process**. Due process is a legal right under IDEA that usually involves the school district violating a legal rule. Examples of these violations include a school district not running an IEP meeting, failing to conduct a triannual evaluation, or failing to implement a student's IEP. Disputes often involve a student's instructional placement, appropriate accommodations or modifications, related services, or changes to IEPs. School districts' due process policies vary depending on the district. IDEA, however, mandates that a **due process legal form** be completed by the parent or legal guardian in order to move forward. This form must be completed within two years of a dispute. **Mediation**, or the process of coming to an agreement before filing due process, can be a solution to the dispute. IEP meetings, even when it is not time for an annual review, are also appropriate options for resolving a dispute before filing due process.

Purpose of Mediation in Lieu of a Parent or Legal Guardian Filing for Due Process

Mediation is a process used to address a dispute prior to a parent or legal guardian filing for due process. The purpose of mediation is to **resolve a dispute** between the parent or legal guardian of a student with a disability and the school district. Disputes occur when the parent or legal guardian does not agree with an IEP component, such as what related services are provided or the way a student's IEP is being implemented. Mediation is not a parent or legal guardian's legal right, but school districts often support mediation to offset a **due process filing**. Mediation involves the attempt to resolve a dispute and includes a meeting between the parent or legal guardian, school district member, and a neutral third party, such as a mediator provided by the state. States have lists of **mediators** available for these situations. Agreements that come out of the mediation process are put into writing and, if appropriate, put into a student's IEP. Disagreements can continue to be mediated, or the decision may be made to file due process. Prior to mediation, parents or legal guardians and school districts have the option of holding IEP meetings (outside of annual meetings) to resolve disputes.

Maintaining Confidentiality and Privacy of Student Records

Similar to the Health Insurance Portability and Accountability Act of 1996 (HIPAA)**,** the **Family Educational Rights and Privacy Act (FERPA)** is a law that protects privacy. However, the FERPA is specific to the privacy of students. The FERPA law applies to any school or agency that receives funds from the US Department of Education. This ensures that schools or agencies cannot share any confidential information about a student without a parent or student's written consent. **Student educational records** can be defined as records, files, documents, or other materials which contain a student's personal information. **IEPs** and **ETRs** are examples of private documents under the FERPA law. The responsibility of a school covered by the FERPA is to maintain confidentiality and privacy. The members of an IEP team, such as special educators, related service professionals, general educators, or other professionals, cannot share any identifying, private information about a student. Information addressing the needs of individual students found on an IEP, ETR, or other identifying document must remain confidential unless express written consent is given by the parent or legal guardian.

PRE-REFERRAL/REFERRAL PROCESS FOR A STUDENT WITH A DISABILITY

The purpose of a pre-referral process for a child with a suspected disability is to attempt **reasonable modifications and accommodations** before the child is referred for special education services. Schools often have **pre-referral teams** whose purpose is to identify the strengths and needs of a child, put reasonable strategies into action, and evaluate the results of this pre-referral intervention. If the results do not show any change, another intervention can be attempted, or the student can be referred for a special education evaluation.

If a child is suspected of having a disability and did not succeed with pre-referral interventions, the school or parent can request an **evaluation**. During the evaluation process, the school compiles information to see if the student needs special education or related services. This information is used to determine if the student's disability is affecting school performance and if the student qualifies for special education. The evaluation lists and examines the student's strengths, weaknesses, and development and determines what supports the student needs in order to learn. An evaluation must be completed before special education services can be provided.

ROLE OF A SCHOOL PSYCHOLOGIST IN SPECIAL EDUCATION

School psychologists are certified members of school teams that **support the needs of students and teachers**. They help students with overall academic, social, behavioral, and emotional success. School psychologists are trained in data collection and analysis, assessments, progress monitoring, risk factors, consultation and collaboration, and special education services. In special education, school psychologists may work directly with students and collaborate with teachers, administrators, parents, and other professionals working with particular students. They may also counsel students' parents, participate in the Response to Intervention process, and perform initial evaluations of students who are referred for special education services. School psychologists also work to improve academic achievement, promote positive behavior and health by implementing school-wide programs, support learning needs of diverse learners, maintain safe school environments, and strengthen and maintain good school-parent relationships.

OVERREPRESENTATION OF STUDENTS FROM DIVERSE BACKGROUNDS

Disproportionate representation occurs when there is not an equal representation of students from different **cultural and linguistic backgrounds** identified for special education services. Students from different cultural and linguistic groups should be identified for special education services in similar proportions. This ensures that no one group is **overrepresented** and **overidentified as having special needs** due to their cultural or linguistic differences. Disproportionality can occur based on a child's sex, language proficiency, receipt of free and reduced lunch, or race and ethnicity. Historically, most disproportionality has been a civil rights issue and due to a child's cultural or linguistic background. Recently, the focus has been on the disproportionate number of students who spend time in special education classrooms instead of being educated alongside regularly educated peers.

The referral process, **Response to Intervention (RTI)**, provides safeguards against disproportionality. The RTI process requires instruction and intervention catered to the unique, specific needs of the individual student. The purpose of RTI is not the identification of a disability or entitlement to services. Instead, it focuses on data used to make educational decisions about individuals, classrooms, schools, or districts. Models like RTI address disproportionate representation, but they are not perfect.

Chapter Quiz

Ready to see how well you retained what you just read? Scan the QR code to go directly to the chapter quiz interface for this study guide. If you're using a computer, simply visit the online resources page at **mometrix.com/resources719/westeearchsped** and click the Chapter Quizzes link.

WEST-E Practice Test

Want to take this practice test in an online interactive format? Check out the online resources page, which includes interactive practice questions and much more: **mometrix.com/resources719/westeearchsped**

1. According to the Assistive Technology Act, assistive devices are:
   a. Electronic devices that support learning such as computers, calculators, student responders, electronic self-teaching books and electronic reading devices.
   b. Any mechanical, electrical or electronic device that helps teachers streamline efficiency.
   c. Any device that could help a disabled student in school or life functions.
   d. Experimental, high-tech teaching tools that teachers can obtain by participating in one of 67 government funded research projects.

2. When writing learning objectives, the acronym "SMART" is often used. What do the letters in "SMART" stand for?
   a. Systematic, measurable, attainable, reasonable, targeted
   b. Specific, measurable, attainable, relevant, time-bound
   c. Systematic, measurable, attainable, reasonable, tested
   d. Specific, measurable, attainable, reasonable, time-bound

3. Augmentative and Alternative Communication (AAC) devices, forearm crutches and a head pointer are assistive devices that might be used by a student with:
   a. Severe intellectual disabilities.
   b. Cerebral palsy.
   c. Tourette syndrome.
   d. Minor skeletal birth defects.

4. A four-year-old child has difficulty sorting plastic cubes, circles, and triangles by shape, doesn't recognize patterns easily, and doesn't understand the relationship between little/big, tall/short, many/few. The child enjoys counting but does not say the numbers in proper order nor recognize the meaning of different numbers. This child most likely:
   a. Has dyspraxia
   b. Is developing within an acceptable range
   c. Has dysgraphia
   d. Has dyscalculia

5. Response to Intervention (RTI) is:
   a. Parents, classroom teacher, special education teacher and other caring persons stage an intervention to express how a student's socially unacceptable behavior upsets them
   b. An opportunity for a student to openly and freely respond to specific interventions without fear of reprimand
   c. A strategy for diagnosing learning disabilities in which a student receives research-supported interventions to correct an academic delay. If the interventions do not result in considerable improvement, the failure to respond suggests causal learning disabilities
   d. A formal complaint lodged by a parent or guardian in response to what they consider an intrusion by a teacher into private matters

6. Jaden is a second-grade student with a diagnosis of ADHD. When conducting a special education evaluation, which of the following behavior rating scales would be most appropriate?
   a. Single-domain scales
   b. Self-report scales
   c. Multidomain scales
   d. Observer/informant scales

7. When transitioning from one subject to another and when she becomes anxious, a student always taps her front tooth 5 times then opens and closes her eyes 11 times before leaving her desk. The child most likely has:
   a. Tic Disorder
   b. Obsessive Compulsive Disorder
   c. Anxiety Disorder
   d. Depression

8. By law, a child with a disability is defined as one with:
   a. Intellectual disabilities, hearing, speech, language, visual, orthopedic or other health impairments, emotional disturbance, autism, brain injury caused by trauma or specific learning disabilities and needs special education and related services.
   b. Intellectual disabilities, emotional disturbance, autism, brain injury caused by trauma or specific learning disabilities who needs special education and related services.
   c. A child who is unable to reach the same academic goals as his peers, regardless of cause, and needs special education and related services.
   d. The term "disability" is no longer used. The correct term is "other ability".

9. Which classroom environment is most likely to support a student with ADHD?
   a. Students with ADHD become bored easily so a classroom with distinct areas for a multitude of activities will stimulate her. When she loses interest in one area, she can move to the next and continue learning.
   b. Students with ADHD are highly aggressive and easily fall into depression. The teacher needs to provide a learning environment in which sharp objects such as scissors, tacks or sharpened pencils are eliminated. This ensures greater safety for both student and teacher.
   c. Students with ADHD are highly creative. A room with brightly colored mobiles, a multitude of visual and physical textures (such as striped rugs and fuzzy pillows) and plenty of art-based games will stimulate and encourage learning.
   d. Students with ADHD are extremely sensitive to distractions. A learning environment in which visual and audio distractions have been eliminated is best. Low lighting, few posters and a clean whiteboard help the student focus.

10. A resource teacher notices one of her students has made the same reading error numerous times the past few days. She decides the student wrongly believes that 'ou' is always pronounced as it is in the word *through*. She corrects this misunderstanding by showing the student word families containing words like *though, ought, ground*. This strategy is called:
   a. Corrective feedback
   b. Positive reinforcement
   c. Consistent repetition
   d. Corrective support

11. A kindergarten teacher has a new student who will not make eye contact with anyone, so she doesn't appear to be listening. She often rocks back and forth and does not stop when asked or give any indication she has heard. She avoids physical contact. Sometimes the teacher must take her arm to guide her from one place to another. Occasionally the student erupts, howling in terror and fury. The most likely diagnosis is:
   a. Conduct Disorder
   b. Obsessive-Compulsive Disorder
   c. Autism
   d. Oppositional Defiant Disorder

12. A special education teacher shows parents of a dyslexic child a study that examined brain scans of dyslexic and non-dyslexic readers. The study demonstrated that dyslexics use (the) _____ side(s) of their brains, while non-dyslexics use (the) _____ side.
   a. Both, the left.
   b. Both, the right.
   c. Left, right.
   d. Right, left.

13. A student with _____ has a great deal of difficulty with the mechanical act of writing. She drops her pencil, cannot form legible letters and cannot decode what she has written.
   a. A nonverbal learning disorder
   b. Dyslexia
   c. Dyspraxia
   d. Dysgraphia

14. Typical cognitive development in a child between the ages of 2 and 6 would consist of which of the following?
   a. A child that manipulates objects
   b. A child that uses perception in their thought process
   c. A child that applies logical reasoning
   d. A child that has abstract thoughts

15. How can reading comprehension and vocabulary best be assessed?
   a. They should be assessed with brief interviews and tests every two months to determine how much learning has taken place. Students learn in spurts, and in-depth assessments of comprehension and vocabulary are a waste of time.
   b. They should be assessed by a rough combination of standardized testing, informal teacher observations, attention to grades, objective-linked assessments, and systematized charting of data over time.
   c. They should be assessed by giving students weekly self-assessment rubrics to keep them constantly aware of and invested in their own progress.
   d. They should be assessed by having students retell a story or summarize the content of an informational piece of writing. The degree to which the material was comprehended, and the richness or paucity of vocabulary used in such work, provides efficient and thorough assessment.

16. A diabetic first grader is very pale, trembling and covered in a fine sweat. The teacher attempts to talk to the child, but the girl's response is confused and she seems highly irritable She is most likely experiencing:
   a. Diabetic hypoglycemia.
   b. Lack of sleep.
   c. Hunger.
   d. Diabetic hyperglycemia.

17. An intellectually disabled teen has been offered a job by an elderly neighbor. The neighbor wants the teen to work alongside her in the garden twice a week. They will plant seeds, transplant larger plants, weed, lay mulch, water, and fertilize. Later in the season, they will cut flowers and arrange bouquets, pick produce, and sell them at the neighbor's roadside stand. The neighbor, the teen's mother, and special education teacher meet to discuss the proposal. The plan is:
   a. Tentatively accepted. Because the teen is excited about having a job, her mother and teacher reluctantly agree. They both know the girl is likely to lose interest quickly and caution the neighbor that if she truly needs help, she may want to look elsewhere. However, no one wants to disappoint the girl, and all decide the experience will be good for her.
   b. Rejected. Despite the teen's insistence she can manage these tasks, her mother and teacher believe she cannot. They fear trying will set her up for failure.
   c. Rejected. The teacher and her mother are very uncomfortable with the neighbor's offer. They suspect the elderly woman is simply lonely or may be a predator who has selected an intellectually disabled victim because such children are particularly vulnerable.
   d. Enthusiastically accepted. The adults discuss a background check and the possibility the teen might discover gardening is not for her and may want to quit. However, this is most likely to happen early in her employment, giving the neighbor sufficient time to find another helper.

18. Dr. Gee reads the following sentence to a group of 5th graders: "The turquoise sky is reflected in the still lake. Fat white clouds floated on the lake's surface as though the water was really another sky. It was such a beautiful day. The students were to write the word "beautiful" in the blank. One student wrote 'pretty' instead. This suggests:
    a. The student doesn't know the meaning of the word 'beautiful'.
    b. The student is highly creative and believes he can substitute a word with a similar meaning.
    c. The student did not know how to spell 'beautiful'.
    d. The student did not hear what the teacher said. He heard 'pretty' instead of 'beautiful.'

19. Autism Spectrum Disorder is also known as:
    a. Pervasive Spectrum Disorder
    b. Asperger's Syndrome
    c. Variable Developmental Disorder
    d. Artistic Continuum Syndrome

20. A third grade boy is new to the school. His teacher has noticed he happily plays with other children, redirects his attention without upset when another child rejects his offer to play and doesn't mind playing on his own. However, the boy doesn't pay attention when academic instruction is given. He continues to speak with other children, draws, or distracts himself. The teacher reminds him repeatedly to listen and follow instruction. When he does not, she moves him to a quiet desk away from the others. When isolated, the boy puts his head on the desk and weeps uncontrollably, or stares at a fixed spot and repeats to himself, "I hate myself, I hate myself. I should be dead." During these episodes, the teacher cannot break through to the student; his disconnection seems complete. The teacher has requested a conference with his parents, but they do not speak English and have not responded to her offer of a translator. The teacher should:
    a. Establish a consistent set of expectations for the child. He needs to understand there are appropriate times for play and for learning
    b. Isolate the boy first thing. His behavior suggests manipulation. By third grade children fully understand they are expected to pay attention when the teacher is speaking. The boy is punishing the teacher with tears and repetitive self-hate, consciously or unconsciously attempting to make the teacher feel guilty
    c. Immediately refer him to the counselor. The boy is exhibiting serious emotional distress suggesting abuse or neglect at home or outside of school
    d. Recognize the child's highly sensitive nature; offer comfort when he acts out self-loathing. Carefully explain why he must learn to pay attention so he will use reason instead of emotion when making future choices

21. A student with Asperger's Syndrome is most likely to display which set of behaviors?
    a. He is confrontational, argumentative and inflexible.
    b. He is fearful, shy and highly anxious.
    c. He is socially distant, focused on certain subjects to the point of obsession and inflexible.
    d. He is flighty, tearful and exhibits repetitive, ritualized behavior.

22. A special education teacher working with a group of third graders is about to begin a unit on birds. She asks the children what they know about birds. They tell her birds fly, lay eggs and build nests. She asks the students to draw a picture of a bird family. Some children draw birds in flight; one draws a mother bird with a nest of babies; another draws an egg with the baby bird inside the egg. These pre-reading activities are useful because:
   a. They help assess prior knowledge
   b. They establish a framework in which to integrate the new information
   c. They create a sense of excitement and curiosity
   d. All of the above

23. **Verbal dyspraxia is:**
   a. A motor skill development disorder that includes trouble with the physical act of writing
   b. A motor skill development disorder that includes refusal to speak
   c. A motor skill development disorder that includes misplacing letters within words
   d. A motor skill development disorder that includes inconsistent speech errors

24. A resource room teacher has a small group of second and third graders who are struggling with reading comprehension. The most effective strategy would be to:
   a. Present a list of vocabulary before students read a particular text
   b. Ask students to create a play about the story
   c. Read a story aloud. Ask students to raise their hands when they hear an unfamiliar word
   d. Have each child keep a book of new vocabulary words. Whenever an unfamiliar word is seen or heard the student should enter the word in her personal dictionary

25. **Tourette syndrome is characterized by:**
   a. Facial twitches, grunts, inappropriate words and body spasms.
   b. Inappropriate words, aggressive behavior and tearful episodes.
   c. Facial twitches, grunts, extreme shyness and refusal to make eye contact.
   d. Refusal to make eye contact, rocking, spinning of objects and ritualized behavior.

26. A second grader finds it impossible to remain in her seat. She wanders around the room, sprawls on the floor, and rolls back and forth when asked to do math problems and jumps up and down when waiting in line. When the teacher tells her to sit down, she rolls her eyes in apparent disgust and looks to other students for support. When she finds a student looking back, she laughs and makes a face. The teacher has noticed when a reward is attached to good behavior, the girl is consistently able to control her actions for long periods of time. When reprimanded without the promise of a reward, however, she becomes angry and tearful and pouts. This child is most likely manifesting:
   a. Tourette's syndrome
   b. Attention deficit hyperactivity disorder
   c. Lack of sufficiently developed behavior and social skills
   d. Psychosis

27. **What would be the best example of negative social influence?**
   a. Conformity
   b. Independence
   c. Compliance
   d. Individualism

28. What would be an example of effective feedback in a lesson plan for a third-grade class?
   a. Selectively choosing students to call on
   b. Immediately calling on a student after asking a question
   c. Reinforcing student behavior
   d. Providing corrective feedback the next day

29. When working as a case manager for students with Individualized Education Programs (IEPs), which role must be taken on as part of that duty?
   a. Ensuring students on the caseload do not fail.
   b. Ensuring students on the caseload attend class.
   c. Ensuring students on the caseload meet IEP goals.
   d. Ensuring students on the caseload access accommodations.

30. What would be the best warm-up for a lesson on adding and subtracting fractions?
   a. Multiplying and dividing fractions
   b. Adding and subtracting fractions
   c. Multiplying and dividing whole numbers
   d. Adding and subtracting whole numbers

31. The Individuals with Disabilities Education Act (IDEA) requires that members of an IEP team include:
   a. All teachers involved with the student, the parent(s) or guardian and the student (if appropriate)
   b. The classroom teacher, a special education teacher, the parent(s) or guardian, a representative of the local education agency knowledgeable about specialized instruction, someone to interpret instructional implications, the student (if appropriate) and other people invited by the parents or the school
   c. The classroom teacher, a special education teacher, the principal or AP and the parent(s) or guardian
   d. All teachers involved with the student, the principal or AP, the parent(s) or guardian and the student (if appropriate)

32. At the beginning of each month, a student reads a page or two from a book he hasn't seen before. The resource teacher notes the total number of words in the section and the number of times the student leaves out or misreads a word. If the student reads with more than a 10% error rate, he is:
   a. Reading with full comprehension.
   b. Probably bored and his attention is wandering.
   c. Reading at a frustration level.
   d. Missing contextual clues.

33. A cloze test evaluates a student's:
   a. Reading fluency
   b. Understanding of context and vocabulary
   c. Phonemic skills
   d. Ability to apply the alphabetic principle to previously unknown material

34. A Kindergarten teacher is showing students the written alphabet. The teacher pronounces a phoneme and one student points to it on the alphabet chart. The teacher is presenting:
   a. Letter-sound correspondence
   b. Rote memorization
   c. Predictive Analysis
   d. Segmentation

35. A resource teacher wants to design a lesson that will help first and second graders learn irregular sight words so all the students can read their lists. She should teach them how to:
   a. Divide sight words into syllables. Considering one syllable at a time provides a sense of control and increases confidence.
   b. Recognize word families. Organizing similar words allows patterns to emerge.
   c. Sound out the words by vocalizing each letter. Using this approach, students will be able to sound out any sight word.
   d. Memorize their lists by using techniques such as songs, mnemonic devices and other fun activities. By definition, irregular sight words cannot be decoded but must be recognized on sight.

36. Phonological awareness activities are:
   a. Oral
   b. Visual
   c. Tactile
   d. Semantically based

37. It is important to teach life skills to students with developmental delays to prepare them for life after school. Which of the following skill sets should these students be taught?
   a. Count money, plan meals, grocery shop, recognize safety concerns
   b. Count money, order delivery meals, dating skills, how to drive
   c. How to drive, style and hygiene tips, social strategies, dating skills
   d. Stock market investment, hairdressing, house painting, pet care

38. A student is able to:
- apply strategies to comprehend the meanings of unfamiliar words
- supply definitions for words with several meanings such as *crucial, criticism,* and *witness*
- reflect on her background knowledge in order to decipher a word's meaning

These features of effective reading belong to which category?
   a. Word recognition
   b. Vocabulary
   c. Content
   d. Comprehension

Refer to the following for question 39:

   A teacher is concerned about three of her students. While they are enthusiastic about writing, they do not always recognize letters, confusing *b, d,* and *p,* or *e* and *o*. They do, however, know which sounds go with certain letters when they are orally drilled. When they write, they appear to be attempting letter–sound associations.

"Now I'm writing *M*," the teacher heard one boy say as he scripted a large *N* in the upper right corner of his paper. He studied it for a moment and added, "Nope, it needs another leg." The student then wrote an *I* beside the *N*. "There," he said. "Now you are an *M*. I can write the word *man* because now I have *M*." The child then moved to the lower left corner of the paper. "M-A-N," he said to himself, slowly pronouncing each sound. "I already have that *M*. Here is where the rest of the word goes." He turned the paper sideways and wrote *N*.

The second child sang to herself as she gripped the crayon and scribbled lines here and there on her paper. Some of the lines resembled letters, but few actually were. Others were scribbles. As she "wrote," she seemed to be making up a story and seemed to believe she was writing the story down.

The third child didn't vocalize at all while he worked. He gripped the paper and carefully wrote the same letter over and over and over. Sometimes the letter was large, sometimes tiny. He turned the paper in every direction so that sometimes the letter was sideways or upside down. Sometimes he flipped it backward. "What are you writing?" the teacher asked him. "My name," the child told her. The teacher then realized the letter was, indeed, the first letter of his name. She gently told him he had done a fine job of writing the first letter of his name. Did he want her to help him write the rest of it? "Nope," he cheerfully told her, "it's all here." He pointed at one of the letters and "read" his full name. He pointed at another letter and again seemed to believe it represented all the sounds of his name.

39. In the above example, the emergent writers are demonstrating their understanding that letters symbolize predictable sounds, that words begin with an initial sound/letter, and that by "writing," they are empowering themselves by offering a reader access to their thoughts and ideas. The next three stages the emergent writers will pass through in order will most likely be:
   a. Scripting the end-sound to a word (KT=cat), leaving space between words, writing from the top left to the top right of the page and top to bottom
   b. Scripting the end-sound to a word (KT=cat), writing from the top left to the top right of the page and from top to bottom, separating the words from one another with a space between
   c. Leaving space between the initial letters that represent words, writing from the top left to the top right of the page and from top to bottom, scripting the final sound of each word as well as the initial sound (KT=cat)
   d. Drawing a picture beside each of the initial sounds to represent the entire word, scripting the end-sound to a word (KT=cat), scripting the interior sounds that compose the entire word (KAT=cat)

40. As defined by the Individuals with Disabilities Education Act (IDEA), Secondary Transition is a coordinated set of activities that are:
   a. Results-oriented and include post-school activities, vocational education, employment support and adult services and considers the individual's strengths, preferences and interests
   b. Socially structured and consider the individual's strengths, preferences and interests and vocational requirements
   c. Designed to support vocational training, results-oriented and have a strong social component
   d. Selected by the parent(s) or guardian because the student cannot choose for himself

41. A resource teacher can facilitate the greatest achievement in emergent writers who are scripting initial and final sounds by:
   a. Suggesting they write a book to build confidence, teach sequencing, and encourage them to deeply explore ideas.
   b. Suggesting they read their stories to other students.
   c. Inviting a reporter to write about her emergent writers.
   d. Inviting parents or guardians for a tea party at which the children will read their stories aloud.

Refer to the following for question 42:

   A teacher is concerned about three of her students. While they are enthusiastic about writing, they do not always recognize letters, confusing *b*, *d*, and *p*, or *e* and *o*. They do, however, know which sounds go with certain letters when they are orally drilled. When they write, they appear to be attempting letter–sound associations.

   "Now I'm writing *M*," the teacher heard one boy say as he scripted a large *N* in the upper right corner of his paper. He studied it for a moment and added, "Nope, it needs another leg." The student then wrote an *I* beside the *N*. "There," he said. "Now you are an *M*. I can write the word *man* because now I have *M*." The child then moved to the lower left corner of the paper. "M-A-N," he said to himself, slowly pronouncing each sound. "I already have that *M*. Here is where the rest of the word goes." He turned the paper sideways and wrote *N*.

   The second child sang to herself as she gripped the crayon and scribbled lines here and there on her paper. Some of the lines resembled letters, but few actually were. Others were scribbles. As she "wrote," she seemed to be making up a story and seemed to believe she was writing the story down.

   The third child didn't vocalize at all while he worked. He gripped the paper and carefully wrote the same letter over and over and over. Sometimes the letter was large, sometimes tiny. He turned the paper in every direction so that sometimes the letter was sideways or upside down. Sometimes he flipped it backward. "What are you writing?" the teacher asked him. "My name," the child told her. The teacher then realized the letter was, indeed, the first letter of his name. She gently told him he had done a fine job of writing the first letter of his name. Did he want her to help him write the rest of it? "Nope," he cheerfully told her, "it's all here." He pointed at one of the letters and "read" his full name. He pointed at another letter and again seemed to believe it represented all the sounds of his name.

42. At what point should the kindergarten teacher in the above example offer the three children picture books and ask them to read to her?
   a. When the three children are all able to script initial sounds, end sounds, and interior sounds.
   b. As each child reaches the stage in which he or she can script initial sounds, end sounds, and interior sounds, the teacher should ask only that child to read to her.
   c. As each child reaches the stage in which he habitually writes from the top to the bottom of the page, moving left to right.
   d. From the first day of school onward

43. How can a teacher teach spelling effectively?
  a. Students who have an understanding of letter-sound association do not need to be taught to spell. If they can say a word, they can spell it.
  b. Students who have an understanding of letter-sound association and can identify syllables and recognize when the base word has a Latin, Greek or Indo-European ancestry don't need to be taught to spell. They can deduce what is most likely the correct spelling using a combination of these strategies. A teacher who posts charts organizing words into their ancestor families, phonemic units and word-sound families is efficiently teaching spelling. The rest is up to the student.
  c. Students who spell poorly will be at a disadvantage for the rest of their lives. It is essential students spend at least 15 minutes a day drilling spelling words until they know them forward and backward. The teacher should alternate between students individually writing a new word 25 times and the entire class chanting the words.
  d. Students should be taught writing is a process. By applying spelling patterns found in word families, the spelling of many words can be deduced.

44. A special education teacher gives a struggling reader a story with key words missing:

  The children were hungry. They went into the _____. They found bread, peanut _____ and jelly in the cupboard. They made _____. They _ _ the sandwiches. Then they were not _____ anymore.

The student is able to complete the sentences by paying attention to:
  a. Syntax. Word order can provide enough hints that a reader can predict what happens next.
  b. Pretext. By previewing the story, the student can determine the missing words.
  c. Context. By considering other words in the story, the student can deduce the missing words.
  d. Sequencing. By ordering the ideas, the student can determine the missing words.

45. Collaborative Strategic Reading (CSR) is a teaching technique that depends on two teaching practices. These practices are:
  a. Cooperative learning and reading comprehension
  b. Cooperative reading and metacognition
  c. Reading comprehension and metacognition
  d. Cooperative learning and metacognition

46. Before being assigned to a special education classroom, a student must:
  a. Agree to the reassignment.
  b. Have an Individualized Education Program developed.
  c. Have an Independent Education Policy developed.
  d. Be seen by an educational psychologist to confirm her diagnosis.

47. A teacher has a child who does not volunteer in class. When the teacher asks the student a question the student can answer, she does so with as few words as possible. The teacher isn't sure how to best help the child. She should:
   a. Leave the child alone. She is clearly very shy and will be embarrassed by having attention drawn to her. She is learning in her own way.
   b. Ask two or three highly social children to include this girl in their activities. She is shy, and she probably won't approach them on her own.
   c. Observe the child over the course of a week or two. Draw her into conversation and determine if her vocabulary is limited, if she displays emotional problems, or if her reticence could have another cause. Note how the child interacts with others in the class. Does she ever initiate conversation? If another child initiates, does she respond?
   d. Refer her to the school counselor immediately. It is clear the child is suffering from either a low IQ or serious problems at home.

48. A special education teacher feels some of his strategies aren't effective. He asks a specialist to help him improve. The specialist suggests he:
   a. Begin a journal in which he considers strategies he has used. Which seemed to work? Which didn't, and why?
   b. Meet with the specialist to discuss the teacher's goals.
   c. Permit the specialist to drop into his classroom unannounced to observe. This will prevent the teacher from unconsciously over-preparing.
   d. Set up a video camera and record several student sessions to review. They can effectively collaborate at that time.

49. A student is able to decode most words fluently and has a borderline/acceptable vocabulary, but his reading comprehension is quite low. He can be helped with instructional focus on:
   a. Strategies to increase comprehension and to build vocabulary
   b. Strategies to increase comprehension and to be able to identify correct syntactical usage
   c. Strategies to improve his understanding of both content and context
   d. Strategies to build vocabulary and to improve his understanding of both content and context

50. Research indicates that developing oral language proficiency in emergent readers is important because:
   a. Proficiency with oral language enhances students' phonemic awareness and increases vocabulary.
   b. The more verbally expressive emergent readers are, the more confident they become. Such students will embrace both Academic and Independent reading levels.
   c. It encourages curiosity about others. With strong oral language skills, students begin to question the world around them. The more they ask, the richer their background knowledge.
   d. It demonstrates to students that their ideas are important and worth sharing.

51. A teacher has shown a mentally challenged student a website that integrates music and video clips with a variety of educational games about a topic the student has shown interest in. The student is initially intimidated and fears interacting with the program might result in her breaking the computer. The teacher reassures her she cannot harm the machine and shows the girl how to manipulate the mouse and keyboard. The teacher reminds the student what she already knows about the subject. As the student becomes more comfortable with the mouse, she focuses on the images and sounds, at times responding to the program conversationally, telling it what she knows about dinosaurs. The teacher is using the computer along with which teaching strategy?

   a. Modular instruction.
   b. Scaffolding.
   c. Linking.
   d. Transmutation.

52. A student has been identified with a cluster of learning disabilities. She will be joining a special education classroom. She is understandably nervous about making the change to a different teacher and group of classmates. In order to help her make the transition, the child should:

   a. Have a party to which her new classmates are invited along with some friends from the fifth-grade class she is leaving
   b. Prepare to begin classes with her new teacher the next day. Once the decision has been made, nothing will be gained by postponing the inevitable
   c. Be brave and understand life will be full of transitions. This is an opportunity to learn new skills that will serve her well in the future
   d. Visit the classroom, meet the teacher and her new classmates and be given the opportunity to ask questions about the change she is about to make

53. A student is taking a reading test. The teacher has blocked out a number of words. Each blank is assigned a set of three possible words. The student must select the correct word from each set so that the text makes sense. The student is taking:

   a. A cloze test
   b. A maze test
   c. A multiple-choice quiz
   d. A vocabulary test

54. A teacher has a student with dyscalculia who has trouble organizing addition and subtraction problems on paper. She can best help him by:

   a. Encouraging memorization of number families. Committing them to memory is the only way.
   b. Demonstrating a problem in different ways. Write a problem on the board: 11 - 3. Gather 11 books and take 3 of them away. Draw 11 x's on the board and erase 3.
   c. Use graph paper to help him organize. Show him how to write the problems, keeping each number in a box aligned with other numbers.
   d. Make a game of addition and subtraction problems. Divide the class into groups and let them compete to see which group can solve the most problems.

55. A child has been losing strength in her muscles over a period of time. The loss is very gradual, but the teacher is concerned and recommends the child see a doctor. The possible diagnosis is:
   a. Cerebral Palsy
   b. Muscular Dystrophy
   c. Muscular Sclerosis
   d. Spastic Muscular and Nerve Disorder

56. A middle school student is preparing to transition from a self-contained special education classroom to a general education classroom. This transition should be made:
   a. With proper preparation. A student this age needs to acclimate socially and can best do so with the same group of students in every class
   b. At the beginning of the next school year so the student doesn't have a stigma when joining the new group
   c. One class at a time with the special education teacher supervising academic and social progress
   d. By transitioning into classes he is most interested in because he is most likely to succeed with subjects he cares about. The confidence he gains from academic success will support him as he transitions into classes he's less interested in

57. The four required activities described by the Assistive Technology Act (AT ACT) of 1998 are a public awareness program, coordinating activities among state agencies, technical assistance and training and
   a. Specialized training for special education teachers and support.
   b. Outreach to underrepresented religious groups, ethnicities and urban populations.
   c. Outreach to underrepresented and rural populations.
   d. New technologies training on a quarterly basis for special education teachers and support.

58. Behavior problems in special education students are most effectively handled with:
   a. Zero tolerance
   b. Positive Behavioral Support (PBS)
   c. Acceptance and tolerance
   d. Positive Behavioral Control (PBC)

59. A teacher suspects one of her kindergarteners has a learning disability in math. Why would the teacher suggest intervention to the child's concerned parents rather than assessment as the first step?
   a. She wouldn't; assessment should precede intervention
   b. She wouldn't; kindergarteners develop new skills at radically different rates. Suggesting either intervention or assessment at this point is premature. The teacher would more likely observe the child over a three month period to note her development before including the parents about her concern
   c. Assessing a young child for learning disabilities often leads to an incorrect conclusion because a student must be taught the subject before it's possible to assess her understanding of it. Intervention teaches the child specific skills to correct her misconceptions. If the intervention fails, assessment is the next step
   d. Assessment at this stage is unnecessary and wastes time and money. Since an assessment that resulted in a diagnosis of a learning disability would recommend intervention to correct it, it is more efficient to proceed directly to intervention

60. IDEA requires that students identified with learning disabilities or other special needs be educated in _____ learning environment appropriate for their needs.
   a. The safest
   b. The least restrictive
   c. The most appropriate
   d. The most desirable

61. Howard Gardner's theory of Multiple Intelligences organizes learners into what types of intelligences?
   a. Verbal linguistic, mathematical, musically attuned, visual special, body embraced, interpersonal, naturalistic, existential.
   b. Emphatic, recessive, aggressive, assertive, dogmatic, apologetic, determined, elusive.
   c. Verbal linguistic, mathematical logical, musical, visual spatial, body kinesthetic, interpersonal, naturalistic, existential.
   d. Dramatic, musical, verbal, mathematical, dance-oriented, sports-oriented, scientific, socially concerned.

62. Lead teaching, learning centers / learning stations, resource services, team teaching and consultation are all used in:
   a. Innovative teaching
   b. Strategic teaching
   c. Collaborative teaching
   d. Self-contained classrooms

63. Jason is a second-grade student with an intellectual disability. Which of the following characteristics would you most expect to impact his educational performance?
   a. Significantly subaverage general intellectual functioning
   b. Concomitant impairments that cause severe educational needs
   c. Disorder in one or more of the basic psychological processes
   d. An injury to the brain caused by an external force

64. Identifying specific skills deficient in special education math students is important so the teacher can decide how to remediate. Problems can include an inability to recall math facts, understand mathematical operations and formulas and how rules are used in solving problems or focusing on attention to details. Such students might be:
   a. Able to solve math problems when they haven't been taught an operation required to do so
   b. Unable to locate errors in their own work
   c. Able to solve math problems in another language
   d. Unable to count higher than 100

65. What steps are taken to identify specific skill deficits in math?
   a. Standardized assessment tests, examining areas of weakness in student work to determine patterns, teacher observations, interviews with the student.
   b. Standardized assessment tests, examining areas of weakness in student work to determine patterns, teacher observations, interviews with parent(s).
   c. Teacher observations coupled with examining areas of weakness in student work are sufficient.
   d. None of the above

66. A fifth-grade lead teacher and the special education teacher have scheduled a parent conference to discuss the behavior problems of the student. They anticipate the boy's mother will be anxious and defensive as she has been at previous conferences. The best approach for the teachers to take is to:
   a. Draw the parent out about issues in her own life so that she will feel reassured and trusting. Point out possible connections between the mother's emotions about her own life and her son's behaviors and reactions
   b. Be very firm with the mother, explain the penalties and disciplines her son can expect if the behavior continues, and stress neither the parent nor the child has input regarding punishment
   c. Stress the teachers will not do anything without the parent's approval since they do not want to face liability issues
   d. Begin by welcoming the mother and telling her about her son's academic improvements. Stress the teachers, the mother and the child share goals for the student's success. Explain the behavior problems and ask if the mother has any insights to share.

67. At the beginning of the week, a special education teacher asked a group of students to generate a list of verbs that make visual or sound pictures. She suggests students think of verbs that mean ways of walking, talking, eating, sitting and playing. The students spend the remainder of the week compiling the list. They notice interesting verbs as they read books, remark on less common verbs they hear in conversation or on television and locate interesting verbs in signs, magazines and other printed materials. One child begins to draw pictures to illustrate some of the verbs. Two children collaborate to create a play in which they demonstrate some of the verbs in a dance. A boy writes a song incorporating the list of verbs. The project is extremely successful. At the end of the week the students have created the following list:

> TIPTOE, SCOOT, MUMBLE, MUNCH, LEAP, SPIN, DIVE, POUNCE, GLIDE, SLITHER, MOAN, WHISPER, GRUMBLE, NIBBLE, SHRILL, HOLLER, PERCH, LEAN, STOMP, MARCH, GIGGLE, HOP, STRUT, SLOUCH, GULP, HOWL, WHINE, SLURP, CROUCH, DRIBBLE, DROOL, HOOT, YELP, YOWL, GROWL, WHISTLE, SHRIEK, SNICKER, INSULT, COMPLIMENT, PLEAD, BARK, WIGGLE, TWIST, SLINK, TODDLE, TRUDGE, WANDER, STROLL.

The teacher's goal is to:
   a. Enhance students' understanding of theme by encouraging them to make connections between categories of verbs.
   b. Enhance students' vocabulary by encouraging them to find examples in the world around them.
   c. Enhance students' understanding of context by encouraging them to explore verbs for contextual clues.
   d. Enhance students' sense of curiosity by directing their attention to a number of different resources they may not have considered.

68. Rebecca has intellectual disabilities and has lived at home with her parents all her life. She has no job skills. Her parents are getting older and would like her to have a job when she finishes school. She has been placed in a group home and a day habilitation training program. Which scenario is most suitable for her?
   a. Attend academic classes in the training center and work in a workshop part-time.
   b. Receive job training in classes at the training center and transition to a workshop.
   c. Be placed in a sheltered workshop immediately instead of in the training center.
   d. Learn work skills at the training center and then have a job at the training center.

69. A classroom teacher has a student with learning disabilities that affect her ability to do math. The teacher consults with the special education teacher and decides she will modify the work the child is given by reducing the number of problems, letting her have extra time to finish, and providing her with a multiplication chart. Which of the following statements on the teacher's actions is accurate?
   a. The teacher is giving the student an unfair advantage. Letting her have extra time should be sufficient.
   b. The teacher is giving the student an unfair advantage. Providing a multiplication chart should be sufficient. With that, she should get her work done on time.
   c. The teacher is making appropriate modifications. Each child is different. In this case, she consulted with the special education teacher and concluded the child needs multiple supports.
   d. The teacher is modifying the student's work because it makes it easier on the teacher. There is less to explain and less to grade.

70. Which of the following would be the responsibility of the school nurse with regard to students who receive special education services?
   a. Serving as the case manager of the IEP
   b. Ensuring that accommodations are put into place
   c. Implementing mental health services
   d. Providing health updates at eligibility meetings

71. The ADA is:
   a. The Americans with Disabilities Act
   b. The Anti-Discrimination Act
   c. The American Diabetes Association
   d. The Alternatives to Discrimination Act

72. Cooperative learning is an important strategy for students with autism. What may be a reason to hesitate to implement this strategy in a general education classroom with students with autism?
   a. General education students may not be accepting of students with autism.
   b. Students with autism may not learn as much through this strategy.
   c. Students with autism may struggle to understand concepts initially.
   d. Cooperative learning may negatively affect the confidence of a student with autism.

73. The development of an IEP is a(n) _____ process.
   a. indirect
   b. collaborative
   c. mathematical
   d. single

74. From the age of 3 years to 5 years, a child's expressive vocabulary will usually:
   a. Double
   b. Increase by 25%
   c. Increase by 50%
   d. Triple

75. Flash cards can be a useful math intervention for students who struggle with math fact calculations. When may the use of flash cards be inappropriate for students to practice?
   a. When memorizing division facts
   b. When students pass their math fact quizzes
   c. When students are too young to read
   d. When reviewing already known facts

Answer Key and Explanations

1. C: Any device that could help a disabled student in education or life functioning. The Assistive Technology Act of 1998 is the primary legislation regarding assistive technology for disabled students and adults. The act funds 56 state programs concerned with the assistive technology needs of individuals with disabilities. Assistive devices include wheelchairs, hearing aids, glare-reduction screens, Braille devices, voice-recognition software, screen magnifiers and a wealth of other tools.

2. B: When writing learning objectives, it is important that they are specific to the needs of the student, measurable or quantifiable, appropriately attainable for the group of students, relevant to the current topic or lesson, and include a timeframe for the student to achieve the goal. Answers A, C, and D are incorrect because they are each missing some of these SMART components.

3. B: Cerebral palsy. Cerebral palsy is an umbrella term that groups neurological childhood disorders that affect muscular control. It does not worsen over time and the cause is located in damaged areas of the brain that control muscle movement. Depending upon the severity of the disorder, a child with cerebral palsy might benefit from an AAC device to help in speaking, forearm crutches to assist in walking or a head pointer for a child whose best motor control is his head.

4. D: The child most likely has dyscalculia. Dyscalculia defines a range of difficulties in math, such as the inability to understand numbers' meanings, measurements, patterns, mathematical terms, and the application of mathematic principles. Early clues include a young child's inability to group items by size or color, recognize patterns, or understand the meaning or order of numbers.

5. C: A strategy for diagnosing learning disabilities in which a student with an academic delay receives research-supported interventions to correct the delay. If the interventions do not result in considerable academic improvement, the failure to respond suggests causal learning disabilities.

6. A: Although all of these choices may be beneficial in targeting specific student behavior, single-domain scales tend to be most beneficial for students with ADHD. Single-domain scales are designed to assess a specific area of concern such as executive functioning. Many students with ADHD will have one main area of concern that the evaluators will focus on. Answer b is incorrect because self-report scales tend to be more beneficial for older students who can accurately report their behavioral concerns. Answer c is incorrect because multidomain scales may make it difficult to target one specific area of concern in students. Answer d is incorrect because observer/informant scales tend to be for students with multiple areas of concern in order to determine the cause of the behavior.

7. B: Obsessive Compulsive Disorder (OCD). Children and adults with OCD typically engage in a series of highly ritualized behaviors that are rigidly performed when they feel stressed. Behaviors include tapping, snapping fingers, blinking, counting and so forth.

8. A: Intellectual disabilities, hearing, speech, language, visual, orthopedic or other health impairments, emotional disturbance, autism, brain injury caused by trauma, or specific learning disabilities who needs special education and related services. Children with one or more of these conditions are legally entitled to services and programs designed to help them achieve at the highest level of their ability.

9. D: Students with ADHD are generally extremely sensitive to distractions. A learning environment in which visual and audio distractions have been eliminated is best. Low lighting, few posters, and a clean whiteboard will help minimize distractions.

10. A: Corrective feedback. Corrective feedback is offered to a student in order to explain why a particular error is, in fact, an error. Corrective feedback is specific; it locates where and how the student went astray so that similar errors can be avoided in the future.

11. C: The most likely diagnosis is autism. Autistic children are typically very withdrawn, avoid eye contact, and are not responsive to verbal or physical attempts to connect. Some autistic children fall into repetitive behaviors that are very difficult to arrest or prevent. These behaviors include rocking, spinning and handshaking.

12. A: Both, the left. Research using MRIs shows dyslexics use both sides of their brains for activities such as reading, while non-dyslexics use only the left side.

13. D: Dysgraphia. Dysgraphic individuals cannot manage the physical act of writing. While many dysgraphics are highly intelligent and able to express themselves cogently, they have extreme difficulty holding a writing implement and shaping letters.

14. B: A child that is between the ages of 2 and 6 will typically start to use perception in their thought process. Children at this age tend to be able to solve simple problems rather than complex, multidimensional ones. Psychologist Jean Piaget proposed that a child's intellectual development progresses through four stages. Answer A is incorrect because a child that is manipulating objects would typically be younger than 2. Answer C is incorrect because a child that applies logical reasoning will likely be older than 7. Answer D is incorrect because a child that has abstract thoughts will likely be 12 or older.

15. B: Reading comprehension and vocabulary cannot be sufficiently assessed with occasional, brief studies. Performing continuous observation, using high-stakes and standardized testing, paying attention to grades, and closely tracking the outcomes of objective-linked assessments are interrelated tools that, when systematically organized, offer a thorough understanding of students' strengths and weaknesses.

16. A: Diabetic hypoglycemia. Diabetic hypoglycemia, also known as insulin reaction, occurs when blood sugar falls to a very low level. It is important to treat it quickly or the diabetic could faint, in which case an injection of glucagon is administered.

17. D: Enthusiastically accepted. The adults discuss a background check and the possibility the teen might discover gardening is not for her and may want to quit. However, this is most likely to occur early in her employment, giving the neighbor sufficient time to find another helper. The teacher is pleased because the girl will learn new skills through modeling and repetition. The mother is pleased because the experience will add to the girl's self-esteem as well as show her that she is capable of learning. The elderly neighbor is pleased because she is both compassionate and truly needs help. The girl is delighted the neighbor recognizes her potential and sees her as valuable.

18. C: The student did not know how to spell 'beautiful'. It is doubtful the student heard "pretty" instead of beautiful since the two sound nothing alike. It is equally unlikely he doesn't know the meaning of the word 'beautiful' since his substitution, 'pretty', is a synonym for beautiful. It is likely this child is creative, but that alone wouldn't be sufficient reason to replace one word with another. The most logical answer is that he simply didn't know how to spell 'beautiful'. He does know that some words mean almost the same thing, and since he already knew how to spell 'pretty', he incorrectly believed a synonym would be acceptable.

19. A: Pervasive Spectrum Disorders (PSD) is another name for Autism Spectrum Disorders (ASD). PSD causes disabilities in language, thought, emotion and empathy. The most severe form of PSD is autistic disorder. A much less severe form is Asperger's Syndrome.

20. C: Immediately refer him to the counselor. The boy is exhibiting serious emotional distress suggesting either abuse or neglect at home or elsewhere. While his behavior may seem manipulative, the fact that the boy is unreachable once he's in the highly charged emotional state in which he repeats, "I hate myself" suggests emotional trauma. The fact the child is socialized with peers, playing with them when invited and not taking rejection personally, suggests his emotional distress may be caused by an adult who has convinced him he is unworthy. A trained counselor is the best choice.

21. C: He is socially distant, focused on certain subjects to the point of obsession and inflexible. Asperger Syndrome is a mild form of autism. Children with this disorder typically do interact with teachers, other adults and sometimes other children; however, the interaction is rather remote and without emotional expression. They are also very focused on subjects of great interest to the abandonment of all others. When asked to redirect focus, Asperger children often become emphatically obstinate, refusing to shift focus.

22. D: This project gives the teacher the opportunity to evaluate what students already know, establishes a scaffold of accessible information to which the students can integrate new information and creates a sense of curiosity and excitement in the students, which encourages them to learn.

23. D: Verbal dyspraxia is a motor skill development disorder which includes speech errors that don't clearly follow a pattern and so appear to be inconsistent. An example is a student who can pronounce /p/ when it is followed by a long i, as in pine, but not when followed by an ou diphthong, as in pout. Verbally dyspraxic individuals are unable to correctly place the tongue, lips and jaw for consistent sounds that can be organized into syllables. Dyspraxia appears to be a brain disorder in which the area that controls production of particular sounds is damaged.

24. B: Asking students to create a play about the story as the teacher reads aloud would be the most effective strategy. This activity grounds the students in the story action as it is occurring. Acting it out ensures understanding; otherwise, the students will most likely stop the teacher and ask for clarification. Furthermore, by acting it out, students are incorporating understanding physically. They will be more likely to retain the story and be able to comprehend the meanings incorporated in it.

25. A: Twitches, grunts, inappropriate words, body spasms. Children and adults with Tourette syndrome are rarely aggressive nor are they reluctant to make eye contact or otherwise engage others. Tourette syndrome is characterized by explosive sounds, sometimes in the form of inappropriate words, more often just as meaningless syllables; muscular twitches of the face or elsewhere in the body and the complete inability to control these spasms. Tourette sufferers often also suffer from Obsessive Compulsive Disorder.

26. C: The child may or may not be hyperactive, but the fact that she can control her behavior for extended periods if a reward is involved suggests the child is overly indulged outside of class. In addition, she appears to act out in an effort to seek peer admiration; this excludes the possibility of Tourette's syndrome and attention deficit hyperactivity disorder. In the first case, she would be unlikely to seek approval. In the second, she would be unlikely to be able to control herself under certain circumstances. There is nothing in her behavior to suggest psychosis.

27. A: Social influences are everywhere around us, from the people we talk with, to social media, to entertainment. Conformity means changing one's behavior to be more like the norm. This can have negative effects. Changing to be like everyone else may mean that a person has changed a part of who he or she is just to fit in. Answers B, C, and D are incorrect because these all tend to be positive effects of social influence. Independence and individualism are the result of thinking for oneself. Compliance is the result of following the rules or guidelines.

28. C: One of the characteristics of an effective lesson plan is positive feedback. Reinforcing student behavior is one of the most effective ways to praise students and provide this positive feedback. Answer A is incorrect because selectively calling on students may create an imbalance of who gets called on. Answer B is incorrect because it is best to give students some time to think before asking a question. Answer D is incorrect because feedback should be provided immediately so they can make corrections.

29. D: It is the responsibility of the special education case manager to ensure that each student on his or her caseload is accessing accommodations and that general education teachers know how to implement them. Answer A is incorrect because it is not the responsibility of the case manager to make sure students do not fail. Answer B is incorrect because it is also not the responsibility of the case manager to make sure students are attending school. Answer C is incorrect because although the case manager will track the progress of students on their IEP goals, it is not their job to make sure they meet the goal.

30. D: When lesson planning, a warm-up is beneficial in that it provides students an opportunity to practice some of the skills they are going to learn in that lesson, which is connected to previous knowledge. To learn how to add and subtract fractions, it would be beneficial to practice adding and subtracting whole numbers. Answers A and B are incorrect because these would be more advanced than the lesson they will be learning. Answer C may be a good warm-up, but it is best practice for the warmup to relate directly to the lesson, so answer D is the best option.

31. B: The classroom teacher, a special education teacher, parents or guardian, a representative of the local education agency knowledgeable about specialized instruction, someone to interpret instructional implications, the student if appropriate and other people invited by the parents or the school. IDEA defines the IEP team as a group of people responsible for developing, reviewing and revising the Individualized Education Program for a disabled student.

32. C: Reading at a Frustration reading level. At a Frustration reading level, a student is unable to unlock meaning from a text regardless of teacher support or strategies. The reader is at this level when he has less than 90% accuracy in word recognition and less than 50% in comprehension, retelling a story is illogical or incomplete and the student cannot accurately answer questions about the text.

33. B: In a cloze test, a reader is given a text with certain words blocked out. The reader must be able to determine probable missing words based on contextual clues. In order to supply these words, the reader must already know them.

34. A: Letter-sound correspondence is the relationship between a spoken sound and the letters predictably used in English to transcribe them.

35. D: The resource teacher should teach students to memorize their lists by using techniques such as songs, mnemonic devices and other fun activities. By definition, irregular sight words do not follow common phonics patterns, meaning teachers should use other techniques to help students recognize them.

36. A: Phonological awareness refers to an understanding of the sounds a word makes. While phonological awareness leads to fluent reading skills, activities designed to develop an awareness of word sounds are, by definition, oral.

37. A: The students should be taught to count money, plan meals, grocery shop, recognize safety concerns. These are among the most basic life skills students with developmental delays must master. Other life skills include specific occupational skills, home maintenance, clothes selection and care, food preparation and personal hygiene.

38. B: Strategizing in order to understand the meaning of a word, knowing multiple meanings of a single word, and applying background knowledge to glean a word's meaning are all ways in which an effective reader enhances vocabulary. Other skills include an awareness of word parts and word origins, the ability to apply word meanings in a variety of content areas, and a delight in learning the meanings of unfamiliar words.

39. A: The next three stages are scripting the end-sound to a word (KT=cat), leaving space between words, and writing from the top left to the top right of the page and from top to bottom. Each of these steps is progressively more abstract. Scripting the end-sound to a word helps a young writer recognize that words have beginnings and endings. This naturally leads to the willingness to separate words with white space so that they stand as individual entities. Once this step is reached, the child realizes that in English, writing progresses from left to right and from the top of the page to the bottom.

40. A: Are results-oriented, includes post-school activities, vocational education, employment support, adult services and considers the individual's strengths, preferences and interests. Additional activities that compose Secondary Transition are instruction, related services, community experiences, the development of employment and other post-school adult living objectives and, if appropriate, acquisition of daily living skills and functional vocational evaluation.

41. B: Suggesting they read their stories to other students. Emergent writers scripting initial and final sounds will gain the most immediate and relevant satisfaction by moving around the room, reading what they've written to other students.

42. D: The teacher should encourage all students to "read" picture books from the first day of school. Talking about the pictures from page to page gives young readers the idea that books are arranged sequentially. Pictures also offer narrative coherence and contextual clues. Emergent readers who are encouraged to enjoy books will more readily embrace the act of reading. Holding a book and turning pages gives young readers a familiarity with them.

43. D: Students should be taught that writing is a process. By applying spelling patterns found in word families, the spelling of many words can be deduced.

44. C: Context. By considering the other words in the story, the student can deduce the missing words. Referring to other words when a reader encounters an unfamiliar or missing word, can often unlock meaning.

45. A: Cooperative learning occurs when a group of students at various levels of reading ability have goals in common. Reading comprehension is achieved through reading both orally and silently, developing vocabulary, a reader's ability to predict what will occur in a piece of writing, a reader's ability to summarize the main points in a piece of writing, and a reader's ability to reflect on the text's meaning and connect that meaning to another text or personal experience.

46. B: An IEP is a requirement of law. The plan, written by a team of individuals including her classroom teacher, the special education teacher, her parents, the student (if appropriate), and other interested individuals, establishes objectives and goals and offers a timeline in which to reach them.

47. C: Until the teacher monitors the child's verbal abilities and habits, she cannot determine if the lack of interaction suggests a learning disability, an emotional problem, or simply a shy personality. The teacher should informally observe the child over a period of time, noting if and when she initiates or responds to oral language, if she is reading with apparent comprehension, if her vocabulary is limited, and the degree to which the child is interested in understanding.

48. B: Meet with the specialist to discuss the teacher's goals. It isn't possible to determine if strategies are effective or determine a future course unless the teacher has a firm grasp of his goals and expectations.

49. A: The student should receive instruction focused on just the areas in which he is exhibiting difficulty, which are comprehension and vocabulary. Improved vocabulary will give him greater skill at comprehending the meaning of a particular text. Strategies focused on enhancing comprehension together with a stronger vocabulary will provide the greatest help.

50. A: Proficiency with oral language enhances students' phonemic awareness and increases vocabulary. Understanding that words are scripted with specific letters representing specific sounds is essential to decoding a text. Students cannot effectively learn to read without the ability to decode. An enhanced vocabulary supports the act of reading; the larger an emergent reader's vocabulary, the more quickly he will learn to read. He will be able to decode more words, which he can organize into word families and use to decode unfamiliar words.

51. B: Scaffolding. Scaffolding is an umbrella teaching approach which offers a multitude of supports. Scaffolding includes prior knowledge, mnemonic devices, modeling, graphs, charts, graphic organizers and information needed prior to starting the lesson such as vocabulary or mathematical formulas.

52. D: Visit the classroom, meet the teacher and her new classmates and be given the opportunity to ask questions about the change she is about to make. When she is able to visualize what the classroom looks like, meet the people that will become her new educational 'family' and have her concerns and questions addressed, she will feel more confident about the transition.

53. B: A maze test is a specific type of cloze test. In a cloze test, words are deleted, and the reader must supply the missing words using contextual clues and vocabulary that is familiar. A maze test is essentially a multiple-choice application of a cloze test.

54. C: Use graph paper to help him organize. Show him how to write the problems, keeping each number in a box aligned with other numbers. This will help him determine which numbers are in the ones group, the tens group, the hundreds group and so on.

55. B: Muscular dystrophy. There are 20 types of muscular dystrophy, a genetically inherited disease that frequently first manifests in childhood. By contrast, muscular sclerosis almost never appears in childhood. Cerebral palsy is not a deteriorating disease, as is muscular dystrophy.

56. C: One class at a time, with the special education teacher supervising his academic and social progress. It is important to make this transition slowly, to permit the special education teacher to remain in the student's life as both academic and emotional support and the student to adjust to her larger classes and students she doesn't know as well.

57. C: Outreach to underrepresented and rural populations. The four required activities of the AT ACT of 1998 are: a public awareness program, coordinate activities among state agencies, technical assistance and training and outreach to underrepresented and rural populations.

58. B: Positive Behavior Support. The Individuals with Disabilities Education Act of 1997 is the recommended method of dealing with behavioral problems in children with disabilities.

59. C: Assessing a young child for learning disabilities often leads to an incorrect conclusion because a student must be taught the subject before it is possible to assess her understanding of it. Intervention teaches the child specific skills to correct her misconceptions. If the intervention fails, assessment is the next step. Many experts recommend such assessment should not be undertaken until a child is at least six years of age.

60. B: Least restrictive. IDEA requires the least restrictive environment (LRE) appropriate to a child's needs is the proper learning environment so children are not unnecessarily isolated from non-disabled children. The student's IEP team is responsible for determining the LRE.

61. C: Verbal linguistic, mathematical logical, musical, visual spatial, body kinesthetic, interpersonal, naturalistic, existential. Harvard Professor Howard Gardner cites his theory of multiple intelligences, also called learning styles, as an answer to how teachers can most effectively reach all their students. It is especially important to recognize the learning styles of students with learning disabilities and design lessons for those students accordingly.

62. C: Collaborative teaching. Classrooms with a lead teacher often include a specialized teacher to listen to the lesson then work with special needs children. Other methods are: learning centers or stations in which collaborating teachers are responsible for different areas, assigning special needs students into a resource room, team teaching and/or consultation by the special education teacher to the classroom teacher.

63. A: A student with an intellectual disability will have a significantly subaverage general intellectual functioning. This will typically be combined with deficits in adaptive behavior and will be manifested during the developmental period. This is something that likely would be noticed in Jason starting from an early age. Answer B is incorrect because a concomitant, or accompanying, disability would fall under the category of multiple disabilities. Answer C is incorrect because a disorder in basic psychological processes would fall under a specific learning disability. Answer D is incorrect because an injury to the brain by an outside force would be in the "traumatic brain injury" category.

64. B: Unable to locate errors in their own work. This is the only logical answer. Answers A, C and D do not make sense in context.

65. A: Standardized assessment tests, examining areas of weakness in student work to determine patterns, teacher observations, and interviews with the student are the typical steps taken to identify specific skill deficits in math. After this, the teacher should be well-prepared to plan instruction.

66. D: Begin by welcoming the mother and discussing her son's academic improvements. Stress that the teachers, the mother and the child share goals for the student's success. Explain the behavior problems and ask if the mother has insights to share. It's important to keep communication open.

67. B: Enhance students' vocabulary by encouraging them to find examples in the world around them. Often children have richer vocabularies than they realize. This project simultaneously encourages students to remember words they already know and to learn other words with similar meanings.

68. B: Taking academic classes would provide no job training and no transition to the workshop. Rebecca would need more training at the workshop to get up to speed. This is not the best plan. Therefore option A is incorrect.

Rebecca can learn job skills first in the training center and then, when she is ready, she can be transitioned to the workshop, where she can actually do work and earn some money. Therefore option B is correct.

If she were placed directly in the workshop, Rebecca would not be prepared since she has no job skills. She needs training first. Therefore option C is incorrect.

A classroom at the training center is a good place for Rebecca to learn some job skills. However, staying there indefinitely would be like staying in school. The workshop, though sheltered for disabled individuals, is still closer to a real workplace than a school, and she can earn money there. After going to school, she should make the transition to having a job. Therefore option D is incorrect.

69. C: The teacher is making appropriate modifications. Each child is different. In this case, she has consulted with the special education teacher and concluded the child needs multiple supports.

70. D: The school nurse may have many roles and responsibilities, but one of them is to provide a health update for each eligibility meeting. It is important that the student's health concerns are updated to determine what impact they might have on a student's access to education. The school nurse may have more involvement for certain students on IEPs than others but is typically involved with each one at some point. Answer A is incorrect because the special education teacher typically serves as the case manager. Answer B is incorrect because the special education teacher also ensures that accommodations are put into place. Answer C is incorrect because the school counselor or social worker will likely implement mental health services.

71. A: The Americans with Disabilities Act. The ADA is a federal act prohibiting discrimination based on disability in the areas of employment, state and local government, public accommodations, commercial facilities, transportation and telecommunications.

72. C: Students with autism often have difficulty with changes in routine and the environment. It may be difficult for them to adjust to a new kind of learning strategy that may affect what they are able to learn. Answer A is incorrect because although not all students are accepting, it is important for students with autism to attempt to engage with everyone. Answer B is incorrect because these students can still learn as much as their peers once they are able to adjust to the new environment. Answer D is incorrect because this kind of learning should actually improve confidence over time.

73. B: The creation of an Individualized Education Plan (IEP) is a collaborative process, in that it involves classroom and special education teachers, family members, the student (if appropriate), and other interested parties who collaborate in the student's best interests.

74. C: From the age of 3 years to 5 years, a child's spoken vocabulary will typically increase by 50% (c). A typical 3-year-old will have a maximum expressive vocabulary of around 1,000 words*; by age 5, this will have increased to around 1,500 words. (*Children develop vocabularies of around 300 to 1,000 words in their first three years; the increase percentage here is based on the high end.) Vocabulary development is more rapid from age 1 to 3 since the child is starting from nothing and has more words to learn. If the child's earlier development has been optimal, the additional increase in spoken vocabulary by age 5 is 50%, making (a), (b), and (d) incorrect.

75. D: If students have already memorized the facts on flash cards, it may be considered a waste of time to continue to review them over and over again. Answer A is incorrect because flash cards can be great to help memorize division facts. Answer B is incorrect because flash cards can still be used with problems students struggled with even if they passed a test. Answer C is incorrect because even if students are too young to read, they can still practice math facts.

How to Overcome Test Anxiety

Just the thought of taking a test is enough to make most people a little nervous. A test is an important event that can have a long-term impact on your future, so it's important to take it seriously and it's natural to feel anxious about performing well. But just because anxiety is normal, that doesn't mean that it's helpful in test taking, or that you should simply accept it as part of your life. Anxiety can have a variety of effects. These effects can be mild, like making you feel slightly nervous, or severe, like blocking your ability to focus or remember even a simple detail.

If you experience test anxiety—whether severe or mild—it's important to know how to beat it. To discover this, first you need to understand what causes test anxiety.

Causes of Test Anxiety

While we often think of anxiety as an uncontrollable emotional state, it can actually be caused by simple, practical things. One of the most common causes of test anxiety is that a person does not feel adequately prepared for their test. This feeling can be the result of many different issues such as poor study habits or lack of organization, but the most common culprit is time management. Starting to study too late, failing to organize your study time to cover all of the material, or being distracted while you study will mean that you're not well prepared for the test. This may lead to cramming the night before, which will cause you to be physically and mentally exhausted for the test. Poor time management also contributes to feelings of stress, fear, and hopelessness as you realize you are not well prepared but don't know what to do about it.

Other times, test anxiety is not related to your preparation for the test but comes from unresolved fear. This may be a past failure on a test, or poor performance on tests in general. It may come from comparing yourself to others who seem to be performing better or from the stress of living up to expectations. Anxiety may be driven by fears of the future—how failure on this test would affect your educational and career goals. These fears are often completely irrational, but they can still negatively impact your test performance.

Elements of Test Anxiety

As mentioned earlier, test anxiety is considered to be an emotional state, but it has physical and mental components as well. Sometimes you may not even realize that you are suffering from test anxiety until you notice the physical symptoms. These can include trembling hands, rapid heartbeat, sweating, nausea, and tense muscles. Extreme anxiety may lead to fainting or vomiting. Obviously, any of these symptoms can have a negative impact on testing. It is important to recognize them as soon as they begin to occur so that you can address the problem before it damages your performance.

The mental components of test anxiety include trouble focusing and inability to remember learned information. During a test, your mind is on high alert, which can help you recall information and stay focused for an extended period of time. However, anxiety interferes with your mind's natural processes, causing you to blank out, even on the questions you know well. The strain of testing during anxiety makes it difficult to stay focused, especially on a test that may take several hours. Extreme anxiety can take a huge mental toll, making it difficult not only to recall test information but even to understand the test questions or pull your thoughts together.

Effects of Test Anxiety

Test anxiety is like a disease—if left untreated, it will get progressively worse. Anxiety leads to poor performance, and this reinforces the feelings of fear and failure, which in turn lead to poor performances on subsequent tests. It can grow from a mild nervousness to a crippling condition. If allowed to progress, test anxiety can have a big impact on your schooling, and consequently on your future.

Test anxiety can spread to other parts of your life. Anxiety on tests can become anxiety in any stressful situation, and blanking on a test can turn into panicking in a job situation. But fortunately, you don't have to let anxiety rule your testing and determine your grades. There are a number of relatively simple steps you can take to move past anxiety and function normally on a test and in the rest of life.

Physical Steps for Beating Test Anxiety

While test anxiety is a serious problem, the good news is that it can be overcome. It doesn't have to control your ability to think and remember information. While it may take time, you can begin taking steps today to beat anxiety.

Just as your first hint that you may be struggling with anxiety comes from the physical symptoms, the first step to treating it is also physical. Rest is crucial for having a clear, strong mind. If you are tired, it is much easier to give in to anxiety. But if you establish good sleep habits, your body and mind will be ready to perform optimally, without the strain of exhaustion. Additionally, sleeping well helps you to retain information better, so you're more likely to recall the answers when you see the test questions.

Getting good sleep means more than going to bed on time. It's important to allow your brain time to relax. Take study breaks from time to time so it doesn't get overworked, and don't study right before bed. Take time to rest your mind before trying to rest your body, or you may find it difficult to fall asleep.

Along with sleep, other aspects of physical health are important in preparing for a test. Good nutrition is vital for good brain function. Sugary foods and drinks may give a burst of energy but this burst is followed by a crash, both physically and emotionally. Instead, fuel your body with protein and vitamin-rich foods.

Also, drink plenty of water. Dehydration can lead to headaches and exhaustion, especially if your brain is already under stress from the rigors of the test. Particularly if your test is a long one, drink water during the breaks. And if possible, take an energy-boosting snack to eat between sections.

Along with sleep and diet, a third important part of physical health is exercise. Maintaining a steady workout schedule is helpful, but even taking 5-minute study breaks to walk can help get your blood pumping faster and clear your head. Exercise also releases endorphins, which contribute to a positive feeling and can help combat test anxiety.

When you nurture your physical health, you are also contributing to your mental health. If your body is healthy, your mind is much more likely to be healthy as well. So take time to rest, nourish your body with healthy food and water, and get moving as much as possible. Taking these physical steps will make you stronger and more able to take the mental steps necessary to overcome test anxiety.

Mental Steps for Beating Test Anxiety

Working on the mental side of test anxiety can be more challenging, but as with the physical side, there are clear steps you can take to overcome it. As mentioned earlier, test anxiety often stems from lack of preparation, so the obvious solution is to prepare for the test. Effective studying may be the most important weapon you have for beating test anxiety, but you can and should employ several other mental tools to combat fear.

First, boost your confidence by reminding yourself of past success—tests or projects that you aced. If you're putting as much effort into preparing for this test as you did for those, there's no reason you should expect to fail here. Work hard to prepare; then trust your preparation.

Second, surround yourself with encouraging people. It can be helpful to find a study group, but be sure that the people you're around will encourage a positive attitude. If you spend time with others who are anxious or cynical, this will only contribute to your own anxiety. Look for others who are motivated to study hard from a desire to succeed, not from a fear of failure.

Third, reward yourself. A test is physically and mentally tiring, even without anxiety, and it can be helpful to have something to look forward to. Plan an activity following the test, regardless of the outcome, such as going to a movie or getting ice cream.

When you are taking the test, if you find yourself beginning to feel anxious, remind yourself that you know the material. Visualize successfully completing the test. Then take a few deep, relaxing breaths and return to it. Work through the questions carefully but with confidence, knowing that you are capable of succeeding.

Developing a healthy mental approach to test taking will also aid in other areas of life. Test anxiety affects more than just the actual test—it can be damaging to your mental health and even contribute to depression. It's important to beat test anxiety before it becomes a problem for more than testing.

Study Strategy

Being prepared for the test is necessary to combat anxiety, but what does being prepared look like? You may study for hours on end and still not feel prepared. What you need is a strategy for test prep. The next few pages outline our recommended steps to help you plan out and conquer the challenge of preparation.

STEP 1: SCOPE OUT THE TEST

Learn everything you can about the format (multiple choice, essay, etc.) and what will be on the test. Gather any study materials, course outlines, or sample exams that may be available. Not only will this help you to prepare, but knowing what to expect can help to alleviate test anxiety.

STEP 2: MAP OUT THE MATERIAL

Look through the textbook or study guide and make note of how many chapters or sections it has. Then divide these over the time you have. For example, if a book has 15 chapters and you have five days to study, you need to cover three chapters each day. Even better, if you have the time, leave an extra day at the end for overall review after you have gone through the material in depth.

If time is limited, you may need to prioritize the material. Look through it and make note of which sections you think you already have a good grasp on, and which need review. While you are studying, skim quickly through the familiar sections and take more time on the challenging parts.

Write out your plan so you don't get lost as you go. Having a written plan also helps you feel more in control of the study, so anxiety is less likely to arise from feeling overwhelmed at the amount to cover.

STEP 3: GATHER YOUR TOOLS

Decide what study method works best for you. Do you prefer to highlight in the book as you study and then go back over the highlighted portions? Or do you type out notes of the important information? Or is it helpful to make flashcards that you can carry with you? Assemble the pens, index cards, highlighters, post-it notes, and any other materials you may need so you won't be distracted by getting up to find things while you study.

If you're having a hard time retaining the information or organizing your notes, experiment with different methods. For example, try color-coding by subject with colored pens, highlighters, or post-it notes. If you learn better by hearing, try recording yourself reading your notes so you can listen while in the car, working out, or simply sitting at your desk. Ask a friend to quiz you from your flashcards, or try teaching someone the material to solidify it in your mind.

STEP 4: CREATE YOUR ENVIRONMENT

It's important to avoid distractions while you study. This includes both the obvious distractions like visitors and the subtle distractions like an uncomfortable chair (or a too-comfortable couch that makes you want to fall asleep). Set up the best study environment possible: good lighting and a comfortable work area. If background music helps you focus, you may want to turn it on, but otherwise keep the room quiet. If you are using a computer to take notes, be sure you don't have any other windows open, especially applications like social media, games, or anything else that could distract you. Silence your phone and turn off notifications. Be sure to keep water close by so you stay hydrated while you study (but avoid unhealthy drinks and snacks).

Also, take into account the best time of day to study. Are you freshest first thing in the morning? Try to set aside some time then to work through the material. Is your mind clearer in the afternoon or evening? Schedule your study session then. Another method is to study at the same time of day that you will take the test, so that your brain gets used to working on the material at that time and will be ready to focus at test time.

STEP 5: STUDY!

Once you have done all the study preparation, it's time to settle into the actual studying. Sit down, take a few moments to settle your mind so you can focus, and begin to follow your study plan. Don't give in to distractions or let yourself procrastinate. This is your time to prepare so you'll be ready to fearlessly approach the test. Make the most of the time and stay focused.

Of course, you don't want to burn out. If you study too long you may find that you're not retaining the information very well. Take regular study breaks. For example, taking five minutes out of every hour to walk briskly, breathing deeply and swinging your arms, can help your mind stay fresh.

As you get to the end of each chapter or section, it's a good idea to do a quick review. Remind yourself of what you learned and work on any difficult parts. When you feel that you've mastered the material, move on to the next part. At the end of your study session, briefly skim through your notes again.

But while review is helpful, cramming last minute is NOT. If at all possible, work ahead so that you won't need to fit all your study into the last day. Cramming overloads your brain with more information than it can process and retain, and your tired mind may struggle to recall even previously learned information when it is overwhelmed with last-minute study. Also, the urgent nature of cramming and the stress placed on your brain contribute to anxiety. You'll be more likely to go to the test feeling unprepared and having trouble thinking clearly.

So don't cram, and don't stay up late before the test, even just to review your notes at a leisurely pace. Your brain needs rest more than it needs to go over the information again. In fact, plan to finish your studies by noon or early afternoon the day before the test. Give your brain the rest of the day to relax or focus on other things, and get a good night's sleep. Then you will be fresh for the test and better able to recall what you've studied.

STEP 6: TAKE A PRACTICE TEST

Many courses offer sample tests, either online or in the study materials. This is an excellent resource to check whether you have mastered the material, as well as to prepare for the test format and environment.

Check the test format ahead of time: the number of questions, the type (multiple choice, free response, etc.), and the time limit. Then create a plan for working through them. For example, if you have 30 minutes to take a 60-question test, your limit is 30 seconds per question. Spend less time on the questions you know well so that you can take more time on the difficult ones.

If you have time to take several practice tests, take the first one open book, with no time limit. Work through the questions at your own pace and make sure you fully understand them. Gradually work up to taking a test under test conditions: sit at a desk with all study materials put away and set a timer. Pace yourself to make sure you finish the test with time to spare and go back to check your answers if you have time.

After each test, check your answers. On the questions you missed, be sure you understand why you missed them. Did you misread the question (tests can use tricky wording)? Did you forget the information? Or was it something you hadn't learned? Go back and study any shaky areas that the practice tests reveal.

Taking these tests not only helps with your grade, but also aids in combating test anxiety. If you're already used to the test conditions, you're less likely to worry about it, and working through tests until you're scoring well gives you a confidence boost. Go through the practice tests until you feel comfortable, and then you can go into the test knowing that you're ready for it.

Test Tips

On test day, you should be confident, knowing that you've prepared well and are ready to answer the questions. But aside from preparation, there are several test day strategies you can employ to maximize your performance.

First, as stated before, get a good night's sleep the night before the test (and for several nights before that, if possible). Go into the test with a fresh, alert mind rather than staying up late to study.

Try not to change too much about your normal routine on the day of the test. It's important to eat a nutritious breakfast, but if you normally don't eat breakfast at all, consider eating just a protein bar. If you're a coffee drinker, go ahead and have your normal coffee. Just make sure you time it so that the caffeine doesn't wear off right in the middle of your test. Avoid sugary beverages, and drink enough water to stay hydrated but not so much that you need a restroom break 10 minutes into the test. If your test isn't first thing in the morning, consider going for a walk or doing a light workout before the test to get your blood flowing.

Allow yourself enough time to get ready, and leave for the test with plenty of time to spare so you won't have the anxiety of scrambling to arrive in time. Another reason to be early is to select a good seat. It's helpful to sit away from doors and windows, which can be distracting. Find a good seat, get out your supplies, and settle your mind before the test begins.

When the test begins, start by going over the instructions carefully, even if you already know what to expect. Make sure you avoid any careless mistakes by following the directions.

Then begin working through the questions, pacing yourself as you've practiced. If you're not sure on an answer, don't spend too much time on it, and don't let it shake your confidence. Either skip it and come back later, or eliminate as many wrong answers as possible and guess among the remaining ones. Don't dwell on these questions as you continue—put them out of your mind and focus on what lies ahead.

Be sure to read all of the answer choices, even if you're sure the first one is the right answer. Sometimes you'll find a better one if you keep reading. But don't second-guess yourself if you do immediately know the answer. Your gut instinct is usually right. Don't let test anxiety rob you of the information you know.

If you have time at the end of the test (and if the test format allows), go back and review your answers. Be cautious about changing any, since your first instinct tends to be correct, but make sure you didn't misread any of the questions or accidentally mark the wrong answer choice. Look over any you skipped and make an educated guess.

At the end, leave the test feeling confident. You've done your best, so don't waste time worrying about your performance or wishing you could change anything. Instead, celebrate the successful completion of this test. And finally, use this test to learn how to deal with anxiety even better next time.

Review Video: Test Anxiety
Visit mometrix.com/academy and enter code: 100340

Important Qualification

Not all anxiety is created equal. If your test anxiety is causing major issues in your life beyond the classroom or testing center, or if you are experiencing troubling physical symptoms related to your anxiety, it may be a sign of a serious physiological or psychological condition. If this sounds like your situation, we strongly encourage you to seek professional help.

Online Resources

Due to our efforts to try to keep this book to a manageable length, we've created a link that will give you access to all of your online resources:

mometrix.com/resources719/westeearchsped